Is God Christian?

Is God Christian?

Christian Identity in Public Theology:
An Asian Contribution

D. PREMAN NILES

FORTRESS PRESS
MINNEAPOLIS

IS GOD CHRISTIAN?
Christian Identity in Public Theology: An Asian Contribution

Copyright © 2017 Fortress Press. All rights reserved. Except for brief quotations in critical articles or reviews, no part of this book may be reproduced in any manner without prior written permission from the publisher. Email copyright@1517.media or write to Permissions, Fortress Press, PO Box 1209, Minneapolis, MN 55440-1209.

Cover design: Rob Dewey

Print ISBN: 978-1-5064-3026-3
eBook ISBN: 978-1-5064-3027-0

The paper used in this publication meets the minimum requirements of American National Standard for Information Sciences — Permanence of Paper for Printed Library Materials, ANSI Z329.48-1984.

Manufactured in the U.S.A.

To the Memory of Ninan Koshy (1934–2015)

friend, colleague and mentor

Contents

Introduction

IS GOD CHRISTIAN?

That question with the assumption that there is a Christian god confronts perhaps even haunts Asian Christians in many and diverse ways. To cite a few instances, in Malaysia there is a legal injunction forbidding Malaysian Christians from using the term "Allah" as a generic name for "God". The assertion is that Allah is the god of the Muslims and has to be separated from a Christian god. More dangerously, the Taliban in Pakistan identify the Christian god as a western god and retaliate on Pakistani Christians when there are US drone attacks on their strongholds. Churches have been bombed during services of worship eliciting the plaintive cry, "We are also Pakistanis." It is presumed that Christians in Pakistan worship a western god who sanctions the dastardly actions of a presumed Christian country. Even after the Liberation Tigers of Tamil Eelam, labelled "terrorists", have been eliminated as a guerrilla fighting force in Sri Lanka, significant parcels of land in the northern and eastern parts of the country, which are traditional Tamil homelands, are still occupied by the armed forces of the majority Sinhala government. Recruitment to the forces continues apace even though there are no identifiable enemies. Consequently, enemies have to be created. Who else but Christians and Muslims viewed as interlopers in an allegedly Buddhist Sinhala land? With the instigation of a fundamentalist minority of Buddhist clergy, Sinhala Buddhist thugs have attacked and vandalised churches and mosques. Though such attacks have diminished with a new government, there is simmering discontent. In the context of virulent religious identity politics in many Asian countries, not only has the answer to the question seem foreclosed for Christians, but their god has also been identified as a *western* god who has to be rejected.

In response, Christian positions have hardened. For many Christians scattered over Asia the answer to the question "Is God Christian?" or "Is there a Christian God?" is a firm "Yes". Such a position is in effect confrontational, and scuppers any possibility of relating meaningfully to followers of other Asian religions. I mention two examples just to illustrate the problem. In the Philippines, Christians (Catholic and Protestant) form the majority. Filipino Christians, by and large, have great difficulty relating to a minority Muslim population in the southern part of the archipelago. Muslim revulsion at being treated as second class citizens has escalated into armed resistance, with which the government of the Philippines has to contend in ways that are not always constructive. In the Republic of Korea (South Korea) Christians are a wealthy and powerful minority with a significant clout in many areas of Korean life. For instance, siding with conservative governments, many Christian churches have time and again refused to countenance communist North Korea thereby stalling efforts to reunify the two Koreas and heal a painful division. The actions of the present North Korean government also do not make a rapprochement easy. These two examples embody the position of many, though not all, Asian Christians that god is not only Christian but is also a god who will brook no rivals.

It is doubtful that authentic answers to the question would emerge if we simply get embroiled in situations of religious and racial conflict either in self-defence or with kneejerk reactions. Rather, what is required is to step back and participate with the many small but significant multi-religious groups that are attempting to find and express alternatives in difficult situations. These too are attempting to get beyond the narrow and exclusive claims of their religions, which extremist groups are using with such deadly effect to pervert justice, legitimise the politics of hate, and subvert any attempt to find and express religious and racial harmony. The seeking for alternatives is a political expression of hope and could therefore be dangerous. It is in such fraught situations that the question, "Is God Christian?" confronts us not simply as a theoretical question but as an existential question that urges us to get beyond narrow Christian claims and attitudes.

The challenge raised by the question is by no means confined to

Asia. It is alleged that more than in any other year, the year 2012 has seen the greatest number of clashes between religious groups not only in Asia but also in Africa and West Asia (the Middle East) with lower levels of intensity in Europe and the continents of the Americas. Not just religion but race also plays a role in these conflicts.[1] Since then, the rise of the fundamentalist jihadist group ISIS, which controls vast swathes of land together with its sympathisers and accomplices, has precipitated different forms of conflict in Asia, Africa, Europe and America. Governments intent on curbing the rise and impact of ISIS and similar fundamentalist groups have inadvertently spawned expressions of Islamophobia. So, while the discussions in this book are located in Asia, the concerns addressed are by no means confined to Asia; and my hope is that what I have to say will resonate with those Christians outside Asia who are also seeking alternatives. "Now is not the time to abandon hope" seems to be their message as they confront the politics of hate.

In a preliminary way, Kim Yong-bock, a Korean colleague and friend from whom I have taken the title for this book, offers an answer to the question, "Is God Christian?" In a personal conversation he said to me that he introduces the doctrine of God in his systematic theology class with a series of questions. "Do you think God is Buddhist?" The class says, "No." "Do you think God is Muslim?" A firm rejoinder that God is not Muslim. "Then do you think God is Christian?" Much hesitation till a feeble voice says, "No." The instructor responds, "Yes indeed. God is the God of all people not just Christians." How do we then relate the god made known to us in Jesus Christ to the many gods of Asia and more importantly to the many peoples of Asia who express their identity as formed through their commitment to these gods?[2] This book reviews the constructive ways in which Asian Christians have responded to this question.

AN ENQUIRY INTO METHODS IN PUBLIC THEOLOGY

This book is a sequel to my previous book, *The Lotus and the Sun: Asian Theological Engagement with Plurality and Power*,[3] and continues the narrative of the social biography of Asian theology.[4] It enters the theological efforts of my generation as a collective enterprise to survey *methods* that in the arena of *public theology* confront and reject the assertion that God is Christian or there is a Christian God among other gods. The Indian Catholic theologian, Felix Wilfred, succinctly states the intention of public theology.

> Asian Public Theology is one in which the accent will be stronger on the "public" than on theology. The focus will be on the issues and questions that affect the people and societies of Asia and which need to be addressed urgently. The theology envisaged here is not the kind that will confine itself within the Christian community, but one which will have an import for the actors in public life. It does not mean that we impose a Christian theology on others which, obviously, will be counterproductive. Rather, Asian Public Theology will be one that will be inherently interreligious in nature.[5]

Following Wilfred's advice, the theological methods to be explored in this book will not be concerned narrowly with problems in Christian theology, but rather with challenges posed for Christian theology in the wider arena of social and political life in Asia.

CONTENDING WITH "COLONIALISM"

As this book examines and evaluates the various approaches employed in the doing of theology in Asia, a term that will keep turning up is "colonialism". The term refers in the first instance to a particular historical period when western dominance in Asia was rife and entangled in that dominance was the assertion that God was not only Christian but also western, leading to attitudes and expressions of Christian triumphalism. In the second instance, colonialism is not only of historical interest but is also typical of ways in which all forms of power attempt to subdue or distort plurality or diversity. In this sense, "colonialism" is a metaphor, a representation, for the continuance of power in new and old forms with which we have to contend.

In *The Lotus and the Sun* I surveyed the various ways in which our Asian Christian forebears attempted to express their identity as both Asian and Christian in responding to Asian realities. Though history was the matrix for the exploration, the main purpose was theological. Besides identifying insights and resources for doing theology in Asia today, the survey also showed that authentic Asian theologies, which attempt to get beyond narrow assertions that God is Christian, accept plurality as intrinsic to creation and would contest any attempt that denies this fact. I used the rhythm of conformity and contestation as a hermeneutical key, a tool for interpretation, to show the conflictual relationship between plurality and power that informs the doing of theology in Asia.

Asian theologians of my generation, who are engaged in issues in the arena of public theology, also accept plurality as *a priori* and contest expressions of power that attempt to stifle or eliminate it. The assumption that underlies their approaches is that there are two or more active partners in responding to Asian realities and that theology in Asia should reflect this fact.

THE PROBLEM OF THE TWO STORIES

Again, I am indebted to Kim Yong-bock for suggesting "the problem of the two stories" as a hermeneutical key for unfolding the various Asian theological responses to the question "Is God Christian?" In a personal conversation he said, "We Asian Christians inherit two stories. It is like marriage, or any partnership between couples. Sometimes together, sometimes apart; sometimes embracing, sometimes repelling." Clearly, no two religious traditions or secular ideologies will totally agree with one another. "The problem of the two stories" reflects this fact. It carries the theme of conformity and contestation from my previous book in a new guise and sets the trajectory of this book as it attempts to relate the story of Jesus the Messiah, which we have received, to the story of our people, which we have inherited; and thus engage in a "triple dialogue", which is a dialogue with cultures, a dialogue with religions, and a dialogue with the poor.[6] Such dialogue involves a two-way process of receiving and giving that cross-textual hermeneutics, implied in the problem of the two stories as a theological method, undertakes.

SETTING THE STAGE FOR AN ENQUIRY
INTO METHODS

First, before moving on to a presentation of theological methods in vogue in Asia today, in the chapters that follow, I propose to examine the various initial attempts to relate the Text (Christian Scripture and traditions) to the Context (Asian Realities) from which present day methods arose as critical responses to them. Such a survey would not only be of historical interest in showing origins, but also, I hope, help those who are still tied to these methods to see the problems inherent in them.

Second, in my previous book, I argued that Christian Scripture by itself is not an adequate basis for relating to people of other faiths or for addressing the problem of the two stories. While there are a few windows permitting the entry of "the nations" into the biblical narrative, the overall concentration is on the God of Israel and then the God of the Church as made known in Jesus Christ.[7] However, when I permit my Asian context to interact with my reading of Scripture,[8] in a paradoxical way I find insights in Scripture to the question "Is God Christian?" that while inchoate yet help to shape a Christian stance as a prerequisite for addressing the problem of the two stories. I present these too in an introductory way to what follows in the main chapters.

RELATING TEXT TO CONTEXT

Foundational for earlier attempts to relate the two stories as an interplay between Text (Scripture and Christian traditions as shaped in the West) and Context (Asian realities) was a statement from the East Asia Christian Conference (EACC), later the Christian Conference of Asia (CCA), which is a regional ecumenical organisation.

> It is out of [the] contemporary necessity to confess the faith that there arises the task for theology for the Churches in Asia. Theology is a living thing, having to do with our very existence as Christians and as Churches. We cannot conceive of it in static or neatly defined final terms. A living theology must speak to the actual questions [people] in Asia are asking in the midst of their dilemmas; their hopes, aspirations and achievements; their doubts, despair and suffering. It must also speak in relation to the answers that are being given by Asian religions and philosophies, . . . secularism and science. Christian theology will fulfil its task in Asia only as the Asian Churches, as servants of God's Word and revelation in Jesus Christ, speak to the Asian situation and from involvement in it. Dogmatic theological statements from a church that stands on the sidelines as spectator or even interpreter of what God is doing in Asia can carry no conviction. *A living theology is born out of the meeting of a living church and its world.*[9]

(A) INDIGENISATION

The first attempt at articulating a contextual theology in Asia was scantier than what the agenda given above envisaged and was called "indigenisation". As the term itself implies, it had to do with importing what is foreign, namely, the core of the Christian faith or tradition as formulated in the West (the Text), and planting it on Asian soil (the Context). One is expected, on the one hand, not to abandon essential aspects of the Christian faith and on the other to avoid thought forms and ideas from a context that may not be congruent with and may even be inimical to the Christian message.

D. T. Niles from Sri Lanka illustrated this process through his famous metaphor of "the potted plant". Christianity has come to Asia as a potted plant that was grown on foreign soil. The task is to break the pot and place the plant in Asian soil so that the plant that grows carries the character not only of the soil in which it first took root but also the soil in which it is growing.[10] In defence of indigenisation it must be said that it was not simply a reaction to accusations that Asian Christianity is simply a foreign import. In the way it was conceived, it was intended to be a way of doing theology using the "incarnation" as a model. The "word" that comes from outside should become incarnate or "enfleshed" in the Asian cultural context and take on Asian characteristics.

However, mostly because of the influence of the Dutch missiologist, Hendrik Kraemer,[11] there was a fear of syncretism. Consequently, most though not all Asian attempts at indigenisation remained at the level of externals. In the life, worship and theology of Asian churches, Asian elements of music, architecture and language were taken and baptised into received Christian faith traditions.

Another factor that featured in indigenisation was the assumption that cultural differences are essentially the result of differing geographical locations and historical accidents, so that beneath the externals one may discern certain congruencies.

Such a view is reflected, for instance, in Robin Boyd's review of Indian Christian theology. He states that for effective Christian witness in India, what is needed is to transfer theology from Chalcedon to India which requires "the re-clothing of the underlying Truth in another set of terms and thought forms, which is already in existence and is as rich and vivid as the original Graeco-Roman context." He then goes on to say:

> Indian and western theologies begin with the same *sruti* (scriptures) while the *anubhava* (experience) of the Damascus road, or of Augustine's garden of Ostia, is fundamentally not different from that of Sundhar Singh in the Punjab. Only the *yukthi* is different, the inference from the facts, and the systematic statement in terms taken from the surrounding cultural environment.[12]

What this viewpoint ignores is the essential connection that is there between what we might call "religion" and "culture". It assumes that religious cultures may be seen as made up of three consecutive, but not too well-defined, circles. At the inner circle there is the body of beliefs that may be called "the core of the faith". The second circle consists of practices, rituals and observances through which the faith is expressed. The third outer circle is the culture—the world-view, language, standards of conduct and so on—that is generated by the first two circles. Since most foreign influences tend to impact on the outer circle, and the outer circle is more susceptible to change than the inner two circles, it was falsely assumed that "culture" may be separated out from the religious matrix to which it belongs.[13]

It is this false assumption that has given rise to certain Christian cognates such as "*khristadvaita*" to communicate "Christian Doctrines" or "Christology" in the Indian context. However, there is a mismatch. The literal translation of the term would be "Christomonism". In which case, one would have serious theological problems with the term, for the implication then would be that only Christ is real and everything else, including the incarnation, would be *maya*, that is illusory, impermanent or secondary. This position would also conflict with the Christian doctrine of creation, the doctrine of the Trinity as well as the historical reality of the incarnation.

It is the failure to discern the problem of the conflict of world views that has led to an uncritical search for Christian cognates based on superficial resemblances in other religious cultures. In a curious way, indigenisation falls into the very trap it strenuously tries to avoid, namely, syncretism understood as the indiscriminate mingling of various religious truths.

Besides ignoring the conflict of world views, indigenisation also assumes that culture is static. It is not seen as dynamic and evolving and changing, so that no real attempt is made to test the current relevance and applicability of the religio-cultural forms and terms it borrows. If one is not careful, it could easily become an antiquarian pursuit.

(B) CONTEXTUALISATION

As a way of setting right in particular the problems created by viewing culture in static terms and in ignoring the social and political dimensions of Asian contexts, the Theological Education Fund (TEF) of the World Council of Churches (WCC), which did much to encourage the development of Third World theologies, presented the concept and process of contextualisation as an advance on indigenisation.

According to the Third Mandate of the TEF (1970), "contextualisation" is defined thus:

> It means all that is implied in the familiar term "indigenisation" and yet seeks to press beyond it. Contextualisation has to do with how we assess the peculiarity of Third World contexts. Indigenisation tends to be used in the sense of responding to the Gospel in terms of a traditional culture. Contextualisation, while not ignoring this, takes into account the process of secularity, technology, and the struggle for human justice, which characterise the historical moment of the nations in the Third World.[14]

In his lecture, "Contextualization as the Way Toward Reform," Shoki Coe from Taiwan, then the Director of TEF, explains the difference between indigenisation and contextualisation with the metaphor of the "potted plant" in mind:

> Indigenous, indigineity and indigenization all derive from a nature metaphor, that is, of the soil, or taking root in the soil. It is only right that the younger churches, in search of their identity, should take seriously their own cultural milieu. However, because of the static nature of the metaphor, indigenization tends to be used in the sense of responding to the gospel in terms of traditional culture. Therefore, it is in danger of being past-oriented. Furthermore, the impression has been given that it is only applicable to Asia and Africa . . . for elsewhere it was felt that the danger lay in . . . an uncritical accommodation such as expressed by culture faiths, the American Way of Life, etc. But the most impor-

tant factor, especially since the last war, has been the new phenomenon of radical change. The new context is not that of static culture, but the search for the new, which at the same time has involved culture itself.[15]

In the same lecture, Coe explains contextualisation as a method:

> By this I mean wrestling with the Text, from which texts are derived and to which they point, in order to be faithful to it in the context; and wrestling in the context in which the reality of the Text is at work, in order to be relevant to it. This "double wrestle" may involve what I call "textual cum contextual" criticism.[16]

Coe correctly sees textual criticism and contextual criticism not as separate activities, but as one and the same activity with two distinguishable moments. Yet for all that, the assumption is that the context is something in which "the reality of the Text is at work". In other words, the Context does not speak for itself to the Text. This position is clearer in the Asian version of contextualisation as set forth in "the Critical Asian Principle". Emerito Nacpil from the Philippines, who was the Director of the Association of Theological Schools in South East Asia during one of its most creative periods, explains the principle in summary form:

> For one thing, it is a way of saying where our area of responsibility and concern is, namely, the varieties and dynamics of Asian realities. We are committed to understand this context both sympathetically and critically. For another thing, it is a way of saying that we will approach and interpret the Gospel in relation to the needs and issues particular to the Asian situation. It functions therefore partly as a hermeneutical principle. Thirdly, it is a way of saying that a theology worth its salt at this time in Asia must be capable, not only of illumining Asian realities with the light of the Gospel, but also of helping manage and direct the changes now taking place along lines more consonant with the Gospel and its vision for human life.[17]

Despite its best intentions, "the Critical Asian Principle" as a hermeneutical method not only attempts to illuminate Asian realities in a Christian way but also of trying to manage the changes taking place in a Christian way. It seems that its intention is to theologise the context. While such a stance may make sense in a Christian country like the Philippines, it would make little or no sense in the rest of Asia, except perhaps Australia and New Zealand.

In a perceptive essay on the movement from indigenisation to contextualisation, Simon Kwan Shui-Man argues that it is not necessary to draw a sharp distinction between indigenisation and contextualisation.[18] He gives examples from Asia, going as far back as 1920 in China and later in North East Asia, in which indigenisation *in practice* included those elements which contextualisation stressed. As the Third Mandate clearly indicates, Kwan sees contextualisation primarily as an attempt to view indigenisation on the broader canvas of Third World theologies. He views the "reform" envisaged in contextualisation not as a shift in paradigm, as David Bosch assumes,[19] but as a change in "discursive practice" made necessary by the shift in location from Asia to the whole of the Third World.

> I suggest taking the emergence of the contextualization discourse as coming out of a new discursive practice, which turns out to be strategically effective, and which was given birth by the entry of the Asian theological discourse to Third World liberation theological discourse, rather than from the rectification of the theological method, namely indigenization.[20]

Kwan uses categories drawn from the philosophy of science (principally Thomas Kuhn), Post-Modernism (Michel Foucault and others) and Postcolonialism, which makes his analysis somewhat difficult to follow. With apologies to him, my intention is to present his argument and recast what he says in language that may be easier to follow, and give the terms and categories he uses in brackets.

The TEF was set up at the meeting of the International Missionary Council in 1958; and it became part of the Commission on World Mission and Evangelism of the WCC. Kwan correctly observes that along with secular political developments as expressed particularly at the Bandung Conference of non-aligned nations (1955), through which the concept of "Third World" nations gained prominence, the WCC was also affected with the ideology of "Third Worldism". This happened with a large influx of churches from the Third World into its membership. Several leaders and theological activists from these churches carried into ecumenical discussions their involvement in the political, economic and social changes in their countries. Terms such as "rapid social change" received attention. The 1966 WCC "Church and Society Conference," as Kwan notes, "was related to the accelerating technological developments, liberation from dominance, struggling for human justice, the growing division between the rich and poor countries, which are not unlike those elements found in the TEF's definition of contextualization."[21] The third mandate of the TEF, which set "contextualisation" as a hallmark for its screening process for funding theological education, in effect reified a language ("discursive practice"), which theological education shared among its Third World members. As Kwan argues, the change from indigenisation to contextualisation was not a radical change calling for a new model ("paradigm shift") for doing theology. It was rather the extension and absorption of indigenisation necessitated by a shift of location ("discursive site") from Asia to the Third World. In effect, as a theological method and emphasis, contextualisation was a political act. Consequently, its language and practice, as Kwan notes, "effectively excluded theological discourses other than contextualization as anomalies."[22]

Besides the factors that Kwan identifies for a change in theological discourse, there were other emerging programmes and emphases in the ecumenical movement that paid special attention to the Third World, and had an impact on the language and focus of the Third Mandate. Principal of these was the setting up in 1970 of the Commission of the Churches' Participation in Development (CCPD) as a programme of the WCC. A concentration on the concerns of the Third World became clearer when in 1976 the WCC Central Committee launched the search for a Just, Participatory and Sustainable Society (JPSS), replacing the earlier model of a Responsible Society.[23] As a programme emphasis, JPSS would serve to present a vision of a new human society that stressed justice (principally an emphasis from Latin America), the participation of all people, not just the elites, with their hopes enshrined in their religious cultures (mostly from Asia) and a sustainable society (environmental concerns raised mostly in Europe and North America). JPSS brought together emphases that the Third Mandate suggested such as rapid social change and the search for a new political language. The argument in JPSS was not so much on whether or not churches and theological educators should participate in the rapid social, economic and political changes that were taking place, but rather on how they may participate in the process of realising the vision for a new human society.

This was also the stance of the EACC/CCA statement quoted above, which speaks of a confessing theology that addresses the actual questions men and women are asking in Asia. Churches and their theological leaders anchored in their faith are viewed as the actors interacting with the context.

Contextualisation as the TEF Third Mandate interpreted it had an impact on the doing of theology in Asia. First, it brought about the realisation that all theologies are contextual in that they arise from specific contexts and are primarily responses to the challenges posed by those contexts. However, some assert that their theological presuppositions and responses are universally valid. As I showed in my earlier book, *The Lotus and the Sun*, this has been the position of theologies within the broad "neo-orthodox" spectrum. Liberation theology from Latin America, especially through the work of the Ecumenical Association of Third World Theologies (EATWOT), also attempted to make a similar claim, which I contested:

> Asian theology is suffering from a crisis of identity, for it is often domi-
> nated by theological thinking in the West and, more recently, by Latin
> American and Black American Liberation theologies. . . . If theology in
> Asia is to have its own identity, it must cease to be merely an extension
> of western theologies, and instead speak meaningfully to and within the
> context of Asian suffering and hope.[24]

I said this at a time when Asian theologians were attempting to make a space for themselves without being suffocated by theologies imposed on them. I was also reflecting the position of most Asian theologians who began to side with Post-modern and Post-colonial critics to reject a "meta-narrative" that purports to cover and address all situations.

On a positive note, contextualisation opened out the possibility of articulating theologies that would concentrate on a specific context and the theology that arises from that context, and identify these as genuine contextual theologies.[25] Some examples are Minjung Theology from Korea, Dalit Theology from India and Homeland Theology from Taiwan. Since many of those who were involved in articulating these theologies were themselves from the contexts concerned, the Context was viewed not just as a passive recipient but also as an active participant in theological articulation.

(C) CONTEXT ADDRESSING TEXT

The contextual theologies mentioned above and other similar theologies began to raise a different set of questions, which I set out in an essay I wrote in 1985, "The Word of God and the People of Asia".[26] In this essay I raised two sets of questions.

> *First.* Is the Context simply a thing – a mere conglomeration of Asian realities to which the Text has to be related? Rather, is not the Context the people themselves who live amongst these realities? What does the Text have to say to them as they relate to these realities and struggle for life in the midst of these realities? Can it speak to them unless it too is a living Word that listens to their word – their story – and speaks to them as a living story – the story of God's compassion for people that is concretely expressed in God's relationship with Israel and in God's self-disclosure in Jesus the Messiah?

> *Second.* Is theology always a matter of relating Text to Context? Is it not also a matter of relating Context to Text so that the Context may speak to the Text? Is Asia only there to receive? Has it nothing to contribute? If it does, then theology can no longer be viewed as a monologue. It is a *dialogue.*[27]

In raising these questions, I was concerned to unpack the demands for a living theology implied in the EACC/CCA statement. Though the predominant mood in that statement is the church addressing the context, it coincidentally concedes that the context is a living thing. The statement identifies two partners for doing theology. Instead of the static concepts of Text and Context, it speaks of a living church and the world of Asian people. A living church is a church that is already contextualised in that it is involved in and has relationships within the context, and therefore can present the gospel in a relevant and credible way. A living church is not just a referee or judge. It is a player or an actor in the arena of everyday life. The other partner is the world of Asian peoples with their religious cultures and histories. It is the encounter between the two—a dynamic two way movement—that is to be envisaged as the locus for a living theology. The assumption is that a living theology will emerge when a living church meets a living world of people. The statement also warns us that the theology or theologies, which emerge from such an encounter, cannot be conceived "in static or neatly defined final terms". In which case, the model or method for a "living theology" should be more illustrative of what is happening rather than prescriptive of what is to be done.

Archie Lee from Hong Kong quotes the questions I raised in my article and proposes "Cross-Textual Hermeneutics" as a method for doing theology in Asia.[28] Such a method would be honest to the fact that as Asian Christians we have two identities—an Asian cultural identity and a Christian identity—and that we live in two worlds —the world of the Bible and the Christian faith and the world of Asian scriptures, cultures and religions. It is a reminder "that we have two texts entrusted to us: the Asian text we have inherited from our own Asian cultural-religious traditions and the biblical text we have received from the Judaeo-Christian communities. The meaning of the term 'texts' includes literary as well as non-literary works. They can be a cultural heritage, historical traditions, religious beliefs, and folk tales."

> Cross-textual hermeneutics gives due attention to the two texts at our disposal for doing theology. It is imperative that the biblical text (text A) has to be interpreted in our own context in constant interpenetration and interaction with our cultural religious texts (text B). The tensions between text A and text B become more apparent when the religious nature of text B is taken into serious consideration.[29]

Instead of the term "cross-textual hermeneutics", which would cover the whole gamut of methods to be explored in this book, I prefer to use "cross-textual reading" to describe an initial foray into exploring the problem of the two stories in chapter one.

IS GOD CHRISTIAN? SOME INSIGHTS FROM CHRISTIAN SCRIPTURE

The Synoptic Gospels (Matthew, Mark and Luke), perhaps incidentally to their main narratives, face this question, and lead us into other scriptural texts that throw light on God's compassion for the nations. In a preliminary way these texts contest the notion that God only favours Christians.

To present this interpretation I avoid placing the texts I have selected in any construal of salvation history. Neither do I view them through the lens of historical criticism of western scholarship. Instead,

I base them on the premise that the God we worship through Jesus Christ is the God of all people; and thus permit my Asian context to interact with Christian Scripture.

To understand better how the gospel writers in their own ways address the question "Is God Christian?" we first need to be aware of the character of their writings. The gospels are confessional documents that are verbal portraits of the historical Jesus. Their primary purpose is not to recount history. Rather, they shape the historical materials available to them to present their particular messages. That is why there are differences in the way each writer of the gospel story uses the same or similar historical incidents, and even adds historical materials from sources peculiar to each of them. Hence, one would be ill-advised to collapse the gospel accounts into a single narrative that would distort the message each writer intends to convey. However, we could permit each account to talk to the other as an exercise in "cross-textual" reading from which we may gain much profit.

I have often wondered why the writers of the gospel story went back to present their portrayals of the historical Jesus after Paul had already declared that though previously Jesus Christ was considered from a human point of view that is no longer the case: "From now on we regard no one from a human point of view (literally, "according to the flesh"), even though we once knew Christ from a human point of view, we know him no longer in that way. So, if anyone is in Christ, there is a new creation: everything old has passed away; see, everything has become new!" (2 Cor 5:16).[30] My assumption is that in presenting their portraits of the historical Jesus, the gospel writers imply that unless one comes face to face with the Jesus of history one cannot really understand the Risen One.

We begin with Mark 7:24–30, Jesus's encounter with a Syrophoenician woman, a gentile. Jesus moves from Israelite territory to foreign territory to the region of Tyre. Though he wanted to escape notice, his presence was detected. A woman from that region comes to Jesus and begs him to cast out an unclean spirit that has taken possession of her daughter. Jesus responds brusquely that it is not good to take the bread belonging to the children and throw it to the dogs. Jews referred to gentiles as dogs. In using this epithet for the gentile woman, Jesus betrays his human limitations as a Jew. Instead of being rebuffed, the woman turns the derisory response of Jesus on to Jesus, and says that even dogs are entitled to the crumbs that fall under the table. Surprised, Jesus says, "Because of this word (Greek: *touton ton logon*) go, the demon has left your daughter."[31] The term "faith" is absent in Jesus's response, which contrasts oddly with his response to the woman with a blood haemorrhage who is cured: "Daughter your *faith* has made you well; go in peace" (5:34). Or, his response to blind Bartimaeus, who receives his sight: "Go your *faith* has made you well" (10:52). Because these two are of the house of Israel, a faith response would make sense; but not to one outside the Jewish household of faith. However, more seems to be implied in Jesus's response. Matthew in his account of this encounter (Matt 15:21–28) gives the explanation that Jesus spoke in this fashion to dismiss the woman because he was sent only to the lost sheep of the house of Israel. That explanation provides a clue for grasping the radical nature of Jesus's response in the Marcan narrative to what the woman said. In saying what she did, in effect the woman was challenging Jesus to move beyond his own limited perception of his messiahship. In so doing she holds up for us also the important role of the outsider in breaking down our confessional prejudices and limitations.

Jesus's encounter with the Syrophoenician woman comes at a crucial point in Mark's narrative. Earlier Jesus upbraids the Pharisees for their myopic interpretation of the law using tradition to subvert the liberative potential of God's law (7:9–13). In so doing, he shows himself as the Messiah sent to the house of Israel. Moving beyond Jewish territory, the encounter with the Syrophoenician woman, who challenges him, stretches his perception of his role as Messiah to embrace the outsider. This enlarged perception finds specific expression when Jesus heals another gentile (7:31–37), which is followed with the feeding of the four thousand on foreign territory where Jesus breaks bread for many (8:1–10). No longer are these perceived as dogs deserving crumbs at best, but as full recipients of the compassion of the Messiah. In a previous account of feeding a multitude, which takes place on Israelite territory, twelve baskets are filled with what is left after all are fed (6:42–44). The abundance of the Messiah's compassion (cf. 6:34) is for the twelve tribes of Israel. In the next episode of feeding a multitude, seven baskets are filled with what is left after all are satisfied. Seven is the number denoting completeness in Hebrew numerology (cf. Gen 2:2), and suggests that the abundance of the Messiah's compassion embraces all God's peoples.

Matthew's account of Jesus's encounter with the Syrophoenician woman has the word "faith": "Woman great is your faith!" (15:28). Matthew provides a different and yet complementary message, which is also found in Jesus's response to the Roman centurion, "Truly I tell you, in no one in Israel have I found such faith" (Matt 8:10). It is a simple yet profound message: do not belittle the faith of the gentiles (nations). Do not discount the faith of those outside. Matthew emphasises this fact when he has Jesus saying that not everyone who confesses him as "Lord" (Hebrew *'adonai* as a rendition of the name of God) will enter the kingdom of Heaven (God) but only those who do God's will (7:21). There is faith out there! That is why it is possible to disciple the nations to do God's will (28:19), which may or may not involve crossing over to the Christian faith.[32]

Luke adds to this mix of insights from Mark and Matthew. Probably the only Gentile writer of books in the New Testament, Luke perceives Jesus as embracing the outsider from the very beginning in the mainstream of his ministry. Of particular importance in this regard is the so-called Nazareth manifesto (4:14–30). Luke bases his narrative on the briefer version in Mark 6:1–5, which explains that Jesus was unacceptable in his hometown because he was perceived as a mere "carpenter" (Greek: *tektōn*) and an upstart. Luke splices into this account his interpretation that Jesus was unacceptable because he included the gentiles as recipients of God's grace.

As David Bosch points out, the radical nature of the Nazareth manifesto is not just in what it says as in what it leaves out.[33] In quoting Isaiah 61:1–2, Jesus omits the last line of the couplet:

> To proclaim the year of the Lord's favour
> and the day of vengeance of our God.

The omission in Luke is striking because the previous lines maintain the couplet structure that is typical of Hebrew poetry.[34] The year of the Lord's favour refers to the Year of Jubilee (the fiftieth year) when all debts are cancelled and those in slavery are freed (Leviticus 25). In implying that the time of release would be similar to the escape from slavery in Egypt (cf. Lev 25:55), the prophet also envisages a punishment on the enemies of Israel like that which was visited on the Egyptians. The belief that the liberation of the Jews would also be a time when God would punish their oppressors was prevalent during the time of Jesus. The implication seems to be that there is no fun in being saved unless someone else is being damned!

By leaving out the day of vengeance, Luke portrays Jesus the Messiah, anointed with God's spirit, as proclaiming the "acceptable year of the Lord" to all nations and not just to Israel. This proclamation is an act of liberation and restoration, and so is a political event. This implication is expanded when Jesus says that there were many widows in Israel but it was to a widow in Sidon that God sent the prophet Elijah at a time of drought; and there were many lepers in Israel during the time of the prophet Elisha but it was Naaman the Syrian whom the prophet healed. No wonder, those who heard Jesus in the synagogue were furious; and they wanted to throw him down a precipice as they would a heretic. But Jesus passed through them and went on his way, because the time for the completion of his ministry had not come.

The references to the widow of Sidon and Naaman are worth exploring further to bring out their import. My reading of both narratives (1 Kgs 17:1–16 and 2 Kgs 5:1–14) would be political rather than religious because the underlying theme is liberation.

The narrative in 1 Kings 17:1–16 introduces a larger narrative that recounts the conflict between Elijah and Queen Jezebel from Sidon who is married to Ahab, King of Israel. The conflict is not so much between two gods as between two differing ideologies of kingship. Coming from Tyre with its particular ideology of kingship, Queen Jezebel had convinced Ahab that as king he was supreme, and he could do anything he desires with impunity. This ideology was at variance with Israel's ideology of kingship which is that the king is responsible to both God and people. A typical expression of this imported ideology that condoned dictatorship is the king's altercation with Naboth whose vineyard abutted the king's palace (1 Kings 21). The king desired the vineyard as an allotment to grow vegetables. In exchange he would give Naboth another plot of land or money. Naboth says that he is not at liberty to trade ancestral property for another however good that alternative might be. In high dudgeon, the king throws himself on his bed, faces the wall and refuses all food and drink. Finding him in this surly mood, Jezebel upbraids him, "Do you now govern Israel? Get up, eat some food, and be cheerful; I will give you the vineyard of Naboth the Jezreelite" (21:7). Jezebel writes letters in the king's name to the elders of the city bringing false accusations against Naboth and has him stoned to death. She then invites the king to take possession of the vineyard. When the king visits the vineyard, Elijah accosts him there and announces the doom that awaits him and his wife as a consequence of this dastardly act.

Resisting dictatorship was one aspect of the conflict. The other has to do with the king's role as the embodiment of the storm god Baal in the fertility rituals that came with this imported ideology of kingship to ensure fecundity. At the ritual at Mount Carmel Elijah proves that the God of Israel, not the king, is supreme and slaughters the prophets of Baal (18:17–40). Jezebel retaliates by threatening dire vengeance on Elijah (19:2), and then persuades the Israelites who had gone over to her side to slaughter the prophets of Israel's God (19:14, cf. 18:13).

As a precursor to this heightened ideological conflict, Elijah says, "As the Lord the God of Israel lives, before whom I stand, there shall be neither dew nor rain these years, except by my word" (17:1), making it clear that it is not Baal but Yahweh who ensures fertility. In making this declaration, Elijah exposes a spurious ideology of kingship.

The drought that followed lasted for some three years. In the midst of this drought, Elijah ekes out a precarious existence at a stream which dries out. He is then sent to a widow in Sidon. The widow is from the same city as Jezebel, showing that the conflict is not between two gods per se or even between two nations as between a true and a false ideology of kingship. The situation is stark when Elijah meets the widow. He finds her gathering a few dry sticks to cook and eat their last meal. Elijah asks her to first bring him a small cake using the meagre rations of flour and oil that she has before feeding themselves. Without demurring, she does Elijah's bidding, sharing what she has. In succouring the prophet of God, a vulnerable widow finds that what would have been a last meal before death overcomes her and her son, becomes in fact food for life. The gift of life in the midst of a life-threatening drought even extends to the prophet reviving her son at the point of death. A measure of flour and a cruse of oil, sufficient for a day (daily bread?!), neither increases nor decreases, and lasts for the whole period of the drought to feed her, her son and God's prophet. I cannot help but interject at this point that God's grace may be boring but it is sufficient—a lesson that a little person in sharing the little that she has conveys.

The episode concerning Naaman, a Syrian general, in 2 Kings 5:1–14, also concerns power relations. In one of its raids the Syrians took a small Israelite girl as slave who served the wife of Naaman.

When Naaman was afflicted with leprosy, which at the time was a generic term for any skin disease, the Israelite slave girl says to her mistress that if only the master would go to the prophet in Samaria he could be healed. Hearing this from his wife, Naaman with the permission of his king, sets out with his army, chariots and horses, and a vast store of silver, gold and garments as gifts. He goes to the palace of the king in Samaria assuming that the prophet he was advised to meet was a court prophet. The king of Israel is dismayed thinking that this was a deliberate provocation to engage him in another war. The king mourns and tears his clothes in agony saying, "Am I God to give life or death?" Elisha sends word that the man is to see him. Naaman turns up with his army and gifts to meet Elisha. Elisha stays inside his house and sends a messenger to Naaman asking him to go wash himself in the river Jordan seven times and then he would be healed. Naaman is furious saying that the least the prophet could have done was to come out and call on the name of his god and wave his hand over the leprous spot and heal him. Was Elisha's action an expression of arrogance or something else? My surmise is that while willing to dispense God's grace to a foreigner and an enemy at that, Elisha wanted to stay clear of power and wealth, which Naaman represented. It is the refusal to meet him face to face that angered Naaman.

Naaman goes away sulking. He grumbles, "Are not the rivers of Syria cleaner than the muddy water of Jordan?" Another small person enters the fray. A servant of Naaman, probably a soldier, says to him, "General! If the man of God asked you to do something difficult would you not have done it? He has asked you to do something simple." So, Naaman dips himself in the river Jordan seven times and is healed.

He returns to meet Elisha and says, "Now I know that there is no God in all the earth except in Israel." This confession needs unpacking. The God of Israel whom Naaman acknowledges, the One who gave him healing, is the God of a small people whom he had defeated many a time in battle. The king of Israel was petrified of him. Yet, he had to acknowledge that it was the God of a small people that was the true God whose grace he had experienced through the healing he had received.

Naaman presses Elisha several times to accept a gift as a token of his gratitude. Elisha refuses and continues to stay clear of power and wealth. Since Elisha would not accept a gift from him, Naaman asks for a gift from Elisha. He asks for permission to take two mule loads of earth from Israel so that he could stand on Israelite soil to worship the God of Israel. At that time, the belief was that gods were territorial (cf. Deut 32:8, Ps 137:1–4). Then there is another request. From time to time Naaman would have to accompany and physically support his king as they go to the house of the Syrian God, Rimmon, to worship there. Would the God of Israel take exception? Elisha seems not to have any problem with this, and says to Naaman, "Go in peace." So much for religious exclusivism!

Where Elisha was careful to stay clear of power and wealth, his servant Gehazi fails. Enticed by what he sees, Gehazi thinks that his master has let Naaman off too lightly. He runs after Naaman to get a gift with a lie that his master has a couple of prophets as visitors and desires some clothing and silver. Naaman sends these gifts through two of his servants, whom Gehazi dismisses at the entrance to the city, and hides what he has received. When he stands before Elisha, Elisha questions him; and he lies knowing that his master would not approve of his act. In dismay Elisha asks, "What have you done? Is this the time to look for wealth?" And the disease from which Naaman suffered and from which he was delivered is visited on Gehazi.

This story is also replete with God's liberating power operating through small people: a slave girl, low ranking soldiers who persuade Naaman to do what the prophet asks him to do, and a prophet of God who spurns power and wealth. But the prophet's servant Gehazi is seduced.

Insights from both introductory discussions will be developed in the chapters that follow.

A NARRATIVE APPROACH

Each method explored in the book reflecting the problem of the two stories has important insights to contribute to an understanding of what constitutes Asian theology. In describing these methods I employ a narrative style. A narrative approach is not only apt for tracking development but it also has the advantage of not always wanting to close the argument. In so doing, my hope is that what I have to say about theology in Asia would open up vistas as well as gaps for readers, including those from other continents, to fill in what is lacking and continue the exploration into what constitutes public theology. Implied in this position is my conviction that no theology should attempt or pretend to have the final say. All theology is theology *en route*.

I will only deal with the thinking of those who I consider are foundational for the methods being explored, and provide dates for the pioneers who have passed on. I will not be exhaustive in describing the theologies that ensue from these methods.[35] Citations in the endnotes provide suggestions for further reading; and the Index of Names is also a helpful guide.

SOME CONVENTIONS USED IN THE BOOK

Because I am not concerned with a Church-centred theology, I have consistently used the term "the church" when referring to churches collectively and avoided using the term "the Church" except when quoting or referring to writers and documents that use the term or when it is part of a proper name. When first mentioned, theologians are identified by name and country and thereafter only by name. The first citation of any writing used in a chapter is given fully in the endnotes, so that readers do not have to comb through endnotes in earlier chapters to find the full reference.

ACKNOWLEDGMENT AND DEDICATION

I am grateful to the Indian painter Jyoti Sahi for permission to use his painting "the Compassionate Guru". The "third eye" in the painting utilises a Hindu motif of god as the all seeing one who weeps with the pain of oppressed people.

As acquisitions editor at Fortress Press for Asian theology, Jesudas Athyal has encouraged me to write and complete this book despite many setbacks. I am grateful to Wesley Ariarajah, with whom I have been able to talk through many aspects of this book and who has graciously given time to read through the manuscript and comment on some of the difficult chapters with alternative readings. Many of my other theological and ecumenical colleagues to whom I owe so much have passed away. So, in a representative way, I dedicate this book to the memory of Ninan Koshy (1934–2015), who urged me to write this book, and provided helpful comments on the sections he had the opportunity to read.

Notes

1. See "Religious Hostilities Reach Six-Year High," Pew Research Center, January 2014.

2. Though I use the term "gods" there are not many gods but one god. It is perhaps best to speak of "many gods" as "focal images", to borrow an expression from Lakshman Wickremesinghe of Sri Lanka, through which various religious persons view reality. See C. Lakshman Wickremesinghe, "Togetherness and Uniqueness—Living Faiths in Inter-relation," *CTC Bulletin* 5, no. 1–2 (April-August, 1984): 6.

3. D. Preman Niles, *The Lotus and the Sun: Asian Theological Engagement with Plurality and Power* (Canberra: Barton Books, 2013).

4. See Niles, *Lotus and Sun*, 4–7, for a fuller desription of this approach.

5. Felix Wilfred, *Asian Public Theology: Critical Concerns in Challenging Times* (Delhi: ISPCK, 2010), xii. For a fuller explanation of what is public theology, see Niles, *Lotus and Sun*, 309–14.

6. I have taken this phrase from the Federation of Asian (Catholic) Bishops' Conferences description of the theological task in Asia from its first plenary assembly in Taipei 1972. See Niles, *Lotus and Sun*, 169–71 for details.

7. Niles, *Lotus and Sun*, 302–3.

8. I firmly believe that there never could be what one might call an "objective" reading of the Bible. All "exegesis" in one way or another involves "eisegesis"; though one may argue that there could be bad eisegesis.

9. *Confessional Families and the Churches in Asia*, Report from a consultation convened by the EACC, Kandy (Redfern, Australia: Epworth, 1965) 20–21, emphasis added.

10. D. T. Niles, *That They May Have Life* (New York: Harper & Brothers, 1951), 80–81.

11. Hendrik Kraemer, *The Christian Message in a Non-Christian World* (London & New York: Harper & Brothers, 1938). See my evaluation in Niles, *Lotus and Sun*, 48–54.

12. Robin H. S. Boyd, *An Introduction to Indian Christian Theology* (Madras: The Christian Literature Society, 1975), 261. Sadhu Sundar Singh was a Sikh convert who previously spurned Christians and publicly burned the Bible. Later, he says that he had a vision of Jesus that led to his conversion, hence Boyd's depiction of his conversion as similar to that of St Paul and St Augustine.

13. For a fuller account of the relationship between religion and culture as understood at that time, see Paul D. Devanandan, "Religion as Creed, Cultus and Culture" in *Selections from the Books of P.D. Devanandan* (Bangalore: CISRS, 1964), 10–13.

14. *Ministry in Context: The Third Mandate of the Theological Education Fund*, ed. TEF Staff (London: TEF, 1972), 20.

15. Shoki Coe, "Contextualization as the Way Toward Reform" in *Asian Christian Theology: Emerging Themes*, ed. Douglas J. Elwood (Philadelphia: Westminster, 1980), 51.

16. Coe, "Contextualization," 49.

17. Emerito P. Nacpil, "The Question of Excellence in Theological Education," *South East Asia Journal of Theology* 16 (1975): 55–58. For an expanded statement, see his "The Critical Asian Principle," in Elwood, *Asian Christian Theology: Emerging Themes*, 58.

18. Simon Kwan Shui-man, "From Indigenization to Contextualization: A Change in Discursive Practice rather than a Shift in Paradigm," *Studies in World Christianity* 11, no. 2 (2005): 236–50.

19. David J. Bosch, *Transforming Mission: Paradigm Shifts in Theology of Mission* (New York: Orbis, 1991), 423: "Contextual theology truly represents a paradigm shift in theological thinking."

20. Kwan, "Indigenization," 243.

21. Ibid., 244.

22. Ibid., 247.

23. See Carl-Henric Grenholm, "Responsible Society," and C.I. Itty, "Just, Participatory and Sustainable Society," in *Dictionary of the Ecumenical Movement*, second edition, ed. Nicholas Lossky, et al. (Geneva: WCC Publications, 2002), 980–81, and 624–25 for succinct descriptions of the two models. Ans van der Bent, *Commitment to God's World: A Concise Critical Survey of Ecumenical Social Thought* (Geneva: WCC Publications, 1995), 58–77, has an excellent discussion of the various models the World Council of Churches proposed for the social engagement of churches.

24. D. Preman Niles, "Toward a Framework for Doing Theology in Asia," in *The Human and the Holy*, ed. Emerito Nacpil and Douglas Elwood (New York: Orbis, 1978), 267. See also James H. Cone and Gayraud S. Wilmore, *Black Theology: A Documentary History*, volume two (New York: Orbis, 2003), 366 where they use this quote to argue for theological space for all third world theologies.

25. For an analytical but rather "flat" account of various models of contextual

theology, see Stephen B. Bevans, *Models of Contextual Theology* (New York: Orbis, 2002).

26. D. Preman Niles, "The Word of God and the People of Asia," *Understanding the Word: Essays in Honor of Bernhard W. Anderson,* ed. James T. Butler, Edgar W. Conrad and Ben C. Ollenburger (Sheffield: JSOT Press, 1985), 281–313.

27. Niles, "Word of God," 282–83.

28. Archie C.C. Lee, "Biblical Interpretations in Asian Perspectives," *Asian Journal of Theology* 7, no. 1 (1993): 35–39.

29. Lee, "Biblical Interpretations," 38.

30. Though the dating of New Testament documents cannot be done with absolute precision, the general consensus of scholars is that the epistles of Paul were written before the gospel accounts. See Marcus Borg, *Evolution of the Word: The New Testament in the Order the Books Were Written* (New York: Harper Collins, 2012) who places New Testament writings in their historical contexts and tracks the development of core ideas of Christianity.

31. I am indebted to the Argentinean theologian José Miguez-Bonino for this insight. In a Bible study he gave on this passage at the assembly of the Council for World Mission in Jamaica (1993) he argued that the real nature of the woman's comeback was challenge rather than just persistence.

32. For a discussion of this position, see Niles, *Lotus and Sun*, 11, 205–6.

33. Bosch, *Transforming Mission*, 110–11.

34. Hebrew poetry employs what is called "parallelism" in which the second line of the couplet expands either positively or negatively what is stated in the first line.

35. For a good survey of theologies in Asia, see Michael Amaladoss, S.J., *Life in Freedom: Liberation Theologies from Asia* (New York: Orbis, 1997).

1.

Cross-Textual Hermeneutics: A Counter-Colonial Approach

Though the entry of Christianity into Asia predates the colonial period, the Bible and the Christian faith as we have them *now* were received in Asia during the colonial period—a roughly four-hundred year period from 1500 to 1900. Even the ancient Church of the St. Thomas Christians was affected by Roman Catholic missions and other western missions during this period.[1] Equally, the whole area of biblical studies, which is concerned with issues of how the Bible is to be read and interpreted, is also an inheritance from this period. Cross-textual hermeneutics, as a way of getting beyond colonial entrapments and making the Bible and Christian traditions meaningful in the contexts of Asia, has been practised for quite some time. The purpose of this chapter is to introduce the character of cross-textual hermeneutics; and in the chapters that follow explore further its important facets.

First, it would be helpful to say something about the complexity of the colonial factor in relation to the Bible and the Christian faith, and show in a preliminary way how cross-textual hermeneutics responds to this factor. *Second*, we will examine three examples of cross-textual hermeneutics. These would be the approaches of Mohandas K. Gandhi of India, Lakshman Wickremesinghe of Sri Lanka, and Ahn Byung-mu of Korea. All three were activists and their varied approaches were shaped by their praxis. Mohandas K. Gandhi

(1869–1948) was a freedom fighter. He was not a Christian, but he read the Bible (actually the New Testament) and the Qur'an together with the Bhagavad-Gita on a regular basis. He speaks of the influence of the Bible in shaping his political engagement. Lakshman Wick-remesinghe (1927–1983) was a bishop of the Anglican Diocese of Kurunagala in Sri Lanka and formatted the articulation of his faith in the context of inter-religious dialogue in a common search for human rights and religious harmony. Ahn Byung-mu (1922–1996) was a New Testament scholar who had his training in Germany, but abandoned much of what he learned in the West when he joined the ranks of the *minjung*[2] theologians in their struggle for human rights and democracy in Korea. *Third*, based on these three examples I will identify some of the characteristics and principles of cross-tex-tual hermeneutics.

THE COMPLEXITY OF THE COLONIAL FACTOR IN RELATION TO ASIAN CHRISTIANITY

An account that Archie Lee from Hong Kong gives of a dialogue between Jewish theologians and Asian theologians in Cochin, India, points to the complexity of the colonial factor in relation to the Bible, biblical studies and the Christian faith in Asia.[3] The choice of Cochin in Kerala as the venue for this dialogue was important because it was and is symbolic of the relations that Asians have with Jews. Cochin is home to an ancient Jewish colony that has received from time to time Jewish immigrants, especially during times of stress in the Mid-dle East and Europe such as the time of the Jewish wars with Rome and the fall of Jerusalem (70 CE) and the Nazi pogroms during the Third Reich.

In the dialogue at Cochin it soon became apparent that the tur-bulent history of the Jews in Europe was not of any real significance in their meeting with Asian Christians. A different and yet common issue surfaced. The Jewish theologians discovered that those who had persecuted them in Europe were also the burden of Asian Christians. Having listened to presentations of the history of Christianity in Asia during the colonial period, the Jewish theologians had this to say,

> If Christianity is foreign to Asian religious tradition, why do you still remain a Christian? Why bother with Christianity after all? Is it not the

aim of Asian Christians to get rid of the Christian faith rather than to try to come to terms with it when it has caused so much suffering and pain as well as carving so deep a scar on the soul of the people? How is the biblical faith relevant to Asian spirituality? In what way does the Bible, an ancient book from another religious tradition, speak to or contribute to Asian realities?[4]

These are searching questions that expose the problem and the complexity of being Christians in Asia. Why not return to the religions of our ancestors that European and American missionaries meddled with? Why remain Christians?

Though some Christians in Asia have reverted to their ancient faith traditions, many have chosen to remain Christian and have responded to this complex problem broadly in one of two ways. One is to continue as European Christians in Asia. These Christians parade the supposed superiority of the Christian religion in one or another of its denominational form drawing spiritual and doctrinal nourishment from the West. They continue a colonial tradition in a post-colonial period either as conservative evangelicals or as European liberals in Asian guise.

The second is to struggle with the problem of what being a Christian in Asia entails with the assumption, if not conviction, that biblical faith is not necessarily opposed to Asian spirituality; and to assert that an ancient book from a Jewish religious tradition together with its Christian addition and interpretation (the "New Testament") adds to rather than detracts from the mix of religious traditions in Asia as borne by their adherents.

In taking this position it is essential for Asian Christians to address the colonial factor, which may be formulated as a question: "How can we be faithful to Jesus Christ in Asia while being unfaithful to the colonial entrapments with which Jesus Christ was brought to Asia?" Underlying this question is the realisation that, ironically, the one who was convicted by an empire was later housed in another empire as one who inhabits and blesses the empire. Thus, the Jesus who came to Asia during the colonial period came as a prisoner of an ideology and its practice, which is "colonialism".

In his play "The Gold-Crowned Jesus," the Korean *minjung* poet Kim Chi Ha,[5] who was imprisoned and tortured for his dissident writings, gives an indication of how Jesus is to be freed from this colonial entrapment. The play alludes to the resurrection. Jesus is a gold-crowned statue in a cathedral. A leper who has come into the cathedral seeking warmth from the winter cold is surprised to hear the statue speaking to him. Jesus begs him to remove the gold crown and free him from the cement in which he is encased and held prisoner. Jesus pleads with the leper:

> You are the only one who can do it. And through your deeds, and with the help of your people, I will establish the kingdom of heaven on earth for all. It is your poverty, your wisdom, your generous spirit, and, even more, your courageous resistance against injustice that makes all this possible. . . . Remove this prison of cement. It is sufficient I keep the crown of thorns. The crown of gold is merely the insignia of those ignorant, greedy, and corrupt people who value only displays of external pomp and showy decorations. Wearing it, I was tarnished, and neither free nor able to speak until you came along. The gold is of no value to me, but can be so to you. Take it and share it with your friends.[6]

The leper demurs saying that he would be accused of stealing. After much persuasion he removes the gold crown from Jesus's head and frees him, but is promptly arrested.

Kim Chi Ha does not address the colonial period (although actually Korea was colonised by Japan), but a situation that arose during the neo-colonial period that carried on many of the tendencies that were evident in the ideology of colonialism. One important strand of this ideology is its pretension that colonialism is good for you. Thus the British Empire claimed to be a "commonwealth"; and the Japanese Imperial depredations into Korea, Taiwan, and China, and later into other Asian countries during the Second World War, were justified as creating "the Greater East-Asia Co-prosperity Sphere". The real interest of colonialists, however, was to subjugate and exploit the colonies. Another Korean Christian activist, Oh Jae-shik, describes how this mind-set was turned into action during the dictatorships that afflicted Asian nation-states during the 1970s and 1980s under the pretext of developing the nation and the people, and often did so with the collusion of religious authorities:

> When the development decade was launched, its declared aim was to tackle questions of poverty and not the poor, hunger and not the hungry. I do not know whether it was a calculated attempt or a latent process to separate the issue of poverty from the person, people. At any rate, it separated the two. The issue of poverty then became a material

matter not a spiritual challenge, a matter of economics not of politics. It was a clear distortion of the issue of poverty. When separated from the individual, the issue of poverty then became that of matter, objectifiable materials and then manageable objects. Insofar as this matter was the only factor that was significant, multiplication and quantification were what were needed. In order to achieve such a goal, implementation of a centrally planned scheme was the prime step. For the sake of the primary goal, elimination of obstacles including people has had the moral blessing not only of the power centers but also of certain religious circles. Development programs pledged to eliminate poverty from the earth have, in many instances, gone against the interests of the poor themselves.[7]

The workers, intellectuals and activists who exposed these dictatorial/colonial mind-sets in Asian countries were severely punished, and some were even assassinated. Colonialism continues in many forms and in several guises even today in several Asian countries and those who expose and resist it are persecuted.

It is the continued and ever changing impact of colonialism, both from the West and from the East, that the umbrella phrase "critical engagement in the Asian context" is expected to address.[8] That is a task for theology in Asia as a whole. In this chapter we will concern ourselves with one part of that larger task, namely, reading the Bible in Asia and the field of biblical studies with a presupposition that we have already surfaced. This is to view the Bible and Christian faith traditions as adding to the Asian religious mix and in the process being critiqued and even freed of colonial encumbrances. What Kim Chi Ha attempted in his play "The Gold-crowned Jesus," interplaying a biblical theme with Korean *minjung* culture, was not peculiar to him. This method was and still is widespread in Asia.[9]

Hence, instead of ploughing critically through the whole history of "historical criticism" as it has been taught and practised in the West as the major component of biblical studies to arrive at what we should be doing in Asia, we will begin with examples of how the Bible was received in Asia and then work backwards to describe approaches appropriate for biblical criticism in Asia and the faith expressions that emanate from them.

THE RECEPTION OF THE BIBLE IN ASIA

Three realities about the Bible, which are usually clouded over by issues of doctrine and Christian tradition, become apparent in the various ways in which the Bible was received in Asia.

The first is that the Bible is in the public domain, and therefore could be received and interpreted in myriad differing ways depending on the standpoint of the receiver. Doctrinal controls on interpretation seldom if ever work.

The second is that the Bible is literature. It is composed of many literary genres, such as narratives, legends, stories or fables, and poetry. It contains myths, historical accounts, legal codes, wisdom sayings, songs, and so on. There are the words of God addressed to people and the words of the people addressed to God. The simplistic position that the Bible is the definitive word of God and has to be accepted as such tends to obscure this fact and ends in confusion. For instance, every time a person adduces a biblical verse in support of a theological position another could find another verse that says something different.

The third is that it is an ancient book, the latest of the writings in it being at least one thousand eight hundred years old. How is this gap to be bridged? In order to make it address us directly as the word of God, attempts are often made to modernise it with interpretative translations that paper over the seams, contradictions and ancient world-views inherent in the Bible. This approach complicates rather than addresses the problems raised by this question.

These three realities either singly or in combination raise several questions for Christian theology. If the Bible is to be understood primarily as literature and recognised as ancient literature, how is it to be understood as the word of God for us today? Given the variety of literary genres and the fact that there are several literary layers in the Bible, how is it to be interpreted? Finally, what is the relationship between the Bible and the doctrines and dogma that are supposed to be derived from it? These are important and complex questions that need to be faced. However, to take an *a priori* stand and then try to impose it on how the Bible is to be received and understood would be misguided. There are no easy answers. Yet, the ways in which the Bible has been received in Asia provide some helpful clues.

MOHANDAS K. GANDHI–JESUS THE SATYAGRAHI

"Mohandas K. Gandhi–Jesus the Supreme Satyagrahi," which is a chapter in M. M. Thomas, *The Acknowledged Christ of the Indian Renaissance*, prompted me to examine Gandhi's cross-scriptural hermeneutics. As a parallel and in some ways a response to Raymond Panikkar's, *The Unknown Christ of Hinduism* (1964), Thomas from India wrote his book to show "how some of the foremost spiritual leaders of the Indian renaissance, especially Neo-Hinduism, sought to understand the meaning of Jesus Christ and Christianity for religion and society in renascent India."[10] Though his book also shows how some of the representatives of the Indian church got entangled with the thoughts of these Hindu activists and were often bested, the real contribution of his book lies along two important lines that provide a perspective for grasping their thinking. First, there is the immediacy of praxis. As he says, "I am deeply concerned with men's reflections on the truth of Jesus Christ in the context of their grappling with the meaning of life in concrete situations."[11] The second line becomes clear in the exchanges between missionaries, who were concerned to maintain the so-called verities of the faith, and these thinkers, who had their own ways of approaching the Bible and Christianity. To borrow a phrase from another Indian theologian, Stanley Samartha, a Hindu response can only be to an "Unbound Christ".[12]

A somewhat similar exchange seems to be taking place today in China between the so-called "cultural Christians" working within the Academy of Social Sciences in Beijing and elsewhere and some of the representatives of the Chinese Church. Instead of griping, our response should be one of celebration that the Jesus whom the church proclaims can and indeed does break free from the dogmatic shackles of the church to speak in ever new and fresh ways. Consequently, we need not be covert and look for Christ incognito or unknown from a Christian standpoint, but rather learn from the Jesus who is incarnated in the thoughts and actions of others. With this perspective, we approach the thinking of Gandhi with particular attention to his cross-scriptural hermeneutics.

As Thomas notes, Gandhi was not a systematic thinker or philosopher. "He was primarily a man of political and social action, inspired by a religious interpretation of human existence."[13] While Thomas is right in saying that Gandhi was inspired by a religious interpretation of human existence as the basis for his political and social action, the concepts of *satya* (truth), *ahimsa* (non-violence) and *satyagraha* (truth-force or soul-force), which formed the essential framework of his religious vision, were not primarily derived from any particular religion, but rather evolved from what he calls *My Experiments with Truth*, which is his autobiography (from childhood to 1921), written in Gujarati.[14] As far as religion goes, he kept his promise to his mother that as a *vaishnavite* he would not veer from being a vegetarian; and time and again speaks of God's guidance in many matters. But the religious concepts that actually guided his thinking and action arose from specific incidents during his extended sojourns in South Africa where he had to contend with discrimination on the basis of colour and class that adversely affected the Indians whom he represented as a lawyer.

Thus, for instance, while the idea of non-violent resistance in dealing with white officialdom in South Africa informed his thinking and actions, he was unhappy calling it "passive resistance". It was much later that "passive resistance" became the more positive "*satyagraha*". In chapter 103 of his autobiography entitled "The birth of Satyagraha" he writes,

> The principle called Satyagraha came into being before that name was invented. . . . In Gujarati also we used the English phrase 'passive resistance' to describe it. When in a meeting of Europeans I found that the term 'passive resistance' was too narrowly construed . . . it was clear that a new word must be coined by the Indians to designate their struggle.
>
> But I could not for the life of me find out a new name, and therefore offered a nominal prize through Indian Opinion [a journal started in South Africa] to the reader who made the best suggestion on the subject. As a result Maganlal Gandhi [his cousin] coined the word 'Sadagraha' (Sat=truth, Agraha=firmness) and won the prize. But in order to make it clearer I changed the word to 'Satyagraha', which has since become current in Gujarati as a designation for the struggle.

The term *ahimsa* was also born in a similar manner. In chapter 86, "A Tussle with Power," Gandhi narrates an incident in which he had occasion to expose and challenge the corrupt practices of two white officials, whose biased actions affected the people of colour in the Transvaal. He gathered enough evidence against them and, with the help of the police commissioner, brought these two to trial. But to Gandhi's chagrin an all-white jury dismissed the charges against them. However, their guilt was so patent that the government cashiered both of them. Later on both could find jobs in the Johannesburg municipality, provided Gandhi did not object; and Gandhi did not. This was but one of many actions in which Gandhi came to practice *ahimsa*. He writes,

> This attitude of mine put the officials with whom I came in contact perfectly at ease, and though I had often to fight with their department and use strong language, they remained quite friendly with me. I was not then quite conscious that such behaviour was part of my nature. I learnt later that it was an essential part of Satyagraha, and an attribute of ahimsa. . . . This ahimsa is the basis of the search for truth. I am realizing every day that the search is vain unless it is founded on ahimsa as the basis. It is quite proper to resist and attack a system, but to resist and attack its author is tantamount to resisting and attacking oneself.

In the last chapter (168 "Farewell"), Gandhi brings together the fruits of his experience, and presents his religious vision:

> My uniform experience has convinced me that there is no other God than Truth. And if every page of these chapters does not proclaim to the reader that the only means for the realization of Truth is Ahimsa, I shall deem all my labour in writing these chapters to have been in vain. . . . The little fleeting glimpses . . . that I have been able to have of Truth can hardly convey an idea of the indescribable lustre of Truth, a million times more intense than that of the sun we daily see with our eyes. In fact what I have caught is only the faintest glimmer of that mighty effulgence. But this much I can say with assurance, as a result of all my experiments, that a perfect vision of Truth can only follow a complete realization of Ahimsa.
>
> To see the universal and all-pervading Spirit of Truth face-to-face one must be able to love the meanest of creation as oneself. And a man who aspires after that cannot afford to keep out of any field of life. That is why my devotion to Truth has drawn me into the field of politics; and I can say without the slightest hesitation . . . that those who say that religion has nothing to do with politics do not know what religion means.

Implicit in this religious vision is a maxim that Gandhi would repeat quite often: "God is Truth" or even "Truth is God." This does not mean that for Gandhi God is simply a non-personal principle. He was a theist. Neither does it mean that Truth is the only quality of God. Such a position would be unthinkable for a Hindu. Many qualities and many names could be attributed to God; and yet God as trans-personal transcends all names and attributes.[15] In social and political action, which was his principal area of commitment, Gandhi perceives God as Truth and the only way to apprehend and realise Truth is through *satyagraha* as the practice of *ahimsa*. It is outside the scope of this chapter, which is primarily concerned with Gandhi's hermeneutical method, to illustrate how this approach was reflected in Gandhi's actions where in the interest of Truth he refused to confront violence with violence, choosing rather to accept violence and counter it with the morality inherent in *ahimsa*. In his *The Life of Mahatma Gandhi*, Louis Fischer[16] gives a good account of Gandhi's political career, and what he accomplished in implementing his religious vision.

His reading of the Bhagavad-Gita gives a clue to his approach to religious texts in general, and his hermeneutical method. In chapter 20 of his autobiography, Gandhi narrates his first encounter with the *Gita*. Two theosophist brothers invited him to read the *Gita* with them. At the time he had not even heard of the *Gita* leave alone knowing it in Sanskrit of which he only had a limited knowledge. However, Sir Edwin Arnold's translation named *The Song Celestial,* gripped him. He was particularly struck by verses in the second chapter: "If one ponders on objects of the sense, there springs attraction; from attraction grows desire. Desire flames to fierce passion. Passion breeds recklessness; then the memory all betrayed lets noble purpose go, and saps the mind, till purpose, mind, and man are all undone." He goes on to say, "[This] impression has ever since been growing on me with the result that I regard it today as the book par excellence for the knowledge of Truth. It has afforded me invaluable help in my moments of gloom."

While the *Gita* fascinated him and he held it as the touchstone for evaluating other religions and their scriptures, he had difficulty with one of its central moments in which Lord Krishna persuades Arjuna to perform his duty as a Kshatriya warrior and engage his evil cousins in battle without giving thought to self. Gandhi could not accept this trace of violence as it conflicted with his religious vision. Spurning traditional orthodox Hindu approaches, Gandhi read the *Gita* neither as history nor as legend but as an allegory, so that the struggle between good and evil, truth and falsehood, were constantly warring in one's soul not on a physical battlefield.[17]

One detects in this approach not only the trumping of a religious vision drawn from contextual experiences over a traditional Hindu reading of scripture, but also the primacy given to reason. Since his initial encounter with other religions, especially Christianity and Islam, was through their religionists, who were at great pains to convert him with their unique claims to salvation, Gandhi subjected all claims to reason. In Chapter 40 of his autobiography, he writes:

> It was more than I could believe that Jesus was the only incarnate son of God, and that only he who believed in him would have everlasting life. If God could have sons, all of us were His sons. If Jesus was like God, or God Himself, then all men were like God and could be God Himself. My reason was not ready to believe literally that Jesus by his death and by his blood redeemed the sins of the world. . . . Thus if I could not accept Christianity either as a perfect, or the greatest religion, neither was I then convinced of Hinduism being such. Hindu defects were pressingly visible to me. If untouchability could be a part of Hinduism, it could but be a rotten part or an excrescence. I could not understand the *raison d'etre* of a multitude of sects and castes. What was the meaning of saying that the Vedas were the inspired Word of God? If they were inspired, why not also the Bible and the Koran?

His close friend and associate, C. F. Andrews an English missionary in India, quotes from a later statement of Gandhi on his Hindu faith, which also has a bearing on the way he read other scriptures:

> I do *not* believe in the exclusive divinity of the Vedas. I believe the Bible, the Quran, and the Zend Avesta to be as much divinely inspired as the Vedas. My belief in the Hindu Scriptures does not require me to accept every word and every verse as divinely inspired. Nor do I claim to have any first-hand knowledge of these wonderful books. But I do claim to know and feel the truths of the essential teaching of the Scriptures. I decline to be bound by any interpretation, however learned it may be, if it is repugnant to reason or moral sense.[18]

Gandhi shunned dogmatic positions and abhorred any form of fundamentalism.

A further aspect, among many, in Gandhi's religious vision helps to understand more fully his hermeneutical approach to other religious texts. That is *swadeshi* (patriotism) based on the *Gita* doctrine of *swadharma* (one's given duty), which Gandhi explains: "The *Gita* has very wisely said that the performance of one's own religious duty is preferable to the carrying out of the religious duty of others."[19]

While *satyagraha* as the practice of *ahimsa* embraces the whole world, *swadeshi* is its practice in a particular location at a particular time. Gandhi's most succinct statement on what *swadeshi* means for him is in his speech to missionaries from the Christian Missionary Society in Madras (1906): "Swadeshi is that spirit within us which restricts us to the use and service of our immediate surroundings to the exclusion of the more remote. . . . In the matter of religion I must restrict myself to my ancestral religion. . . . If I find my religion defective I should serve it by purging it of its defects."[20] When C. F. Andrews, to whom Gandhi recounted his address to the missionaries, pressed him to elucidate his position, he answered,

> Our present existence is a discipline which has to be lived within certain rules suited to this present age. We cannot choose at this stage, for instance, our own parents, or own birthplace, or our own ancestry. Why, then, should we claim as individuals the right during this present brief life-period to break through all the conventions wherein we were placed at birth by God Himself?[21]

Andrews interprets,

> The careful study of [his] address on Swadeshi throws light on certain important details in Mahatma Gandhi's own religious position. It is not of the type that ever looks forward (if I judge him rightly) to a single World Religion and a single World State, but rather to separate units working out their individual destiny in cordial, harmonized, friendly relations. There will always be impassable barriers between them which appear to him divinely ordained. . . . Holding strongly a belief in reincarnation, he seems to have no anxiety about reaching any further stage of unification in the present cycle of existence.[22]

To summarise: First, as C.F. Andrews notes, there is an implicit affirmation of plurality in Gandhi's religious vision. According to Gandhi all religions are both equally true and equally imperfect. "For me the different religions are beautiful flowers from the same garden. . . . Therefore, they are equally true, though being received and interpreted through human instruments, equally imperfect."[23] Second, Gandhi's ethics was context specific without getting lost in generalities. Neither was it so context bound as to admit of no change.

Defects had to be purged in the practice of *ahimsa* as the search for truth. Third, while affirming one's contextual standpoint, it was possible to learn and incorporate perspectives from other religious visions to enrich one's perspective: "My approach to other religions . . . is never as a fault-finding critic but as a devotee hoping to find the like beauties in other religions and wishing to incorporate in my own the good I may find in them and miss in mine."[24]

These three aspects underlie his approach to the Bible and Christianity. As a promise to a Christian friend, he read the Bible. He found the Old Testament boring and parts of it even repulsive. He was instead drawn to the figure of Jesus.[25] For Gandhi, Jesus was a supreme *satyagrahi* who practised what he taught in the Sermon on the Mount; and it was that sermon that endeared Jesus to him. Summarising Gandhi's various statements comparing the Sermon on the Mount with the Gita, Anand T. Hingurani writes,

> The message of Jesus Christ, which is essentially the message of Love, is contained, according to Gandhi, in his *Sermon on the Mount*. The same message, i.e., the message of Love, is argued out in the *Bhagavad Gita*. To him it seemed that what the *Sermon* described and in a graphic manner, the *Gita* reduced to a scientific formula. He derived equal joy and comfort from both. The spirit of the *Sermon on the Mount*, he said, competed in almost equal terms with the *Bhagavad Gita* for the domination of his heart.[26]

Gandhi interpreted the person of Jesus as embodying the law or principle of non-violence: "If Jesus represents not a person but the principle of non-violence, India has accepted its protecting power."[27] He speaks of Jesus as one "who came almost to give a new law",[28] which could be understood as a *dharma* that eschewed retaliation and emphasised forgiveness, and promoted a willingness to accept suffering as an inevitable part of the life and practice of non-violence. In taking this position he turned away from placing importance either on the historical Jesus or the atoning work of Jesus. For him the historical Jesus, other than as one who embodied the law of non-violence, was irrelevant: "I should not care if it was proved by someone that the man called Jesus never lived . . . for the Sermon on the Mount would still be true to me."[29]

He dismissed the atoning work of Jesus as something that ethically undercut human responsibility and inculcated indulgence, which he saw as a failing in many though not all Christians.[30] Yet he could speak of himself as a Christian:

> Though I cannot claim to be a Christian in the sectarian sense, the example of Jesus' suffering is a factor in the composition of my underlying faith in non-violence, which rules all my actions, worldly and temporal. Jesus lived and died in vain if he did not teach us to regulate the whole of life by the eternal Law of Love.[31]

Placing the teaching and figure of Jesus within a Hindu framework, Gandhi saw the relevance of Jesus not in a non-repeatable historical event but in its repetition. Addressing Christians, he said,

> God did not bear the Cross only nineteen hundred years ago, but He bears it today, and He dies and is resurrected from day to day. It would be poor comfort to the world, if it had to depend upon a historical God who died two thousand years ago. Do not then preach the God of history but show Him as He lives today through you.[32]

M. M. Thomas summarises Gandhi's position in these words:

> Gandhi in affirming the primacy of the Principle over the Person indicates his conviction that the fulfilment of the moral law of *ahimsa* was an attainment of moral striving and that doctrines of divine atonement and justification in the final analysis probably cut the nerve of moral effort by becoming excuses for sin.[33]

Gandhi often played down the role of preaching and proclamation asserting that truth communicates itself and needs no artful acts of persuasion.[34] Instead, he called for a Jesus-lived life from Christians that would spurn the accoutrements of western Christianity, which were being imposed on Indian Christians. He decried Indian Christianity that required converts to wear western clothes and have a bottle of brandy in one hand and a piece of beef in the other.[35] He was particularly impressed with Kali Charan Bannerjee, who kept his Bengali cultural identity though he had become a Christian.[36] Colonialism had to be countered even in its religious guise. Andrews provides a letter from Rabindranath Tagore to a missionary intending to proceed to India, as a good illustration of a position that Gandhi would also endorse:

Do not be always be trying to preach your doctrine, but give yourself in love. Your Western mind is too much obsessed with the idea of conquest and possession; your inveterate habit of proselytism is another form of it. Christ never preached himself or any dogma or doctrine; he preached the love of God. The object of a Christian should be to be like Christ.[37]

Despite the strenuous efforts of Christians of many denominational affiliations to convert him to Christianity, he resolutely remained a Hindu. He held that Jesus does not belong just to one religious group but to all people; and his main criticism of Indian Christians was that they do not live by the Sermon on the Mount but have been seduced either by western colonial civilisation and missions or the sop of material advancement offered by the British Raj.[38]

While one may not totally agree with the way in which Gandhi harmonised the teaching of Jesus with his ascetic life-style, his hermeneutical method, which was shaped by his praxis, has much to offer. Principal in his approach is the rejection of all forms of fundamentalism and the importance given to reason, refusing to accept any interpretation of any religious text that was repugnant to moral sense. Rejecting any competition between religions that would lead to the collision between their adherents,[39] he also shunned any attempt to collapse all religions into the mush of an assumed world religion. Realising that all religions are true but imperfect because of the human agency involved, he advocates that we learn from one another seeking the best in every religion. His argument that western Christianity, by and large, has misconstrued both the figure and message of Jesus is well taken. Conversion, if it arises out of genuine conviction, he would argue, should not mean denationalisation. He recovers Jesus as an "Asiatic" who can and does break free from colonial interpretations to speak in ever fresh and new ways.

LAKSHMAN WICKREMESINGHE—
CHRISTIANITY MOVING EASTWARDS

Gandhi read the Bible from a Hindu standpoint. Lakshman Wickremesinghe read Hindu scriptures from a Christian standpoint and used his reading of Hindu scriptures to reformulate the Christian faith.

Wickremesinghe was a rather complex character. A few biograph-ical notes may help to understand both his concerns and his approach. At the university he scored a brilliant first class honours degree in political science and economics. With his academic achievement he could have entered any lucrative secular profession of his choice. Instead, he trained for the priesthood in England (Keble College, Oxford), and was ordained a priest there. He returned to Sri Lanka to become the chaplain of the University at Peradeniya.

In 1962, at the age of 35, he was consecrated Bishop of the Kurunagala Diocese, which his predecessor, Bishop Lakdasa de Mel, had created in the heyday of indigenisation. Given his family back-ground and education, the Kurunagala Diocese was quite a challenge. He came from an affluent family. His father was a well-known intel-lectual and was the first native regional governor, and was personal advisor to the first prime minister of independent Ceylon (later Sri Lanka). His mother was a descendent of one of the old Sinhala aris-tocratic families. Yet, he had to learn to be a shepherd of a diocese that had Sinhala aristocrats as well as those from the Sinhala lower castes, the so-called "untouchables". His diocese also covered the hill country where there were descendants of indentured Tamil labour-ers, whom the British colonial government brought to Sri Lanka from India to work in the tea estates. Some of these were Christians and belonged to his diocese. Political differences cut across all these groups. The diocese was a bewildering social and political mix. With toughness and good humour he held all together. It was not unusual at diocesan meetings (at a few of which I was present as a guest) for some to address him as "Lord Bishop" and others of a different polit-ical bent to address him as "Comrade Bishop". He had good rela-tions with the Buddhist clergy and intelligentsia in his area; and made Buddhist practices, such as meditation or contemplation (*bhavana*), an integral part of his spiritual discipline. Yet, as an Anglo-Catholic, he also embraced that rich liturgical tradition.

His praxis extended beyond the work in his diocese to participate in the trade union movement in Sri Lanka, especially through the work of the Christian Workers' Fellowship, which he helped to found, and to deal with human rights issues through the Civil Rights Movement. Equally important were his experiences in interfaith dia-logue as well as in the participation of movements to secure the rights of the minority Tamil community in the country. Following the racial confrontation in July 1983, when many Tamils lost their lives and property, he visited Tamil people in refugee camps to listen to and to comfort those in pain and even receive their anger at the majority Sinhala community. Towards the end of that year his health collapsed, and he died of a heart attack.

Eclectic, mystic and activist, I began to understand his theological approach especially through two of the many conversations I had with him. The first was during the 1970s when as young theologians from all parts of Asia we met in the Commission on Theological Concerns of the Christian Conference of Asia. At that time we were heavily influenced by the approach of the Taiwanese theologian Choan Seng Song who argued in his article, "From Israel to Asia—A Theological Leap: A Methodological Enquiry,"[40] that it was necessary to break free from the Greek and Teutonic captivity of Asian theology and do theology in Asia using Asian resources based on Asian experiences. Wickremesinghe countered this approach saying to me, "You fellows think that by ridding theology in Asia of its foreign influences you would have pure Asian theology. This is not possible, and even if possible is not desirable. We inherit from many sources—Jerusalem, Athens, London, Benares and many other places. The issue is not a matter of a theology purged of foreign influences but a theology rich with many traditions that speaks to and receives from the contexts in which we live."

The second conversation had to do with the experiences out of which theology should arise. Wickremesinghe upbraided me with the limited approach of some Asian theologians: "The trouble with you people [Protestants] is that God is only in your head. You have no understanding of the popular experience of the Divine as blessing through visual and tactual worship. Neither do you have any understanding of the mystic experience of the Divine as the Cosmic Christ."

Only in 1979, after eighteen years as bishop and four years before he died, did he begin to bring together his experiences and ideas in some important articles. One was the D. T. Niles Memorial Lecture entitled "Living in Christ with People" in which he admits that "one's class position, cultural environment, ecclesiastical inheritance, biblical perspective and personal temperament shapes one's inner perceptions."[41] In this essay, he draws heavily on Hindu mythology and presents complex ideas that may have found better expression in book form. Yet, it provides enough of an insight into his method.

He takes the story of Markandeya, a mighty sage, from the *Matsya Purana* as a parable for presenting the history of the Asian Church. The *Matsya Purana* (the ancient chronicle of Matsya or Fish) narrates the story of one of the ten major avatars or incarnations of the god Vishnu. It is a composite work probably written around 500–250 BCE. Markandeya is an ancient rishi or sage and figures as a legend in many Hindu scriptures. Wickremesinghe uses the story in the *Matsya Purana* as an interpretative tool to treat the theme of "people" under three headings: first "people" in the sense of multitudes (*ochlos*) as opposed to the elite; second "people" in the sense of nations (*ethnē*) with each nation having its own religio-cultural tradition; and third "people" in the sense of the Christian community (*laos*).

The *Matsya Purana* narrates the experiences of Markandeya in the interval between the dissolution and recreation of the universe.[42] He is in the body of the god Vishnu, which reclines on the primordial waters of chaos. Wandering around within the body of Vishnu, the sage beholds the ideal vision of what the created world should look like—each caste working in its appointed place and the four stages of life[43] operating with full effect in human lives. He experiences order and is filled with confidence. He then falls out of the slightly open lips of Vishnu into the primordial waters of chaos and is bewildered, afraid and confused. He is taken up into the body of Vishnu and wanders in it, but falls out again into the acosmic watery womb. However, this time as he struggles to stay afloat to re-enter the cosmic order, he is able to behold the body of Vishnu from outside in a series of archetypal images: first as the cosmic man (*narayana*) reclining on the acosmic waters, symbolising elemental chaos; then as a cosmic gander, the sound of whose melodic breathing, *ham* (inhale)-*sa* (exhale), is the melody of the creation and dissolution of the universe; and finally as a luminous divine child at play who is untroubled by the watery chaos on which he reclines. After narrating the story in greater detail than given here, Wickremesinghe introduces his approach:

> This experience of immersion in the elemental waters of fear, chaos and potential disintegration, and the three visions of Vishnu in different archetypal symbols as seen by someone reared within the

socio-economic and religio-cultural traditions of Hinduism will be the framework for my theological reflections on the theme of "Living in Christ with People" in the three aspects I have previously mentioned.[44]

Markandeya within the cosmic order that is congenial to his nature and style of life is like that of the Asian churches during the colonial period. Their self-assurance, however, collapsed during the post-colonial period with the unexpected immersion into the elemental waters of fear and confusion with possible disintegration as they lost their position of privilege. There was a loss of morale and a sense of direction in the churches when there was a revival of indigenous religions and the renaissance of ancient cultures derived from them to speak to life in the present through new ways in art, drama and politics. Markandeya's re-entry into the cosmic order, as it would be for the Asian churches, is infused with the experience of being immersed in the acosmic waters with its potential for destruction and dissolution: "His self-understanding of life in its totality is now ambivalent, because his experience of what is real is a mixture of the overt vision of constructive harmony and the underlying fear of destructive chaos." When Markandeya slips into the watery chaos for a second time,

> What dominates his attention now and guides his struggled swimming in the acosmic waters is the vision of this gigantic man glowing with wonderful luminosity. His ambivalent self-understanding of life remains, but is now illumined and empowered by the dominant vision of what is *human*, both as a person and humanity in its totality.[45]

In using this myth, what Wickremesinghe attempts to bring out is the clash between cosmos and chaos, which is not only a theme of a creation story, as it is in the Judaeo-Christian tradition, but is an ever recurring human experience as an interplay between certitude and ambiguity and between conviction and confusion. In this situation of ambiguity, in which inaction is not an option, there is given a heavenly vision of all contradictions being held together as in the vision Krishna vouchsafes to Arjuna as he hesitates to engage his unrighteous cousins in battle (Bhagavad-Gita).[46]

From this essay I select one of the several instances he gives of how this method operates. It has to do with political engagement, which he deals with under the category of solidarity with the *ochlos*. He cites two ideologies imported from the West but now indigenised in Asia, namely indigenous welfare capitalism and indigenous Marxian socialism. He rejects the ideology of welfare capitalism as it only reifies elitism and privilege and offers no liberation for the disadvantaged. Instead he opts for indigenous Marxian socialism. He argues that socialism has to be influenced rather than dominated by Marxism, because class analysis alone will not deal with issues of racism and sexism. Nor will it positively and adequately acknowledge the role of religion in the lives of people.

Having taken this option he is also conscious of the demonic aspects inherent in this ideology as in any ideology, which introduces an element of ambiguity that novelists and dramatists in Sri Lanka have explored. Yet for him as for them the option for indigenous Marxian socialism remains, but in his case is informed by a Christian perspective:

> [Indigenous Marxian socialism] means giving concrete priority to the image of Jesus as prophetic contestant and martyr. But we are also constrained to hold this image in dialectical tension with the image of Jesus as companion and rehabilitator of sinners and outcasts, and also as the self-sacrificing satyagrahi converting enemies with the soul-force of vicarious suffering love . . . Christ-centred theory and social action must creatively interact upon each other.[47]

He sees this happening with M.M. Thomas of India, Edicio de la Torre in the Philippines and Kim Chi-ha in Korea, and I would add also in Wickremesinghe's sacrificial ministry within the church and the broader community.

With an extended treatment of Markandeya's experience in perceiving the cosmic gander, when he was in the acosmic waters for a second time, Wickremesinghe expounds its implications for experiencing God (the Cosmic Christ) as mystery through mystic contemplation. "The inward rhythmic breathing of the Supreme Self is made to become concurrent with the disciplined rhythmic breathing of the yogi [Markandeya] who . . . finally becomes aware of identity with the Supreme Self." In the midst of uncertainty and turbulence, mystic contemplation is avenue for equanimity, which is essential for social involvement and action as selfless service. In drawing on the theme of people as *ethnē*, from whom we receive so much as Asian

Christians, he says, "Theology is coloured by metaphysics as much as by ideology."[48]

Since my primary concern is not so much with his theology as his method, I will only pay attention to some of the important methodological points that he makes in this and other essays.

First, in a lecture on ecclesiology in Asia, he states that our primary concern in dealing with our heritage is not to be imitative or even adaptive but innovative, so that there is a creative interplay between the Judaeo-Christian tradition and Asian religious traditions.[49]

Second, in working out this interplay it needs to be remembered that the focal images with which the various religious traditions view transcendent reality and its relation to spatio-temporal reality are both different and exclusive. Yet, it is within the context of conflicting truth claims that inter-religious dialogue takes place. In this praxis, where disagreement need not be the cause for conflict, participants agree that while the focal image of each is central, unique and normative for all, it is not complete. There could be a meaningful borrowing from other traditions arising out of the experiences and encounters that take place in dialogue.[50]

His basic position and plea is that we need to broaden the mythological pool of Christianity in Asia if we are to respond both theologically and pastorally as we engage critically in the contexts of Asia. It is this process of decolonisation and broadening that he has in mind when he speaks of "Christianity moving eastwards."[51]

For Wickremesinghe, as for the Asian theologians who draw from their indigenous religious heritages, these themes are not mere window dressing to present Christian ideas, as it would be for those who are concerned with indigenisation. Rather, these are heuristic tools for opening out and augmenting Christian theological concerns and providing new perspectives not always obvious in the Judaeo-Christian tradition.

AHN BYUNG-MU—JESUS AND
THE MINJUNG MOVEMENT

The third example of reading the Bible in the context of Asia comes from one of the many Korean scholars who joined a broad coalition of movements to try to bring to an end the string of dictatorships, which President Park Chung-hee initiated, and to install democracy in Korea.

Under the somewhat innocuous heading of "the mission of the church in Korea", I was responsible as executive secretary for theological concerns of the Christian Conference of Asia (CCA) for arranging a theological dialogue in Seoul from 22–24 October, 1979. Around fifteen Korean theologians met with about the same number of other Asian theologians. All of the Korean theologians present at this dialogue had decided to explore the possibilities of *minjung* culture for doing theology in Korea to give depth to their political commitment. It was at this symposium that the term "Minjung Theology" was coined to signify what was emerging as an indigenous Korean theology.

A day after the meeting, President Park Chung-hee was assassinated. His assassination, though only an attempt at an internal military coup, set off a number of popular uprisings. After a time, when victory seemed assured, the armed forces intervened to put down with much brutality the movements for democracy. Of these the most vicious was the massacre of civilians in the southern city of Kwangju. Several *minjung* theologians who were involved in these protests were also arrested and dismissed from their teaching positions.

During this period, when the Korean theologians were imprisoned, the papers presented at the symposium were translated, however inadequately, and smuggled out. The failed attempt for a coalition for democracy in Korea and the suffering that ensued coloured the rewriting and editorial shaping of the papers. I was the ghost editor. I went back to Korea and had all the edited, and even rewritten, papers read and approved by the authors after they came out of prison; and the collection was published under the title *Minjung Theology: People as the Subjects of History*.[52] This is a thumbnail sketch of the immediate context.

But, if we are to understand Ahn's method we also need to have some idea of the broader context out of which Minjung Theology arose. Two distinguishable strands of religio-political culture, each with its own social base, seem to operate in Korea. One strand, with its roots in the aristocracy (*yangban*) and the ruling elite of Korea, is driven by Confucianism and state-recognised Buddhism. The other is the religio-political culture of the masses or *minjung*, which has its

roots in Shamanism and several forms of popular religions including popular Buddhism. The Korean term "*han*" is used to describe
the situation of the *minjung*. The term has no real English equivalent.
Generally speaking it could be described as an intense and indescrib-
able oppressive feeling of injustice and subjugation that is the experience not only of individuals but also of a whole subaltern society.
Han is something that has accumulated over generations. In the case
of individuals it could lead to all kinds of maladies and tendencies
towards self-destruction. Shamans are then called upon to release the
han through various ceremonies (*han-puri*).[53] *Han* could also be chan-
nelled creatively into drama and dance through which the *minjung*
tell their story. It could also be harnessed as a socio-political force in
movements for liberation.[54]

The Christian response to both cultures is somewhat mixed. When
the missionaries came to Korea in the early nineteenth century,
attempts to influence the aristocracy, with the premise that if the
leaders were converted the masses would follow, failed. So, work
started among the *minjung* and yielded results. As was normal missionary practice, the Bible was translated into the country's language.
However, it was not translated using Chinese characters, which are
best suited for expressing metaphysical and philosophical ideas, but
the phonetic Korean script, *Hangul*, which was better suited for narration and stories and which the *minjung* could read. Consequently,
Korean converts seized on biblical narratives and the parables as vehi-
cles for expressing their stories and feelings. For instance, the story of
the exodus was historicised in a Korean way in which Egypt became
Japan and the people of Israel became the people of Korea. Despite
the urgings of missionaries to stay clear of politics, Korean Christian messianic movements joined forces with other peoples' messianic
movements for liberation as in the Donghak Revolution in 1894 and
more importantly in the 1919 March First Independence Movement
to rid Korea of the colonial and military rule of the Japanese empire.[55]

This part of Korean Christian history lies buried under later developments. Following the usual tendency to move upwards socially,
Christians were later attracted to the culture of the *yangban*, which
now sways the majority of Korean Christians. This trend utilises a
theology of release from personal sins (*han*) through the sacrificial
death and resurrection of Jesus Christ. It is a personalised religion
of atonement. Minjung Theology, however, refused and still refuses

to follow this trend, and seeks to base itself on the early history of Christianity in Korea and the religio-political culture of the *minjung* and their condition of *han* as an unresolved, internalised "lump" in their being and existence. It is against this total social and historical background of Korean *minjung* culture that Ahn Byung-mu read and interpreted Mark and the other two synoptic gospel accounts in Matthew and Luke.[56]

The linking with Korean *minjung* culture and history was neither a natural evolution from the past nor was it a result of scholarly research. Korean theologians in one way or another were shocked into embracing *minjung* culture and in doing so rediscovered their past. In the preface to his book *Jesus of Galilee*, Ahn speaks of his own experience of "conversion".

Following the predilection for history and narrative in early Korean Christianity, his primary interest had always been the historical Jesus. With this interest in view, he studied in Germany. He read all the material he could find both in German and in English, but his quest to find the historical Jesus failed. With the use of form criticism and the history of traditions, Ahn found that Rudolf Bultmann had fractured "the traditional, metaphysically formulated images of Jesus." But his methodology ended up putting forward the "Kerygmatic Christ" (the Jesus Christ of the church's proclamation), but left in limbo the search for the historical Jesus. Should not there be a historical core within the Kerygmatic Christ? Though Bultmann's students, Günther Bornkamm, with whom Ahn studied, and Ernst Käsemann raised this question, Ahn discovered that they could not proceed much further than Bultmann. They too were wedded to the methodology of form criticism and attempted to find the historical Jesus through the Kerygmatic Christ. Redaction criticism, succeeding form criticism, prevented the shredding of the gospel narratives, and instead highlighted the theological concern of each writer. But it went no further in finding and elucidating the historical Jesus who lay behind all the Kerygmatic traditions and theologies. Ahn summarises his encounter with German biblical studies: "My attempt to search for Jesus with the Western theological paradigm brought me nothing but agnosticism toward historical Jesus." Yet, his attachment to the historical Jesus remained. So, returning to Korea, he found himself moving along two parallel tracks: "the Jesus who motivated me" (the preaching track) and "the Jesus of [Western] hermeneutical conclusion" (the teaching track).[57]

The shock event that propelled him from academic study fashioned in the West into dealing with Korean reality was the death of Jeon-Tae-il in November 1970. He was a factory tailor who studied the labour laws of the country, and organised his fellow workers and fought for better working conditions. He failed; and in despair immolated himself in a market place as a public act of protest. Already touched by the many tragic events happening in Korea, Ahn viewed Jeon Tae-il as representative of the plight of the *minjung* and his self-immolation as a self-transcending act. Ahn then joined the movement for democracy, and was dismissed from his professorship and later imprisoned in 1976.[58]

For Ahn, as for all *minjung* theologians, Jesus the crucified and risen Messiah was not just someone who was releasing them from sin to join a party of pilgrims on the way to the promised land (read "heaven"), but one who was calling them to follow him into historical engagement in the here and now. It was this conviction that made Ahn return to the quest for the historical Jesus who was alive and active in the *han*-ridden history of the *minjung*. As he puts it:

They [Westerners] have raised questions based on their own cultural value system including theologies formulated from Christianity. We belong within radically different cultural boundaries. We have suffered also from the different socio-political contexts. Thus our questions cannot be the same as Westerners. The more faithful we are to our own historical context, the more genuine our questions will be.[59]

Suffocated by the long traditions of western Christianity, it took him a long time to realise that only through an immersion into the reality of Korea would help him to raise the right questions in his search for the historical Jesus.

In submitting himself to this process, Ahn did not jettison wholesale the historical critical methods that he had learned. Neither did he ignore the writings of western New Testament scholars. He refers to some with approval, challenges the positions of others, and amplifies the conclusions of still others. His writings are replete with footnotes to their works. The problem was not so much with the method as with the subject using the method. Bultmann provided him with an insight into the whole process of biblical studies. It is that the way a question is shaped determines the answer. Till the point of his "conversion" he had simply accepted both the theological questions and answers fashioned in the West in western terms as his own. Consequently, "I—a historical being—was omitted in my questioning about Jesus." Immersion in the reality of Korea made him ask questions about the historical Jesus in a different way. In seeking answers he found that he could reuse methods that he had learned, but had to reshape them to answer the questions he was raising.[60]

Form criticism, which seeks the original life-setting (*Sitz im Leben*) of pericopies, Ahn felt would simply lead him back to the scepticism he had earlier experienced in his search for the historical Jesus. This problem is inherent to form criticism. Martin Noth, a well-known German scholar of the Old Testament, who used form criticism and the history of traditions for historical research, is often sceptical about the historical reality of Israelite figures. For instance, after examining the traditions about Moses, he comes to the conclusion that Moses was not originally connected with the Exodus, Sinai or Wilderness traditions, but only in a peripheral way was related to the Occupation tradition. It was in the history of traditions that he came to occupy the position of being a great Israelite leader.[61]

Ahn found redaction criticism more promising but recognised that traditional redaction critics simply pointed to editorial links between pericopies, but did not take these editorial statements as historically, sociologically and theologically significant. To demonstrate his divergence from traditional redaction critics, he takes Mark 1:14–15 as a key passage for his exposition of Mark's gospel account: "Now after John was arrested, Jesus came into Galilee, preaching the gospel of God, and saying, 'The time is fulfilled, and the Kingdom of God is at hand; repent and believe in the gospel'." Commenting on this passage he says that most western scholars take verse 14 as an editorial introduction and verse 15 as the core statement about Jesus's ministry. For Ahn, verse 14 is important and provides two important points:

> It introduces a political event that John the Baptist, the pioneer of Jesus, was arrested. It also indicates that Jesus went to Galilee ruled over by Herod Antipas, the very king who arrested John the Baptist, at the moment of John's arrest. Only based on this pre-understanding can one realize how radical Jesus' proclamation of the Kingdom of God is and how clearly it may reveal the truth about Jesus.

He then goes on to say that it is the *ochlos*, the crowds or multitudes that show the truth about Jesus:

> At first, I considered *ochlos* in Mark as just the oppressed who are poor, weak, and powerless, and as the object of other's help. But after I carefully examined them, I discovered that they are the ones who bear powers that made Jesus be Jesus.[62]

In a revealing comment he made during the discussion at the theological symposium in October 1979, Ahn introduced the avenue for his search for the historical Jesus: "Jesus is not the key for understanding the *ochlos* but rather the *ochlos* is the key for understanding Jesus." In other words, it is only through the *ochlos* that one could discover the historical Jesus. This was the insight he received as he identified himself, both physically and intellectually, with the *minjung* of Korea. This immersion led him to question assumptions implicit in projections about the Kerygmatic Christ. He is convinced that the Kerygmatic Christ is the construction of the church to bolster its position of privilege using such attributes as Jesus being descended from King David and assertions that he was the son of God. As Ahn points out, in the synoptic tradition Jesus neither used nor claimed this title, preferring the title "son of man" that stressed his humanity. Furthermore, in this tradition Jesus was from Galilee, which was a place of outcasts—the *minjung* of Galilee.[63]

Using his immersion in the Korean historical reality as a key, he asks questions that he is convinced would lead him to the historical Jesus thereby bypassing discussions about the Kerygmatic Christ. Why did Mark write his narrative about Jesus, after Paul had written his letters to the many Gentile churches of his time? Paul's concern was both apologetic and didactic. In writing to the Gentile churches, Paul was not so much concerned with "Jesus after the flesh" (the Messiah) but the crucified and Risen One (the Christ). Mark's interest was different. In essence his concern was to address a historical situation of crisis during the Jewish wars with Imperial Rome when the people were being driven hither and thither like sheep without a shepherd. He finds that the story about Jesus, who was an insignificant figure both from a Jewish and a Roman point of view, was preserved by the *minjung* or *ochlos* of Galilee as one who proclaimed and embodied the kingdom of God as an alternative reality of hope that was crystallised in the resurrection of Jesus. To comment on what Ahn has to say: the resurrection was not a public event; neither was it just the personal experience of a few individuals. Rather, it was the collective bodily experience of the *minjung* who followed him.

For Ahn, the Jesus *minjung* movement was neither something of the past nor geographically confined. Taking this position, he gives a clear statement of his method:

> The history of Jesus' minjung movement has continued until today. This fact can be discovered in world history as a whole. In particular we are experiencing this history of Jesus' movement in Korean history, especially in the recent minjung movement in which we participated directly.
>
> Hence, I have posed the questions that arose from the minjung events in Korea, as the theological questions of this work [Ahn's research and writing]. And I have searched for the answers in Jesus' minjung movement. At the same time, I have tried to re-illuminate the Jesus-events in [terms of] today's minjung movements. Since the situation of Korea is particular, the questions are also particular. Nevertheless, particularity is connected to universality. Therefore, the answers will by no means be useful only to Korea, but also, I think, to others in the world, as they permeate into history.[64]

If we were to ask whether Ahn's presentation of Jesus is historically plausible, the answer would be, in all probability, yes. Because, coming at the same issue with social, economic and political analyses of the time of Jesus, scholars such as John Dominic Crossan have shown that as a carpenter (Greek, *tektōn*; cf. Mark 6:3; Matt 13:55) Jesus fell outside the Roman social structure of patronage and privilege, and as a *tektōn*, also a term of derision, he would have been seen as one who belonged to a group of "expendables", that is, those who were socially and economically of no consequence. From such a position, the message and deeds of Jesus in befriending and giving prominence to the outcasts would have been viewed as sedition.[65] Yet, for all this research, one is still only in the realm of historical probability. Outside the gospel accounts and Christian tradition there are no safe historical records of the life and ministry of Jesus. How could there be? From a Jewish point of view he was uneducated, even though he was well-versed in the Hebrew Scripture, and really did not deserve the title of Rabbi, because he did not maintain Sabbath and purity laws, and was the friend of sinners and tax-collectors. He could not even be labelled a zealot—a revolutionary, though he had zealots in his entourage. From the point of view of Rome he was irrelevant, just another troublemaker who had to be done to death.

If, however, we were to pursue the historical reality of Jesus in and through the Jesus *minjung* movement, as does Ahn, the answer would be a clear "yes". For it is in historical engagement with the *minjung* that one comes to grasp the historical reality of Jesus, the crucified and risen one.

CHARACTER AND ASSUMPTIONS
OF CROSS-TEXTUAL HERMENEUTICS

Instead of consigning these three presentations of cross-textual hermeneutics to the past and treating them as historical oddities, it is important that we identify their character and their universal appeal for the doing of theology in the present, especially in Asia.

Despite their differences, all three practitioners of cross-textual hermeneutics point to certain commonalities. *First*, all three go through something of a traumatic experience (Gandhi in South Africa, Wickremesinghe and Ahn in their homelands) that jettisons them from the comfort of received or inherited circumstances to an orientation with "the people" which we might term the *ochlos* (marginalised) and *ethnē* (nations). We might even call it a "conversion-experience". *Second*, the conversion-experience leads to a particular praxis. The specifics of the praxis urge and shape the engagement with biblical material and Christian traditions. For Gandhi the specifics of his praxis required him to utilise the method of *satyagraha* in the struggle for India's independence. His primary concern was with ethics, so that Jesus comes to him as one who practised non-violence as soul-force for realising truth. Consequently, the historical Jesus was of little or no consequence for him. For Wickremesinghe, the praxis was with social and political engagement in the broad forum of inter-religious dialogue in Asia's struggle for full humanity. His interest was the Cosmic Christ whose address to the present situation could be grasped only by widening the pool of mythological resources for biblical interpretation and action. Ahn was engaged in a particular historical struggle to subvert the history shaped by the *yangban* with the historical memory of the *minjung*. His primary attention was on the historical Jesus who is discoverable only through the Galilean Jesus *minjung* movement interpreted through the Korean *minjung* movement. *Third*, all three refuse to get bogged down with western debates on the course of biblical studies that argue for the so-called "correct method" for interpreting the Bible and thus presenting the Christian faith. For each of them Asian approaches to biblical studies are not only desirable but also essential for making the Bible speak to us today. In taking this position, either implicitly or explicitly, they consider western approaches to biblical studies as attempts to answer questions shaped in the West, which they consider to be of little or no consequence in and for critical engagements in the contexts of Asia.

From the character of these three concrete examples, we could identify some of the principles with which cross-textual hermeneutics operates.

First and foremost, despite the valiant efforts of missionaries to wean us away from our previous religious and cultural heritages, cross-textual hermeneutics asserts that as Asian Christians we inherit two traditions, which is a fact to be celebrated not negated with attempts to kill off the second tradition. Each inherited Asian religious and cultural tradition is therefore not viewed as a dead context to which the Christian tradition or message has to be related. Rather, it is valued as a living text that functions as an interlocutor and makes its own contribution. The hybrid character of Asian Christianity becomes apparent in the usage of terms from Asian languages to translate biblical terms. A typical example would be the terms chosen to translate the word "God"[66] by which a bridge is created between western biblical interpretations and Asian religious worldviews resulting in a constant to and fro traffic of myths, symbols and terms. Another illustration of such two-way traffic is the drawing on Asian religious traditions to express Asian Christian piety in poetry (songs/lyrics) and in art. For instance, the three principal attributes of Brahman—*Sat* (being), *Chit* (intelligence or consciousness) and *Ananda* (bliss)—are used in Indian Christian lyrics to express the Christian Trinity. Another is the use of *Mukti* for salvation in Indian Christian piety. These are not feeble nativistic attempts to return to a vernacular past, as postcolonial critics allege.[67]Rather, instead of always trying to use western and Judaic mythological imagery and religious concepts, which sit uneasily in the vernacular and often carry no real meaning, these draw on a pool of imagery for the

Divine in Asian religious traditions to express Asian Christian piety in Asian languages, The important point to note here is that there is a reverse flow of insights and emphases from Asian religious traditions that both critique and augment biblical perceptions, so that these are not to be treated as simple equivalents of theological terms fashioned in the West.

Second, basing itself on the fact that Asian Christians are by and large religious hybrids, cross-textual hermeneutics addresses "the problem of the two stories" in a particular way. It skirts pointless and even frustrating debates on syncretism, and asserts that what we have inherited through our Asian religious traditions is an authentic repository of God's dealing with Asian people. While taking this position, cross-textual hermeneutics also recognises a problem that is inherent in relating the two traditions, because they do not easily dovetail into each other. In fact, the two are quite often antagonistic because they begin with different focal images of the Ultimate and with different ways of perceiving reality. For example, in Christianity God is thought of as personal whereas in Hinduism and Buddhism the Ultimate is transpersonal. In Christianity reality is perceived largely in historical and anthropocentric terms while in Hinduism and Buddhism perceptions are holistic and cosmic. Hence, not just the confluence but also the tensions between the two need to be recognised and respected.

Instead of a collision between the two, which would result either in the abolition of one of the two stories or falling into the trap of saying "all paths lead to the same goal", there is a stress on sensitive listening to the second tradition in its own terms. This makes it possible to use each tradition to illuminate the other in fresh ways, as we have seen in some detail in the three cases of cross-textual hermeneutics examined above.

Third, cross-textual hermeneutics also assumes that in juxtaposing the Christian biblical tradition with Asian religious and cultural traditions its colonial encumbrances could be shed so that it may speak in a fresh way to Asian realities and be a valid contribution to Asian spirituality.

In the next chapter we will examine some examples of cross-textual reading as typifying assumptions inherent in cross-textual hermeneutics in general; and in the chapters that follow look at other models that exemplify the assumptions inherent in cross-textual hermeneutics in different ways.

Notes

1. See D. Preman Niles, *The Lotus and the Sun: Asian Theological Engagement with Plurality and Power* (Canberra: Barton, 2013), 249–96, for a fuller presentation.

2. In Korean, the term "*minjung*" is used to differentiate the common people from the elite classes called the "*yangban*". More will be said to describe the *minjung* later in this chapter and in chapter 5.

3. Archie C. C. Lee, "Biblical Interpretation as Dialogical Process in the Context of Religious Pluralism," in *The Bible Speaks Today, Essays in Honour of Gnana Robinson*, ed. Daniel J. Muthunayagam (Delhi: ISPCK, 2000), 201–9.

4. Lee, "Biblical Interpretation," 201.

5. Kim Chi-ha, *The Gold-Crowned Jesus and Other Writings*, eds. Chong-sun Kim and Shelly Killen (New York: Orbis, 1978), 85–131.

6. Kim, *Gold-Crowned Jesus*, 124.

7. Oh Jae-shik, "Mission and Development," in *Mission in the Context of Endemic Poverty*, ed. Lourdino A. Yuzon (Singapore: CCA, 1983), 19–20.

8. I prefer this phrase to the over-worked and over-used term "contextualisation". For my argument on this matter see D. Preman Niles, *Critical Engagement in the Asian Context: Implications for Theological Education and Christian Studies* (Hong Kong: Asian Christian Higher Education Institute of the United Board for Christian Higher Education in Asia, 2005), 51–52.

9. For the sake of convenience I would refer the reader to the many essays that employ the method of cross-textual reading in Philip Wickeri, editor, *Scripture, Community, and Mission: Essays in Honour of D. Preman Niles* (Hong Kong: Christian Conference of Asia, London: Council for World Mission, May 2003 second printing).

10. M.M. Thomas, *The Acknowledged Christ of the Indian Renaissance* (Madras: The Christian Literature Society, 1976), xiii.

11. Thomas, *Acknowledged Christ*, xiii.

12. Stanley Samartha, *The Hindu Response to the Unbound Christ* (Madras: C.L.S., 1974).

13. Thomas, *Acknowledged Christ*, 194.

14. Mohandas K. Gandhi, *My Autobiography: The Story of My Experiments with Truth*, translated by Mahadev Desai in 1940. Since several editions are available, I am not giving page numbers but only headings of chapters, which are very brief.

15. Robert Ellsberg, editor, *Gandhi on Christianity* (New York: Orbis, 1991), 71 ("The Nature of God"). In order to reach as wide a readership as possible, Gandhi published his ideas in various journals he founded. Many of these are not easily accessible. Ellsberg has done a great service by going through these journals and collecting what Gandhi had to say on his relationship with Christians and Christianity. Equally useful are two other compilations: *M.K. Gandhi: The Message of Jesus Christ*, Anand T. Hingurani, editor, (Bombay: Bharatiya Vidya Bhavan, 1971) and *M.K. Gandhi: What Jesus Means to Me*, R. K. Prabhu, compiler, (Ahmedabad: Navajivan Publishing House, 1959).

16. Louis Fischer, *The Life of Mahatma Gandhi* (London: Harper Collins, 1997).

17. Fischer, *Mahatma Gandhi*, 47–48.

18. Charles F. Andrews, *Mahatma Gandhi's Ideas Including Selections from His Writings* (London: George Allen & Unwin Ltd, 1929), 36. (Citations are taken from a cheap edition published in 1931.)

19. Andrews, *Gandhi's Ideas*, 129.

20. Ibid., 120.

21. Ibid., 129.

22. Ibid., 127–28.

23. Ellsberg, *Gandhi*, 65.

24. Ibid., 69.

25. Gandhi, *Autobiography*, chapter 20.

26. Hingurani, *Gandhi's Message*, v.

27. Ibid., 63–64.

28. Ellsberg, *Gandhi*, 21–22.

29. Hingurani, *Gandhi's Message*, 65–66.

30. Gandhi, *My Experiments with Truth*, chapter 36. Arguing against the religion of the Plymouth Brethren who said that they have been freed from sin and its consequences, Gandhi said, "I do not seek redemption from the consequences of my sin. I seek to be redeemed from sin itself, or rather the very thought of sin. Until I have attained that end, I shall content to be restless." See also Ellsberg, *Gandhi*, 7.

31. *Harijan: A Journal of Applied Gandhism* (New York & London, January 7,

1939); Ellsberg, *Gandhi*, 26, and R. K. Prabhu, *Gandhi: What Jesus means to Me*, 10.

32. Ellsberg, *Gandhi*, 42.

33. Thomas, *Acknowledged Christ*, 202.

34. Ellsberg, *Gandhi*, 53.

35. Ibid., 38–39.

36. Ibid., 39.

37. Andrews, *Gandhi's Ideas*, 356.

38. Ellsberg, *Gandhi*, 55.

39. Ibid., 64–65.

40. Choan Seng Song, "From Israel to Asia—A Theological Leap: A Methodological Enquiry," *Mission Trends No. 3: Third World Theologies*, eds. Gerald H. Anderson and Thomas F. Stransky, C.S.P. (Grand Rapids: Eerdmans, 1976), 211–22.

41. C. Lakshman Wickremesinghe, "Living in Christ with People," *CTC Bulletin* 5, no. 1–2 (April–August, 1984): 17–34. This lecture was prepared for the 1981 assembly of the Christian Conference of Asia, which had the theme "Living in Christ with People." Marshal Fernando, editor, *The Visionary Wisdom of a People's Bishop* (Colombo: Ecumenical Institute for Study and Development, 2009) has brought together all Wickremesinghe's writings and speeches.

42. *Matsya Purana* 167, 13–66. Wickremesinghe follows in large measure Heinrich Zimmer's interpretation in his *Myths and Symbols in Indian Art and Civilization*, ed. Joseph Campbell (New Jersey: Princeton University Press, 1973), 35–45.

43. In Vedantic Hinduism, human life is believed to be in four stages called "*ashramas*". The first is *brahmacharya* (a celibate learner), *grihastha* (marriage and procreation), *vanaprastha* (the hermit devoted to meditation), *sanniyasa* (the wandering ascetic who moves towards death).

44. Wickremesinghe, "Living in Christ," 18.

45. Ibid., 19.

46. Ibid., 19–20.

47. Ibid., 21.

48. Ibid., 26.

49. C. Lakshman Wickremesinghe, "Ecclesiological Issues Emerging from Asian Manifestations of the Life, Worship and Witness of the Church," *CTC Bul-*

letin 5, no. 1–2 (April–August 1984): 35–38.

50. C. Lakshman Wickremesinghe, "Togetherness and Uniqueness—Living Faiths in Inter-relation," *CTC Bulletin* 5, no. 1–2 (April–August 1984): 9.

51. C. Lakshman Wickremesinghe, "Christianity Moving Eastwards," *CTC Bulletin* 5, no. 1–2 (April–August 1984): 58–68.

52. CTC–CCA, editor, *Minjung Theology: People as the Subjects of History* (Singapore: Christian Conference of Asia & New York: Orbis, 1983).

53. Shamans who are called upon to perform *han-puri* are usually women. For a detailed treatment of *han* and *han-puri,* see Yvonne Lee Young-ja, *Religion, Culture of Han and Han-puri, and Korean Minjung Women: An Interdisciplinary and Post-Colonial Religio-Cultural Analysis of the Indigenous Encounter with the Colonial Religions in Korea* (Denver, Colorado: Iliff School of Theology and Denver University, 1999).

54. See Suh Nam-dong, "Towards A Theology of *Han,*" in *Minjung Theology,* 55–69.

55. See Choo Chai-yong, "A Brief Sketch of Korean Christian History from a *Minjung* Perspective," and Kim Yong-bock, "Korean Christianity as a Messianic Movement of the People," in *Minjung Theology,* 47–119. More information is available in David Suh, *The Korean Minjung in Christ* (Hong Kong: CCA, 1991) and Kim Yong-bock, *Messiah and Minjung* (Hong Kong: CCA, 1992).

56. Ahn Byung-mu, "Jesus and the *Minjung* in the Gospel of Mark," in *Minjung Theology,* 138–52. Ahn Byung-mu, *Jesus of Galilee,* (Hong Kong: Christian Conference of Asia & Seoul: Dr Ahn Byung-mu Memorial Service Committee, 2004). See also his essays, "The Transmitters of the Jesus-event," *CTC Bulletin* 5, no. 3, and 6 no. 1 (December 1984–April 1985): 26–39; "Jesus and People (Minjung)," *CTC Bulletin* 7, no. 3 (December 1987): 7–13 republished in *Asian Faces of Jesus,* ed. R. S. Sugirtharajah (London: SCM, 1993), 163–72.

57. Ahn, *Jesus of Galilee,* 1–5.

58. Ibid., vii–viii.

59. Ibid., 2.

60. For a fuller treatment of Ahn Byung-mu's personal and theological journey with personal interviews, see Volker Küster, "Jesus and the Minjung," in his *A Protestant Theology of Passion: Korean Minjung Theology Revisited* (Leiden: E.J. Brill, 2010), 59–78.

61. Martin Noth, *A History of the Pentateuchal Traditions,* trans. Bernhard W. Anderson (Englewood Cliffs, NJ: Prentice-Hall, 1972), 156–75.

62. Ahn, *Jesus of Galilee*, xii.

63. Ahn Byung-mu, "The Riddle of Jesus" in his *Jesus of Galilee*, 6–30.

64. Ahn, *Jesus of Galilee*, 4.

65. John Dominic Crossan, *Jesus: A Revolutionary Biography* (San Francisco: Harper San Francisco, 1994); Stephen J. Patterson, *Beyond the Resurrection: Rethinking the Death and Life of Jesus* (Minneapolis: Fortress Press, 2004), 13–38.

66. Archie C. C. Lee, "Naming God in Asia: Cross-Textual Reading in Multi-Cultural Context," *Quest* 3, no. 1 (April 2004): 21–42.

67. R. S. Sugirtharajah, *Asian Biblical Hermeneutics and Postcolonialism: Contesting the Interpretations* (New York: Orbis, 1998), 12–14.

2.

Cross-Textual Reading:
Demonstrating A Method

Since several approaches with their underlying assumptions are usually herded together under the rubric "cross-textual reading" as a facet of cross-textual hermeneutics, it would help to separate these out and illustrate them to understand the process better. As a postscript, the chapter ends with a critical appraisal of "comparative theology", which is both similar and dissimilar to cross-textual reading.

CROSS-TEXTUAL READING BETWEEN TWO
SCRIPTURAL TEXTS

Instead of a collision between two scriptural texts, there is a stress in cross-textual reading on sensitive listening to the second tradition on its own terms. To illustrate this point, I will expand on the encounter between Krishna and Arjuna in the Bhagavad-Gita, which Gandhi uses and to which Wickremesinghe alludes, and read it cross-textually with Exodus 33:12–23.

Taking the episode in the Bhagavad-Gita first, the warrior prince Arjuna finds himself in the unenviable position of having to engage his cousins in battle. Such action would violate family relationships (*kula-dharma*). In his debate with Lord Krishna, who is his charioteer, Arjuna expresses his reservations about the ethics of war in general and doubts about his personal duty in the given situation. Krishna, however, urges on him the need to do his duty in this situation both as a matter of practical policy and as a principle of human destiny. What in effect Krishna tells Arjuna is that in discharging his human responsibility selflessly, which is his *karma*, he also fulfils his appointed destiny, which is his *dharma*. As chapter 2 verse 38 states, "Treat joy or sorrow, gain or loss, victory or defeat with equanimity, and then engage in war. By doing so, you will not incur sin." Lord Krishna voices the essential theme of the Bhagavad-Gita which is *nishka-makarma* (literally: to act without desire). It is to perform one's given duty without any ulterior motive or any thought of personal gain. This is the principle Gandhi sought to exemplify.

Even after listening to the arguments of Krishna, Arjuna is still troubled by the contradiction between given loyalties and appointed destiny, and therefore seeks confirmation for his action in a total vision. He beseeches Krishna:

> As thou hast declared Thyself to be, O Supreme Lord, even so it is.
> [But] I desire to see Thy divine form, O Supreme Person.

Krishna responds:

> But thou canst not behold Me with this [human] eye of yours;
> I will bestow on thee the supernatural eye.
> Behold My divine power.
> Having thus spoken . . . the great lord of yoga then revealed to
>   Partha [Arjuna] His Supreme and Divine Form . . .
> There the Pandava [Arjuna] beheld the whole universe,
>   with its manifold divisions gathered together in one,
>   in the body of the God of gods.[1]

No human eye can behold the divine form. For a fleeting moment, Krishna bestows on Arjuna the capacity to see the transcendental vision. In it he sees all the contradictions and paradoxes of the universe held together as one undivided whole. Through it he also receives the assurance that his particular obedience, in spite of its contradictions, would find its ultimate meaning in the Divine One who urges him to discharge his appointed task now. The stress in the Bhagavad-Gita is on right motives, which is encapsulated in the "incarnation" or "bodying forth" of Krishna:

Whenever there is a decline of righteousness
and rise of unrighteousness,O Bharata [Arjuna]!
Then I send forth (incarnate) Myself.
For the protection of the good,
for the destruction of the wicked
and for establishment of righteousness ,
I come into being from age to age.[2]

Exodus 33:12–23 breathes a different air though there are certain commonalities with the Bhagavad-Gita episode. In both there is the uncertainty about discharging an appointed task; and in both there is a request for a confirming vision of God that would make sense of a specific obedience.

The biblical account, which needs to be read in its total narrative context in the books of Exodus and Numbers, presents Moses's predicament. God has appointed him to lead the people of Israel to the land of promise. However, because of the recalcitrance of the people, their incessant murmuring and grumbling at the hardships in the wilderness of Sinai, and hankering after the flesh-pots of Egypt, recounted in Numbers 11, God refuses to accompany them to avoid destroying them (Exod 33:3). Instead, God would send a substitute ("an angel") to go before them. Given the awkwardness of the journey, the ever present possibility of the disobedience of the people, and the unreliable Aaron, his assistant, who instigated by the people made a golden calf for them to worship and be their god (cf. Exodus 32), Moses is not certain that he could fulfil his appointed task.

Two parallel requests, "let me know your ways" in 33:12–17 and "let me see your glory" in 33:18–23 bring together these two pericopes or narrative units.

Since God has not told him about who is to accompany him and the people on the journey to the land promised, Moses deftly interweaves two considerations to present his request, "Let me know your ways." One consideration is that though the people could provoke God to anger they are still God's people not Moses's people. Moses is only their leader. The other is that Moses has found favour in God's sight. Then, Moses should not be left to stumble alone on the journey that lies ahead. So, he asks for a blueprint or a map of what lies ahead for what could be a hazardous journey. Instead of a blueprint, Moses is assured of God's supporting presence: "My presence will go with you, and I will give you rest." Acknowledging that he would not be bereft of God's supporting presence, Moses responds blending the two considerations into a rhetorical question: "For how [else] shall it be known that I have found favour in your sight, I and your people, unless you go with us?"

Moses wants to make God's assurance doubly sure. So, in 33:18–23, he seeks a confirming vision of both God's presence and intention, implied in God's glory: "Let me see your glory, I pray." The request is to meet God face to face and not just shrouded in a "pillar of cloud" (cf. Exod 33:9). God responds that no one can behold the divine presence face to face and survive. Instead, God's goodness will pass before Moses, as God proclaims the divine name, "Yahweh, and I will be gracious to whom I will be gracious; and show mercy on whom I will show mercy" (33:19).

An earlier parallel account of the revealing of the divine name to Moses in Exodus 3:13–15 sheds light on how the proclamation of the divine name in Exodus 33:19 is to be understood. On the one hand, the name of God is revealed to Moses in response to the question that the people would ask regarding Moses's authority: "Who is this presumed god of our ancestors who has sent you?" (Exod 3:13). The name of God is given as an assurance of God's presence with Moses in delivering Israel from bondage and leading them to the land of promise (Exod 3:16–17). On the other hand, there is an emphasis on divine freedom, which is implied in the cryptic, *'ehyeh ašer 'ehyeh* in Hebrew, which is usually translated "I will be who I will be," as the meaning of God's name. Moses is to tell the people that *'ehyeh*, as the presumed first person singular of the third person "*yahweh*", has sent him. While divine presence is assured through the revealing of God's name, divine freedom is not compromised.

A similar reticence is also reflected in the proclamation of the divine name in Exodus 33:19: "I will be gracious to whom I will be gracious; and show mercy on whom I will show mercy." No one can encounter God face to face and survive. Divine freedom is not compromised. Yet, God's presence is assured. The experience of God's goodness in the past to the ancestors of Israel (cf. Ps 22:4) is the assurance of God's presence in the present and in the future. As the narrative puts it pictorially, "While my glory passes by I will put you in a cleft of the rock, and I will cover you with my hand until I have passed by; then I will take away my hand, and you shall see *my back*, but *my face* shall not be seen" (33:21–23, emphasis added).

Juxtaposing the two episodes, in different ways God is shown to be both accessible and inaccessible. No human eye can behold the divine form or totally comprehend God (Hindu perspective). No one can grasp the totality of God's purpose or nature (Judaeo-Christian perspective). Both episodes wrestle with the contradictions implicit in a specific obedience. Within this commonality different perspectives emerge. On the one hand, the Judaeo-Christian perspective places its emphasis on history, which is reflected in a longer retelling of the narrative as indicated above. In a historical sweep of events, a particular action or obedience has meaning within a total divine purpose, which though not fully divulged is yet discernible when one contemplates God's faithfulness in the past. God's *name* carries this historical perspective. It complements the Hindu perspective, which envisages the cosmos as a series of evolutions and devolutions, so that there is no final historical goal to be reached. On the other hand, the Hindu perspective supplements a Judaeo-Christian perspective that can so easily preclude larger relationships to the whole cosmic order with its primary interest in the goals of human liberation and development. God's *form* carries this cosmic perspective with its emphasis on *correct motives* that are to be selflessly undertaken in the pursuit of justice. As Mahatma Gandhi who regularly read the Bhagavad-Gita would say many a time, "The moment there is suspicion about a person's motives, everything he does becomes tainted." It is not just the action, but also the motives prompting the action that are important. It is wrong if the action is intended to accomplish selfish ends. It is right if the action is undertaken in a cause that is higher than one's self. The implication is that right motives will result in right results.

In an unpublished lecture, Francis D'Sa, SJ, from India made a comment on cross-scriptural reading in general, which is also pertinent for the reading we have done above:

In such a context we cannot meaningfully employ the principle of "either-or" but that of "both-and", since for a comprehensive understanding of the mountain of Ultimate Meaning all possible perspectives have to be taken into consideration. If one keeps this in mind, then one will seek an organic and harmonious integration of all the complementary perspectives; one will want to find out too the interrelationship between them and the reasons for their differences. Certain aspects will be enhanced by one perspective but certain others pushed into the background. Perhaps this enhanced aspect will challenge the other perspectives to search for less prominent details which have been totally overlooked or neglected.[3]

The encounter between Moses and Arjuna with their respective experiences requires that in evaluating the aptness of an action we should hold together, despite their tensions, a "spirituality for combat" that is needed to accomplish a given goal with a "spirituality in combat" that critiques motives.

CROSS-TEXTUAL READING BETWEEN CREATION NARRATIVES

The assumption in this form of cross-textual reading is that the mythological material Israel borrowed from other religious traditions probably offers a better and more profitable basis for cross-textual reading than just historical narrative texts that deal with motifs such as redemption and being a chosen people, which are utilised in constructions of "salvation history". This approach puts into practice the maxim of Wickremesinghe that theology is shaped as much by mythology as ideology. The inclination to juxtapose mythological texts is observable not only in the work of Asian scholars but also in the approach of Bernhard W. Anderson, a renowned scholar of the Hebrew Scriptures. In his lecture, "Creation Theology as a Basis for Global Witness,"[4] he utilises biblical material on the motif of creation together with related Wisdom literature to present the Christian message in dialogical form in an increasingly plural religious world. We will utilise some of his insights on the motif of creation to augment Archie Lee's reading of the biblical motif of creation cross-textually with Chinese creation myths.[5]

In his cross textual reading between creation narratives in the Bible and Chinese literature, Archie Lee is particularly concerned to theologically rehabilitate "the dragon" which is a benevolent symbol in Chinese culture but receives a bad press in the Bible. "The God introduced by the missionaries," says Lee, "was a slayer of the dragon, which in the minds of the Chinese was a beneficent being worshipped by many ordinary people." He had "a shattering experience" of the clash between these two perceptions of the dragon when he and his family became Christians.

I still remember that the pastor and the "army" of Christians of the church marched to our house and demanded that all art and literature and household items . . . that bore the dragon image be surrendered . . . and were then burned completely in front of the house. What a drama! These "Christian soldiers" won a triumphant battle in destroying the symbol of the dragon that once represented blessing and good omen in the culture of the new converts but which was regarded as evil and superstitious in the Western Christian teaching of that time.[6]

This antagonism presents Chinese Christians with a problem. The problem becomes apparent in Chinese translations of the Bible, which by and large avoid the use of *"lung"*, the Chinese word for dragon, to translate the biblical dragon-serpent. One translation uses the term but qualifies it with the adjective "perverse". With the widespread use of the symbol of the dragon in Chinese culture, Lee contends that Chinese Christians would want to re-examine the biblical message on creation with its heavy emphasis on the dragon as a symbol of chaos.

In Ancient Near Eastern creation myths, from which biblical writers borrowed, the dragon-serpent symbolises the chaotic waters that have to be conquered. In the creation myth from Mesopotamia, Marduk slays *Tiamat* (the deep) and cleaves its carcass into two, one part forming the earth and the other the heavens. In the Canaanite fertility cult, there was the annual ritual of Baal conquering the chaos monsters *Yam* (sea) and *Nahar* (river) to herald the beginning of Spring and the beginning of fertility. Borrowing from these myths, the Hebrew Bible uses several names for the chaos monster such as Rahab, Leviathan, Tehom, Tannin, Yam and Nahar (cf. Ps 74:12–14); and portrays God's battle with and conquest of the chaos monster not just as a once for all event at the beginning in creation, but as a continuous battle to keep chaos in check. In this sense, says Lee, "Creation is then seen not so much in the cosmological sense as the founding of the physical world, but more significantly in the socio-political sense as the formation and maintenance of the human world."[7] That is why a recounting of Yahweh's saving deeds follows Yahweh's victory over the chaos monster. A good example is Isaiah 51:9–11, in which the prophet uses the mythological language of creation to depict the historical return of Israel from exile:

Awake, awake, put on strength,
   O arm of the Lord;
awake as in the days of old,
   the generations of long ago.
Was it not thou that didst cut Rahab in pieces,
   that didst pierce the dragon (*tannin*)?
Was it not thou that didst dry up the sea (*yam*),
   the waters of the great deep (*tehom*);
that didst make the depths of the sea (*yam*) a way
   for the redeemed to pass over?
And the ransomed of the Lord shall return
   and come to Zion with singing;
everlasting joy shall be upon their heads;
   they shall obtain joy and gladness
   and sorrow and sighing shall flee away.

Yahweh establishes his throne on the foundation of justice and right-eousness (Ps 89:14); enters into a covenant with his people; and establishes the earthly king who is called God's son (Pss 2:7; 89:26–27) to maintain the order of justice and righteousness (Ps 72:1-2). After examining Ancient Near Eastern and biblical accounts of creation, Lee contends

> The "dragon-serpent" in the Bible has nothing to do with the Chinese *lung*. The former is the great sea-monster in the mythology of the Ancient Near East, which is a symbol of chaos and evil. It is presented as the opponent of the creator God in the context of creation theology.[8]

This is another instance of superficial resemblances leading to hasty comparisons with invidious results. Instead, Lee sees a "theology of ordering" implicit in the biblical creation accounts, which could function more profitably as a hermeneutical key in the cross-textual reading with Chinese creation myths.

Lee admits that in Chinese culture the dragon is an ambivalent symbol. On the one hand, it could represent the authority of the emperor and later the authority of the state and is a static, perhaps even oppressive, symbol. On the other, in folklore the dragon is a river-god. There are popular rituals, in some ways similar to the Baal fertility rituals, to enact the periodic ascent of this river-god into the clouds to bring down the beneficial rain. It is this popular and active perception of the symbol of the dragon that figures prominently in many Chinese creation myths.

The most popular of these has to do with Yu the Great. In this myth the deluge, which covered the earth for some ten years, is not perceived as punishment for sin, but is viewed as a natural state. The flood was infested with reptiles harmful to humans. What Chinese people fear most, says Lee, are "fierce floods and savage beasts". It is these that need to be equated with the biblical "dragon-serpent". The flood with its infestations had to be conquered if human civilisation were to be possible. This task was assigned to Yu who worked tirelessly at it. He was assisted by a winged dragon, which marked out with its tail the places where channels could be dug to drain the water. These became the great rivers of China through which the floodwater flowed into the sea; and Yu drove the reptiles into marshy places.

While remaining a beneficial symbol in Chinese creation myths and in popular rituals for the coming of rain, the dragon is also perceived as a mysterious composite figure made up of the features of many animals. It eludes total human comprehension and precise definition.

The myth of Yu clearing the earth of "fierce floods and savage beasts" with the assistance of the dragon also needs to be read as a continuous battle to keep chaos in check. Implied in it is an understanding of creation as a socio-political happening in which the draining of the flood makes for a settled agricultural society. Like the biblical creation myth, it has to do with the management of order. So, here too the myth is historicised. Yu was awarded kingship in recognition of his feat; and he is viewed as the founder-emperor of the Hsia dynasty (2783–1751 BCE).

Lee concludes:

> The symbol of the dragon reminds us of our cultural heritage, whose descendents we are. The symbol of Yu motivates us to do what we ought to do. It also invites us to identify with Yu, as remarked by someone at the time of Hsun Tze: "The man in the street could become a Yu. How about this?" To this Hsun Tze gave a positive answer that every human being in the street can become a potential Yu.[9]

Lee's remarks lead us back to the biblical creation accounts in the Primeval History (Genesis 1–11), which we now read cross-textually with the democratisation of the Chinese creation myth that everyone could be a potential Yu. The Genesis account sheds all allusions to Israel as a chosen people, and instead focuses on humanity as central to the motif of creation. In Genesis 1:26–30, God creates 'ādām (humanity), male and female, in the "image of God" and the "likeness of God". These two expressions occur again in Genesis 5:3 where it is said that Adam became the father of Seth who was in the image and likeness of Adam. Besides denoting the relationship of parent to progeny, these expressions are not really explained in the Hebrew Scriptures.

Scholars have noted that the first creation account in Genesis (1:1–2:3) reflects other creation accounts from the Ancient Near East but with significant changes.[10] So, Bernhard Anderson reads this text cross textually with Ancient Near Eastern texts where these expressions occur. In these the reference is to the function of a king. For instance, the deity addresses Pharaoh Amenophis III: "You are my beloved Son, produced from my members, my image which I have established on the earth. I have made you rule the earth in peace." Anderson explains,

> Here the emphasis is on the king's role in the royal office, his function is ex officio. Analogously, in the biblical texts the image is not something in human nature (reason, will conscience, immortal soul), but refers to the bodily, social role of 'ādām, consisting of male and female. Viewed in this perspective, 'ādām is not an autonomous being, at liberty to rule the earth arbitrarily or violently. On the contrary, human dominion is to be expressed wisely and benevolently so that God's dominion over the earth may be manifest in care for the earth and in the exercise of justice.[11]

While accepting Anderson's argument that the role of the king created in the image of the deity has been democratised to refer to humanity as a whole, the interpretation that such dominion is to be expressed wisely and benevolently and not arbitrarily runs into a slight problem in that the Hebrew verb rādāh translated "to have dominion" carries harsh connotations, such as "subdue". It is also used to tread out the wine in a wine press (Joel 3:13; Hebrew text 4:13). Clearly, a firm perhaps even ruthless control is intended so that creation may not misbehave and revert to chaos. Yet, the harshness is tempered by the fact that the intended diet for humanity is vegetarian! God gives them the fruit of the plants and trees for food. It is this toning down of the harshness of "to have dominion" that permits the interpretation that humanity's rule over creation has to embrace care for the earth and the pursuit of justice. To borrow language from Gandhi, *ahimsa* (non-violence) not *himsa* (violence) is to be the character of humanity's rule over creation.

Genesis 9:1-7 rehearses the earlier creation narrative. After the devastation wrought by the flood, creation is renewed in a covenant with Noah and his progeny, who are to exercise dominion over creation and continue the blessing given in creation to humanity to be fruitful, multiply and fill the earth. There is a significant change in this account in that meat is added to the human diet, but blood as the bearer of life may not be consumed: "Only you shall not eat flesh with its life, that is its blood" (9:4). Furthermore, there should be no needless shedding of blood of either animals or human beings (9:5–6). *Ahimsa* should continue to be the rule of life.

CROSS-TEXTUAL READING BETWEEN A TEXT AND A LIVING CONTEXT 1

Cross-scriptural reading is one aspect of cross-textual reading where both are written texts. In another form of cross-textual reading, the second text could be a political or social happening that raises fundamental faith questions. In other words, these are "living" texts" that address questions to the biblical text.

In his article, "Mothers Bewailing: Reading Lamentations," Archie Lee presents an historical incident as a "social text":

> The conventional historical critical approach generally adopted in academic circles is inadequate for understanding the complicated reality of cries of lament as they are articulated and textualized in the book of Lamentations. The reason for this is that historical criticism largely deals with recovering the historical scenario behind the text, focusing on the tragic fate of the holy city Jerusalem and what its chosen people did to bring calamity upon themselves. This preoccupation with the theological themes and concepts of sin, punishment, forgiveness, and hope of redemption has been so rigidly formulated that the significance of lament in human life is undermined as a result. The agonizing experience of YHWH turned enemy of the people, the latter personified in the female character of Jerusalem, is also not given its due. What I am

attempting, therefore, is to reread the book of Lamentations in the light of the contemporary experience of bewailing mothers at the Tiananmen Square Massacre of 1989. Cross-textual reading, which acknowledges the encounters of different texts in the reading of the Bible, is proposed here as an alternative mode of interpretation that seeks to enhance these two textual formulations of the deep human quest for meaning in the midst of great grief and pain. It is my hope that the confluence of these two texts will enable the understanding of human responses to suffering through the "crossings" made in the process of "cross-textual reading".[12]

In essence, Lee's argument is that the Hebrew/biblical penchant for seeing Yahweh as the source of both good and bad (in later biblical literature, as in Job, Satan takes on the role of being the author of bad things), while presenting a particular argument for the plight of Mother Jerusalem during and after the exile, acts as a shroud to muffle if not distort the place and role of lament. He reads the book of Lamentations alongside the massacre at Tiananmen Square on 4 June, 1989, which led to a group of mothers bewailing the fate of their children. The "Tiananmen Mothers Campaign" has resisted the official verdict that these students were counter-revolutionaries and that the soldiers who opened fire on the students should be honoured as people's heroes. The demand of the mothers for justice for their children has been denied and continues to be denied. Their right to mourn publicly and peacefully is also being suppressed. Yet, the lament continues.

When it is used as a heuristic tool to open up the Book of Lamentations, it strips it of its facile theological assumptions so that the pathos and poignancy of Mother Jerusalem's lament for her dead children stands out in stark relief.

> In Lamentations 1:1, Zion, here personified as a woman, does not seem to be given dignity and respect. She is only portrayed as "the female other", framed within the context of the national crisis of Israel brought about when the capital city fell captive to the Babylonians. The devastated woman has lost her husband and children. She sits alone, condemned of all the sins committed by the predominantly male leadership.[13]

The Book of Lamentation ends with the despairing cry, "Why have you forgotten us utterly, forsaken us for so long" (5:20–22).

As Lee points out, lament expresses a desolate woman's right to be heard on her own terms and not treated as an "other" or as a scapegoat.

To expand on Lee's argument, the lament of bereaved mothers, seeking justice for their children, refuses to let the silenced remain silenced. Thus, lament in this context is not just grieving. It is a political act. There are many more examples of the role of lament as a political act, as in the case of the campaign of the Mothers of Plaza de Mayo in Argentina, seeking vindication for their lost loved ones, and presently, in the cry of Tamil women in the north and east of Sri Lanka for their lost husbands and children. In most if not all of these instances, not only do the authorities attempt to suppress the cries of these women, they also put forward alternative "official" positions in attempts to nullify the cries for vindication. The cries of desolate women find an echo in the haunting cry with which Matthew ends his account of the heinous crime of Herod murdering innocent children to safeguard his power:

> A voice was heard in Ramah, wailing and loud lamentation,
> Rachel weeping for her children; refusing to be consoled
> because they are no more (2:18, cf. Jer 31:15).

Like Ahn Byung-mu, Lee ends his cross-textual reading of the Book of Lamentations with the Bewailing of the Tiananmen Mothers to raise questions about the adequacy of traditional historical critical methods. These methods, Lee contends, reinforce rather than critique the colonial and patriarchal tendencies implicit in the biblical account and furthermore present a vengeful rather than a compassionate God who hears the cry of distress:

> It [the historical-critical method] has not helped to penetrate into the realms of human pain and suffering, social injustice, human violation, and the cries for vindication. The tradition of lament is more about the articulation of grief than about seeking a rational explanation for catastrophic calamities. In the crossings between Text-A and Text-B, then, the voice of the disgraced widow, the representation of human struggles for justice, and the fight against oppressive powers and principalities can be heard more loudly and clearly in the residual cries of the mothers, even though they are thousands of miles and generations apart.[14]

CROSS-TEXTUAL READING BETWEEN A TEXT
AND A LIVING CONTEXT 2

Archie Lee reads Lamentations cross-textually with a particular living context. I propose to read Mark's Gospel account cross-textually with the living contexts of Asia to which I drew attention in the Introduction. What I intend to present is a Christian perspective as we engage with other religionists in seeking alternatives to the dire political situations in which we find ourselves. The seeking for alternatives, as I have already said, are political expressions of hope and therefore could encounter danger. Mark's Gospel account has much to say to us as we read it as a perspective of hope in the dangerous quest for alternatives.

When Mark's narrative is compared with the other two synoptic gospel accounts, one is struck by the fact that there is no comparable call to mission or discipleship at the end as in Matthew (28:18–20) and Luke (25:45–49; Acts 1:8). As most scholars and early church fathers agree, 16:9–20 is a later addition. However, it does not take long for a reader of Mark to realise that the whole gospel account is itself a call to discipleship in a very unusual and troubling way.

Mark ends his narrative at 16:8 saying that the women "went out and fled from the tomb for terror and amazement had seized them." They were so terrified that they said nothing to anyone. Why Mark chose to end his narration in this way no one knows. No other undisputed ending from the hand of Mark has ever been found.

However, what has to be said has already been said. There is a sort of call to discipleship in chapter 13, which is an apocalyptic depiction of the end-time. In 13:10, the disciples are told that they will be arraigned in hostile courts and forums. But they are not to worry because the Holy Spirit will prompt them. So, before the End comes, "the good news must first be proclaimed to all nations." In his description of his own suffering Jesus had predicted that he would rise from the dead, and would go before his disciples to Galilee (14:28). The young man dressed in white sitting in the empty tomb tells the women to tell the disciples, especially Peter, that he is going before them to Galilee.

Yet for all that, the ending is abrupt and perhaps even unsatisfactory. This ending has elicited two broad responses. One response is that Mark expected his readers to supply endings or better to work on sequels, as did Luke and Matthew and the early church.[15] The second response is that Mark uses the dramatic device of "unresolved conflict", as for example the parable of the two sons. Did the older brother go in or not? So the ending is with us. How do we respond? This is the basic position of Donald Juel.[16]

Juel illustrates his point with an incident that happened in his local church. It was customary to have a dramatic reading of Mark's Gospel account during Passiontide. At the first performance, the narrator ended with Mark 16:8, and looked at the audience. The ensuing silence impelled him to say, "Amen!" There was applause. Realising that this was not exactly the response that was needed, on the next day he ended with Mark 16:8, looked at the audience, and quietly and slowly walked off-stage. There was no applause, but as the people left they turned to each other to share the impact that the ending had on them. How does the story end for you and me?

The answer to this question depends on recognising a very simple and yet a very profound truth that is central to Mark's Gospel account. The opposite of faith is not unfaith but fear at a fearful time. Fear could make us do the unfaithful thing. After stilling the storm, Jesus turns to his frightened disciples and asks, "Why are you afraid? Have you no faith?" (4:40).

Keeping this insight in mind, we will explore five related issues. *First*, there is the challenge of Empire in Mark's time as well as in our time. What is to be our response? *Second*, we will explore the challenge posed by this question in the way Mark positions the disciples in the polarity between the "crowds or multitudes" (*ochlos*) and the political and religious authorities. *Third*, we will see how Jesus defines his messiahship against the background of the *ochlos*. *Fourth,* within the *ochlos* there is a group of women who provide a window into what discipleship entails at a fearful time. Perhaps, Mark intends them to be a model to us.

THE CHALLENGE OF EMPIRE IN MARK

Scholars are generally agreed that Mark's Gospel account is the earliest of the three synoptic gospels. Mark seems to have written his account sometime between 64 CE, the end of the persecutions under Nero, and 75 CE before Matthew and Luke wrote their gospel accounts. According to the historian Eusebius, Papias who was a bishop (ca. 140 CE) used to say, "Mark, indeed who became the interpreter of Peter, wrote accurately, as far as he remembered them, the things said or done by the Lord, but not however in order" (*Church History* III.39.15). Early church tradition has it that Peter perished during the persecutions under Nero. Besides the tense relationship between the Christian church and the Roman Empire, there was also the tension between Israel and Rome, which provided the background against which Jesus proclaimed the "Kingdom of God" as an alternative. The headlong collision between Israel and Rome led to the ill-fated war with Rome and the destruction of the Jerusalem temple (70 CE). The Jews were dispossessed of their land and dispersed.

The reality and terror of Empire was prominent when Mark wrote his gospel account. It was indeed a fearful time. In this situation Mark calls for a form of costly discipleship that should break through, confront and even transcend the reality and demands of Empire.

In taking this position Mark faithfully reflects what Jesus would have meant in speaking of the *basileia* of God. The King James Version translates the Greek *basileia tou theou* as "Kingdom of God", a translation that has been followed since, leading to two diverse interpretations. On the one hand, this phrase has been wrongly combined with Matthew's Kingdom of Heaven, where Matthew following Jewish convention avoids using the name of God, and has been spiritualised to refer to another worldly domain, i.e. heaven. On the other, those who find the male orientation in "kingdom" offensive have translated *basileia* variously as "rule", "reign", and "realm". Both these interpretations miss the challenge implicit in what Jesus proclaimed. In his time both friend and foe would have recognised "*basileia tou theou*" as directly confronting the *basileia* of Rome and therefore understood it as "the Empire of God". Jesus deliberately took a political concept to express "the good news" that spoke of an alternative empire in which those who were excluded and treated as "expendables" in the Empire of Rome and its *Pax Romana* would be welcome. In a word, the Empire of God invited and welcomed "the dirty people" and offered a different kind of peace.[17]

Today too the predominant challenge is the global reality of Empire. The imperial power of the USA, Great Britain and their allies is attempting to reorder the world. Asian nation-states, such as China and India, have also become expressions of Empire or allies of Empire.[18] Economic globalisation with the support of military power is an important tool in this process. Those who neither provide nor consume in the global market are excluded. Nation states are being drawn into the political and economic global reality that is being created,[19] and respond or react in the many diverse ways that have created the complex living contexts of Asia.

In this situation we too feel helpless like the *ochlos*—the multitudes, the sheep without a shepherd—to whom Jesus held out the promise of the Empire of God as an alternative. It is a promise that can be understood and received only as one takes into account the plight of those who are treated as expendable, or in the language of today's conflicts "unavoidable collateral damage". Innocent civilians, especially peasants, women and children, suffer the most, and are being killed often in "targeted bombings". Countervailing armed responses, often-labelled "terrorism," are equally indiscriminate. We are in a situation of crisis that calls for a change in perspective—an epistemological shift—and its consequent praxis. The choice is clear. Do we go the way of the Empire or do we go the way of the Suffering Messiah who proclaimed the Empire of God as an alternative that holds out the promise of life for all beginning with the least? With this question in mind we continue our reading of Mark's Gospel account.

THE AUTHORITIES, THE OCHLOS
AND THE DISCIPLES IN MARK

Mark uses two sets of characters to set out the tension between the two poles of faith and fear at a fearful time. On the one side there are the Jewish and Gentile authorities. These have status, power and security, but are essentially insecure. They are afraid because their authority and power are not necessarily legitimate. They are the tenants of the vineyard who are even willing to kill the son and heir to keep what they have wrongfully acquired (12:1–12). They will devour the houses of widows (12:38–40). They will do anything to protect their self-interest. Those who want to protect themselves and what is theirs are always afraid.

To cite an example from the past which would still be pertinent today, Bishop Julio Xavier Labayan, OCD, from the Philippines made an off the cuff remark during his address to the assembly of the Christian Conference of Asia at Penang in 1977. It was a time when the Philippines was suffering under the dictatorship of Ferdinand and Imelda Marcos. Other countries, notably Korea, were also under martial law. Labayan said in almost apocalyptic language, "It is because these dictators are so powerless that they are most dangerous" (cf. Rev 12:12).

Returning to Mark's text, the religious and political authorities show fear. They are afraid of Jesus and the crowds (12:12). They are afraid of Jesus because he strikes hard and to the point. Jesus was popular with the people because he said what the people knew to be true but were afraid to say to the face of the religious and political leaders. He was therefore dangerous. So they wanted to kill him (15:10).

On the other side are the ordinary people, the *ochlos,* the crowds or multitude. In chapter 1 we have the words "they" or "all" (1:22, 27). It is an amorphous group of people. However, beginning with chapter 2, the term *ochlos* appears as the "they" and the "all" interact with Jesus and find expression as an identifiable group. Mark makes very creative use of this term, and is followed by Matthew and Luke but not as consistently as Mark. It is interesting that Mark avoids the term *laos* for "people" used some two thousand times by the Greek Jewish Bible known as the Septuagint. *Laos* occurs in a quotation from the Old Testament (7:6) and in the mouth of the Jewish authorities (14:2).

Why does Mark prefer this term *ochlos?* In 70 CE with the fall of Jerusalem and the persecution in Israel, people had lost their identity and were driven hither and thither as sheep without a shepherd. As the *ochlos* begins to take shape in Mark certain characteristics begin to appear. Unlike the authorities, whose self-interest is all too evident, these act largely to help others and make enormous attempts. They bring a paralytic to be cured (2:3). They bring a deaf and dumb man and beg Jesus to cure him (7:32). They bring a blind man and beg Jesus to touch him (8:22).[20]

In between these two groups are the disciples, largely drawn from the *ochlos*, but with visions of grandeur. Who is to be the greatest among them? (9:33–34). James and John want to sit on thrones on either side of Jesus when he comes in his glory (10:35–40). These two try to pre-empt the others who become very angry (10:41). All of them would aspire to be the leaders in the coming Empire of God.

The disciples also show fear. They are afraid of the storm on the lake (4:40). They are anxious about feeding the people (6:34–37; 8:4). They are afraid to ask Jesus about his death (9:34). Finally, one betrays him, another tries to stand by him but under threat of exposure denies him, and the others flee in fear.

When Jesus speaks of his own suffering and the rejection he will face from the authorities, his execution and then resurrection, the disciples are confused. Peter admonishes him, "Don't think like this." Jesus responds, "Get behind me Satan. For you are thinking the thoughts of human beings not of God" (8:33). It is doubtful that Jesus was imputing satanic or demonic characteristics to Peter, as we would understand the term "Satan" now. It seems to be rather the basic meaning of being an adversary, as one who stands in front and prevents something happening. A good example is Numbers 22:32–34 where God's messenger stands in front of Balaam as an adversary (Satan) to prevent him from doing what would have been against God's will, namely, to curse Israel as was the wish of the king Balak. In asking Peter to get behind him, Jesus was in effect saying, "You are standing in the way and preventing me from accomplishing my God given mission."[21] The second time Jesus speaks of his suffering he speaks in a general way (9:12) and the third time, the disciples don't understand (9:30–32). They argue as to who is the greatest among them. The fourth time he speaks about his suffering, rejection and death (10:33–34), James and John look at the future glory of the Messiah and ask for the important places (10:35). All of us would like to skip the agony of the crucifixion and get to the glory of the resurrection!

The challenge to the disciples is "Which way will you go?" Would you want to go with the authorities or the way of the ordinary people? With whom will you show solidarity at a fearful time?

JESUS, THE SERVANT MESSIAH—THE MESSIAH OF THE "ORDINARY PEOPLE"

To show the ways of God, Jesus does two things. First, he picks up the demeaned values and characteristics of the *ochlos* and presents them as the alternative values of the Empire of God. He who wants to be the greatest must be the servant of all (9:35). A child, a slave, the widow giving her small coin (12:42)—these are the ones who are valued. The dependence on wealth, position and power as the basis for judging human value is condemned. The rich young ruler is told that he lacks one thing—give up your wealth! What is required is not accumulation and acquisitiveness but denial of self. These values from the *ochlos* (living for others, serving others) are held up to oppose the rich and the powerful and as requirements to those who would follow Jesus.

These values are not imposed on the suffering poor themselves. Feminist theologians have rejected the metaphor of the servant, which has been used by men to prescribe the role of women. Often servitude is tied to caste and lowly status. The disciples are told that it is in being part of the *ochlos*, that they can truly exhibit the values of the Empire of God.

Second, he shapes his Messiahship in his interaction with the *ochlos* and in terms of Old Testament prophecy. Jesus consistently refers to himself as the Son of Man (Dan 7:13). There are five important points. (i) "I saw one like a human being" says Daniel. It is the humanity of Jesus the Messiah that is stressed. "Are you the Messiah?" Jesus responds with the quotation from Daniel. (ii) However, the demons recognise and confess him: "The Holy One of God" (1:24); you are the son of God (3:11); the Son of the Most High God (5:7). But he kept shutting up the demons and would not allow them to talk (1:34) lest the real purpose and character of his messiahship be misunderstood. (iii) To the authorities he says, "The Son of Man is lord of the Sabbath" (2:28). He has the authority to forgive sins (2:10), to demonstrate the fact that Jesus has power to release people from whatever holds them in bondage. The authorities argue with him and lose every time. (iv) The revealing of his real identity as the suffering servant of God is through the affirmation he receives at the time of his baptism—"my beloved son in whom I am well pleased" (1:11); and at the transfiguration—"This is my beloved son listen to him" (9:7). Finally, (v) it is the centurion who makes the real identity of Jesus public: "This indeed was the Son of God" (15:39). Not King of the Jews but the Son of God. So, it is at the end, not so much at the beginning, that the identity of Jesus as the Son of God is revealed. It is from the perspective of suffering humanity that one may understand the role of the Messiah as the Suffering Servant, which in turn reveals the divinity of Jesus.

Third, he takes the self-sacrifice and compassion shown by the *ochlos* and gives it the highest possible value through his own life and ministry. The title ascribed to Jesus at the beginning of Mark says two things. On the one hand, it is the "opposition" that realises and makes the confession. On the other, the disciples of Jesus gradually come to know who God really is and that Jesus is indeed the Son of God. It is not acts of liberation, feeding, etc. by themselves that can truly reveal that Jesus is the Son of God. It is that final self-giving, the execution, that reveals Jesus as the self-giving God. This was a dangerous confession at a time when Caesar was proclaimed as the son of God.

To characterise this self-giving, Mark uses another Greek word, which is also used by the other two synoptic gospels, Matthew and Luke. The word is *splanchnizomai*, "to have compassion". The verb, *splanchnizomai*, is with possibly one exception used only to describe the emotions of Jesus and in the parables Jesus told to describe the Empire of God. It denotes a strong emotional, physical response. Its literal meaning is "to be moved in one's bowels". Or to put it in our language, it is to say that it is a "gut-wrenching experience and response". It is in some ways a very maternal image—the anguish a mother feels in her very womb for a wayward child. It is not just a mental attitude—to have pity or to feel sorry for people. It is a physical response to human conditions that leads to action. It is the response of Jesus when he sees the crowds or multitudes.

A good example of the compassion of Jesus is found in Mark 6:30–44. Jesus tried to get away from the crowds to a lonely place to rest awhile. He got into a boat with the Twelve and moved away to another part of the shore of the Sea of Galilee. Seeing him leave, the crowds ran along the shore to the place where he was to land. "As he landed he saw a great *crowd* and *he had compassion on them*, because they were like sheep without a shepherd; and he began to teach them many things."

Jesus's compassion found expression in his teaching. Through the stories or parables Jesus presented to the "crowds" the Empire of God as a reality made known in him and through his ministry. They were invited to repent—to return and come home to God and to the place where God reigns—and be forgiven and restored. For them, the Empire of God was good news (cf. Matt 5:3–10).

Jesus's compassion found expression in his healing. As Jesus was leaving Jericho for Jerusalem, two blind men sitting by the roadside heard that Jesus was passing by and cried out: "Lord have mercy upon us, Son of David." The crowd rebuked them. But Jesus called them to him and asked: "What do you want me to do for you?" They said:

"Lord, let our eyes be opened." And Jesus *had compassion on them* and touched their eyes; and they received their sight (Matt 20:29–34).

Compassion could also find expression in anger. Jesus told a parable comparing the Empire of God to a king who wished to settle accounts with his servants. One of these owed him much money. The king ordered him to be sold with his family and possessions to recover what was owed. The servant fell on his knees and implored the king to have patience with him and promised that he would eventually pay back everything. The king *had compassion on him* and released him and forgave his debt. The same servant found another servant who owed him money, and demanded repayment. The other servant in turn asked him for patience and a time for repayment. But he refused, and put the man in prison till the debt was repaid. His fellow servants in distress reported what had happened to the king. Then the king summoned the servant and scolded him: "You wicked servant! I forgave you all the debt because you pleaded with me; and should not you also have shown mercy on your fellow servant as I had mercy on you?" And in great anger the king delivered him to the jailers till he paid all that he owed (Matt 18:23–34).

The compassion of Jesus expressed as anger resisted the unjust demands that the religious authorities placed on the people. Listen to this: "But woe to you, scribes and Pharisees, hypocrites! Because you shut the kingdom of heaven against people, for you neither enter yourselves, nor allow those who wish to enter to go in. Woe to you scribes and Pharisees, hypocrites! For you cross sea and land to make a single convert, and when he becomes a convert you make him twice as much a child of hell as yourselves" (Matt 23:13–15). This is strong language, and there are many more instances in the gospel accounts of Jesus crying and weeping in anger and anguish.

In him and through him, the compassion of God was expressed in the strongest of terms. Furthermore, his compassion (solidarity), to the dismay of the religious leaders of his time, made Jesus break a line of "untouchability". He had table fellowship with the *ochlos* (2:15–17; cf. Luke 15:1–2). He crossed a boundary to create community. In him and through him, it was also revealed that compassion is the quality of the Messiah.

It was this close identification with the crowds—the victims of injustice, the prostitutes and sinners, and those on the periphery of society—expressed in his compassion for them that led to his death on the cross. Jesus kept bad company and created a dangerous community.

What he did was dangerous. It opened up dimensions of hope for those who were considered to be unclean and those on the periphery of society. Through Jesus the Messiah, the compassion of God expressed itself in affirming the human dignity of those whom society treated as outcasts. The compassion of Jesus, expressed in acts of love for the people and as resistance against those who shut the gates of the Empire of God in the face of the people, was seen as dangerous political activity. This was why he was executed. Jesus was not stoned to death as was Stephen who was accused of blasphemy—a religious offence. Rather, Jesus was crucified for an alleged political offence. For sure, the religious authorities, whom Jesus questioned and resisted, participated in the arrest and trial of Jesus. They found him dangerous and were convinced that he could imperil the nation in the eyes of Rome (cf. John 11:47–52). But it was Rome that was finally responsible.

The charge against Jesus was a political interpretation of what he did for and with the people (*ochlos*). In proclaiming the "Empire of God" Jesus opened up avenues of hope for the people. But for Rome that was sedition. He was indicted for calling himself or permitting himself to be called the King of the Jews. The execution was ordered and carried out by the authorities of the Roman Empire. In other words, Jesus was crucified not because he was considered to be a bad theologian, but because he was perceived to be a political menace!

The challenge of the Messiah: "If anyone would follow me, let them deny themselves and take up their cross and follow me. For those who try to save their lives will lose their lives. But those who lose their lives for my sake and for the sake of the gospel will save their lives" (8:34-35).

Why did Jesus stick to the *ochlos*? Because those who suffer the most have the *capacity* to care the most. But these were also afraid. They forsook him. They were fickle. The authorities could turn them against Jesus. Yet, he stuck to them.

THE WOMEN IN MARK

There is another group between the *ochlos* and the male disciples. These are the women, some of whom are named. As women belonging to the *ochlos* they were doubly oppressed and had developed mental conditions that kept them in bondage. The severity of what Mary Magdalene suffered is described as being possessed by seven demons. Jesus released them from their bondage and healed them. They in turn served him and his followers. These were also afraid, but they ministered to the Messiah. They watched the death of the Messiah from afar while the disciples were nowhere to be seen. They lay the body of the Messiah in a tomb, and were ready to come at the end of the Sabbath to prepare the body for burial.[22] It is to them that the message of the resurrection is given and entrusted. But they were so petrified that they said nothing to anybody.

Hyun Younghak, a Korean *minjung* theologian, suggests a possible clue to the silence of the women. In his article, "Theology as Rumour-mongering,"[23] he says that rumour, as idle gossip, is harmless. But not so with rumour as political activity which is dangerous. Political authorities are always worried about such rumours and attempt to quash them. An interesting example is the comment of Tacitus, the Roman historian, about the rumour of Jesus with reference to the great fire of Rome in 64 CE:

> Consequently, to get rid of the report, Nero fastened the guilt and inflicted the most exquisite tortures on a class hated for their abominations, called Christians by the populace. Christus, from whom the name had its origin, suffered the extreme penalty during the reign of Tiberius at the hands of one of our procurators, Pontius Pilatus, and a most mischievous superstition, thus checked for the moment, again broke out not only in Judæa, the first source of the evil, but even in Rome, where all things hideous and shameful from every part of the world find their centre and become popular. (*Annales* 15.44)

It is possible that through their silence the women spread the story of Jesus, passing it from mouth to mouth. The content of the rumour may have been something like this: "The Jewish authorities have one version and the Roman authorities another, but this is what actually happened." They were witnesses to everything. Perhaps Mark took this rumour and constructed his (or her?) gospel account. Silencing, silences and open endings are characteristic of Mark's narrative. Mark invites imagination and our active participation in a frightening story at a fearful time. It is to indulge in imagination as fidelity to the Word.[24]

EVALUATING APPROACHES
IN CROSS-TEXTUAL READING

In cross-textual reading there is actually no right method or wrong method. Given the variety of approaches, it is perhaps better to speak of a good approach or a bad approach. Aloysius Pieris, SJ, from Sri Lanka distinguishes between a good approach and a bad approach calling the one right and the other wrong.

A recognised text scholar of Buddhist and Christian Scriptures, Pieris has been engaged in cross-scriptural reading as a component of cross-textual hermeneutics for several decades in the context of Buddhist–Christian dialogue. He sets out some of the principles for a good method in his essay, "Cross-Scripture Reading in Buddhist–Christian Dialogue: A Search for the Right Method."[25]

It is not possible to present the wealth of detail that he gives in his comprehensive essay on the way cross-scriptural reading functions. All that is possible is to set out the bare bones of his argument. He sees three broad ways in which cross-scriptural reading takes place: "the extra-textual confrontation", "the liturgical appropriation", "the symbiotic encounter".

The first approach tends to ignore the fact that the two texts in question inhabit different worlds of meaning, so that superficial similarities are utilised: "de-contextualized texts are read as conveying an identical message or, worse still, odious comparisons are made between the two religions on the basis of decontextualised reading of their scriptures."[26] He alleges that the first method has an irenic agenda while the other has a polemical intention.

The second approach he sees in Hebrew Scriptures where prayers from other nations have been drawn in and offered as prayers to Yahweh through a liturgical appropriation. A similar process is also evident with wisdom literature from outside seeping into the faith expression of Israel. This process was mimicked at a liturgy celebrated at the Theological College of Lanka (where I was a lecturer for some time), in which Buddhist and Christian texts with the overriding theme of hope were juxtaposed. He says that something new was created in the context of worship. Discarding "syncretism" and "synthesis" as what happened in this experiment, he sees evidence of "symbiosis". This is "a living encounter of the texts within the encounter of religions, resulting in a further articulation of implicit meanings, which these texts would not reveal unless they are mutu-ally exposed to each other's illuminating disclosures."[27]

From this experience he proposes the third method for cross-scrip-tural reading that he calls the symbiotic exposure of texts, which "is the procedure most conducive to reciprocal spiritual nourishment among members of the multi-religious communities." He quotes with approval the writings of Lynn de Silva[28] as good examples of the symbiotic exposure of texts. Pieris goes on to say that in expos-ing biblical texts to the Buddhist doctrine of *anatta* (no-soul) de Silva recovers the biblical emphasis on the human being as body and God-given spirit (cf. Gen 2:7, Ps 104:30) rather than the overlaid Greek understanding of a human being as made up of a body and an eter-nal soul. Commenting on de Silva's cross-reading of the Bible with the Buddhist Triptikas, Pieris says, "Now this exegetical exercise has not been a mere intellectual luxury for de Silva; it was also a source of spiritual nourishment. A personal appropriation of the Buddhist and biblical doctrines of *anatta* constitutes the journey towards lib-eration along the Eight-fold path and the Way of the Cross, two forms of *self-denial* advocated by the Two Masters, as the *sine qua non* of ultimate release from the vale of tears (*samsāra*)."[29] Pieris gives other examples from his own experience of the symbiotic exposure of texts through cross-textual reading in which he juxtaposes biblical teachings with Buddhist teachings especially on spiritual and material poverty, and comments:

> It is noteworthy that the Buddhist Tripitaka, as seen from the context of the Christian Bible, confirms a doctrine very strongly advocated in the latter: the strong demand for "poverty in spirit" (*appicchatā*) as con-dition for discipleship does not imply a religious justification of mater-ial poverty (*dāliddiya*) among the masses, as if to imply that the rich can remain complacent about their riches without sharing it with the needy as long as they are "spiritually" detached from their wealth, and that the poor should remain in their poverty and misery without allowing their minds and hearts to hanker after riches. The Tripitaka does not endorse such a view.[30]

Pieris ensures that while the two texts are enriched and hidden mean-ings are made to surface, one reading does not intrude into and dis-tort the other. He concludes:

Cross-scriptural exegesis of the symbiotic type is quite an innovative exercise in inter-religious dialogue. For here the seminal teaching in the scriptures of one religion, sown and buried in the texts, when exposed to the warm light that comes from the teachings of another religion's Sacred Writ, sprouts forth and grows into a fruitful source of new insights. In this "symbiotic" approach, no room is left for diluting or distorting the basic teachings of either religion; and no effort made to indulge in easy equations or odious comparisons.[31]

COMPARATIVE THEOLOGY: A CRITICAL APPRAISAL

Under the rubric "Comparative Theology", other scholars follow a method similar to cross-textual reading. This is a burgeoning field of study that has drawn in Catholic and Protestant scholars mostly from North America. It would not be possible to cover the whole water-front in this brief section, but an examination of the work of Francis X. Clooney, SJ, who in many ways is the pioneer of the practice of Comparative Theology, would help to show differences with cross-textual reading as illustrated above.

In his *Comparative Theology: Deep Learning Across Religious Borders*, Clooney describes the method he follows in bringing together Christian texts and texts from other traditions, especially Hindu texts, in response to religious diversity to enhance and enrich Christian theology:

In our religiously diverse context, a vital theology has to resist too tight a binding by tradition, but also the idea that religious diversity renders strong claims about truth and value impossible. Comparative theology is a manner of learning that takes seriously diversity and tradition, openness and truth, allowing neither to decide the meaning of our religious situation without recourse to the other. Countering a cultural tendency to retreat into a private spirituality or a defensive assertion of truth, this comparative theology is hopeful about the value of learning. Indeed, the theological confidence that we can respect diversity and tradition, that we can study traditions in their particularity and receive truth in this way, in order to know God better, is at the core of comparative theology.[32]

The desire to get beyond the narrow confines of comparative religion, mostly a Christian enterprise to show the excellence of one's own faith over against another, should be applauded. However, limitations become apparent when one notes location or the context in which comparative theology is done and the constraints under which it works.

Clooney admits that he enagages in comparative theology as an American Jesuit theologian who is deeply indebted to that tradition and the experiments of Jesuit missionaries such as Francis Xavier and Robert de Nobili who emersed themselves in the study and appropriation of Hindu traditions to converse with Hindus.[33]While their major aim was the convesion of the Hindu, Clooney's intention is to follow in the footsteps of Anselm of Canterbury in a project of "faith seeking understanding" in the context of a diversity of religions, especially through an encounter with texts from several Hindu traditions.[34] In this enterprise, Clooney finds his inspiration in the Vatican II document *Nostra Aetate* (the conciliar document on world religions).[35] As the document states in paragraph 2: "The Catholic Church rejects nothing that is true and holy in these religions. She regards with sincere reverence those ways of conduct and of life, those precepts and teachings which, though differing in many aspects from the ones she holds and sets forth, nonetheless often reflect a ray of that Truth which enlightens all men. Indeed, she proclaims, and ever must proclaim Christ "the way, the truth, and the life" (John 14:6), in whom men may find the fullness of religious life, in whom God has reconciled all things to Himself." In brief, what is "best" in other religions "reflect a ray of that Truth", which is found in its fullness in Jesus Christ. *Nostra Aetate* states more positively what Augustine of Hippo stated centuries earlier that the best in other philosophies/religions comes from God and rightfully could be used to set out the reasonableness of the Christian faith from truths purloined from other religious philosophies.[36]*Nostra Aetate* in fact does not deviate from received Catholic theology, and sets the parameters for Comparative Theology.

While engaged in learning from other religions to know God better is at the heart of comparative theology, its main intention is to come to a more wholesome appreciation of Jesus Christ in the midst of religious diversity:

> Comparative theology . . . can lead us back to our core commitments; the wider learning need not undecut faith's particularity. It has been my particular commitment to Jesus Christ that energizes most deeply my vision of comparative theological practice as a disclosure of the widest

meaning in the most particular instance. If my comparative theology leads anywhere, it should lead (back) to Christ.[37]

In essence, comparative theology as a project of faith seeking understanding in the context of religious diversity is concerned to illuminate in fresh ways core commitments and amplify received (Catholic) traditions. However, the possibility of core commitments being transformed through an encounter with other religious traditions is absent because the scholar is firmly in control of the religious traditions with which the conversation takes place. As Clooney admits, "I usually give preference to similarity over difference, preferring to foster theological conversation between specific Hindu and Christian theological disourses that seem in harmony with one another."[38] The problem of the two stories, with which cross-textual hermeneutics in general and cross-textual reading in particular has to wrestle, because there is a second partner involved, is avoided. As a method, comparative theology is a reading strategy[39] that is academic and perhaps even elitist, which demands that the scholar has a good knowledge of the languages of primary sources, as does Clooney who knows both Sanskrit and Tamil that are the classical languages of Hindu traditions.

In contrast, cross-textual reading either explicitly or implicitly engages the partner who lives by these traditions rather than just the traditions themselves. In brief, it is to be open to receiving from and being transformed by other religious perspectives. This is the method Lakshman Wickremesinghe and others engaged in cross-textual reading advocate. Their position, as stated particularly by Wickremesinghe, is that while partners engaged in interreligious dialogue in the search for justice, peace and religious harmony hold that their particular focal religious images are normative, they concede that these images are not complete, and are open to receiving from and *being transformed* by other religious perspectives.[40]

The main purpose of this comparison is not to disparage comparative theology, but rather for readers to be mindful of its limitations and not expect more of it than it can deliver. Incidentally, this comparison also serves to highlight in summary form the salient features of cross-textual reading.

Notes

1. *Bhagavadgita* chapter 11:3, 8, 9, 13. From S. Radhakrishnan, *The Bhagavadgita with Translation and Notes* (New Delhi: Harper Collins, 1993), 319, 322, 325.

2. Chapter 4:7, 8. Radhakrishnan, *Bhagavadgita*, 178, 180.

3. For a fuller statement, see Francis X. D'Sa, SJ, "How is it that We hear, Each of Us in our own Native Language? A tentative cross-textual reading of the Incarnation (John 1) and Avatara (Bhagavad-Gita 4)," in *Scripture, Community and Mission*, ed. Philip L. Wickeri, (Hong Kong: CCA & CWM, 2003, second printing), 127–51.

4. Bernhard W. Anderson, *Creation Theology as a Basis for Global Witness* (New York: General Board of Ministries of the Methodist Church, 1999).

5. Archie C. C. Lee, "The Dragon, the Deluge, and Creation Theology," in *Frontiers in Asian Christian Theology*, ed. R.S. Sugirtharajah (New York: Orbis, 1994), 97–108. Archie C. C. Lee, "Genesis 1 from the Perspective of A Chinese Creation Myth," in *Understanding Poets and Prophets: Essays in Honour of George W. Anderson*, ed. A Graeme Auld (Sheffield: JSOT Press, 1993), 186–98.

6. Lee, "The Dragon," 100–101.

7. Ibid., 102.

8. Ibid., 101–2.

9. Ibid., 106. Hsun Tze or Xunzi (312–230 BCE) was a Confucian philosopher.

10. For a brief evaluation of scholarly opinions on the use of Ancient Near Eastern creation myths, especially the Babylonian creation myth *Enuma Elish*, see Bernhard W. Anderson, *From Creation to New Creation* (Minneapolis: Fortress Press, 1994), 42–45.

11. Bernhard W. Anderson, *Contours of Old Testament Theology* (Minneapolis: Fortress Press, 1999), 91.

12. Archie Lee, "Mothers Bewailing: Reading Lamentations," in *Her Master's Tools*, eds. Caroline Vander Stichele and Todd Penner, (Atlanta: Society of Biblical Literature, 2005), 195.

13. Lee, "Mothers Bewailing," 201.

14. Ibid., 209.

15. Dennis MacDonald, *The Homeric Epics and the Gospel of Mark* (New Haven and London: Yale University Press, 2000), Appendix 3: "The Endings of Iliad and the Gospel of Mark," 198–200.

16. Donald Juel, *The Gospel of Mark*, (Nashville: Abingdon, 1999), 167–76.

17. For a convenient and comprehensive summary of this view, propounded especially by the scholars in the Jesus Seminar, see Stephen J. Patterson, *The God of Jesus: The Historical Jesus and the Search for Meaning*, (Harrisburg, Pennsylvania: Trinity Press, 1998), 60–87.

18. In his article, "US Pact Draws India into Muddy Waters," (*Asia Times Online*, October 7, 2014), Ninan Koshy shows how India as a junior partner is being drawn into a partnership with the imperial pretentions of the USA.

19. See Ninan Koshy, *The War on Terror: Reordering the World*, (New Delhi: Leftword, 2003).

20. On Mark's use of "*ochlos*" see especially the writings of Ahn Byung-mu: "Jesus and the *Minjung* in the Gospel of Mark," in *Minjung Theology*, 138–52; *Jesus of Galilee*, (Hong Kong: Christian Conference of Asia & Seoul: Dr Ahn Byung-mu Memorial Service Committee, 2004). See also his essays, "The Transmitters of the Jesus-event," *CTC Bulletin* 5, no. 3—6, no. 1 (December 1984–April 1985): 26–39; "Jesus and People (Minjung)," *CTC Bulletin* 7, no. 3 (December 1987): 7–13 republished in *Asian Faces of Jesus*, ed. R.S. Sugirtharajah (London: SCM, 1993), 163–72.

21. For a useful tracing of the character of Satan in the Bible, see George B. Caird, *Principalities and Powers: A Study in Pauline Theology*, (Oxford: Clarendon, 1956), chap. 2, "The Great Accuser."

22. Mark 15:40–41. See also Luke 8:2–3 and 23:49 and Matthew 27:55–56.

23. See Hyun Young-hak, "Theology as Rumormongering," *CTC Bulletin* 5, no. 3—6, no. 1 (December 1984 –April 1985): 40–48.

24. Bernhard W. Anderson, *The Living Word of the Bible* (Philadelphia: Westminster Press, 1979), Chapter 1: "Word of Imagination." See also the discussion on the role of imagination in Biblical Hermeneutics in D. Preman Niles, *From East and West: Rethinking Christian Mission* (St. Louis: Chalice, 2004), 10–11 and 127–28.

25. Aloysius Pieris, S.J. "Cross-Scripture Reading in Buddhist-Christian Dialogue: A Search for the Right Method," in *Scripture, Community, and Mission*, (Hong Kong: CCA & CWM, 2003, second printing) 234–55.

26. Pieris, "Cross-Scripture Reading," 235.

27. Ibid., 244.

28. See also my discussion of Lynn de Silva's theological contribution in *The Lotus and the Sun: Asian Theological Engagement with Plurality and Power* (Canberra: Barton, 2013), 83–84.

29. Pieris, "Cross-Scripture Reading," 245–46.

30. Ibid., 249–50.

31. Ibid., 253.

32. Francis X. Clooney, S.J., *Comparative Theology: Deep Learning Across Religious Borders* (Chichester, West Sussex, UK: Wiley-Blackwell, 2010), 8–9. Clooney distinguishes comparative theology from other disciplines such as comparative religions and theologies of religious pluralism and deals largely with Catholic forebears of comparative theology.

33. Clooney, *Comparative Theology*, 27–29, 70.

34. Ibid., 4, 70.

35. Ibid., 17.

36. Augustine of Hippo, *De Doctrina Christiana,* chapter 40, section 60. See also my discussion in D. Preman Niles, *The Lotus and the Sun*, 167–68.

37. Clooney, *Comparative Theology*, 107.

38. Ibid., 75–76.

39. Ibid., 59–60.

40. C Lakshman Wickremesinghe, "Togetherness and Uniqueness—Living Faiths in inter-relation," *CTC Bulletin* 5, no. 1–2 (April–August 1984): 6–7.

3.

Postcolonial Hermeneutics: Confronting Colonialism

On reading postcolonial writings in general, one could easily get put off with the convoluted arguments and new verbal constructions that characterise these writings. Yet, for all that, postcolonialism remains a useful tool in exposing and confronting colonial attitudes imprinted in literature and in the interpretation of texts not only in the West but also in the former colonies. It continues the argument already presented in cross-textual reading as a counter-colonial approach, and rigorously scrutinises colonial approaches and attitudes. The premise in postcolonialism is that literature does not simply reflect reality but in actual fact governs one's perception of reality. In the case of colonialism, which it seeks to confront, postcolonialism holds that attitudes were first shaped in literature before they found expression in conquest, expansion and domination.

The term "postcolonialism" does not refer to a period after colonialism, when it would be spelled with a hyphen as "post-colonial", but rather to a stance or a critical method that follows after and contests colonialism. As critical language postcolonialsm has been fashioned principally by Third World émigrés in western academic institutions, mostly from departments of cultural studies. It arose as an interpretive strategy largely out of an experience of being "othered". I give an example of a Ceylonese (now Sri Lanka) scholar in England to illustrate what it means to be "othered". At a time in the previous century when not too many students from the colonies were studying in England, a Ceylonese student at the University of Oxford went for a walk in the Oxfordshire countryside. An English lady met him on his walk and asked ingenuously, "How many of you natives are studying here?" The young man replied, "Madam, I am the only foreigner, all the others are natives!" Either with good humour or rather more sullenly many Asians in western countries have parried expressions of what is now called "orientalism". Today, the experience of orientalism is more likely to be that of persons from the former colonies living in western countries rather than those living in the former colonies, who may not be aware of the impact of orientalism on them. One may either deflect expressions of orientalism or absorb it into one's behaviour and thinking (reverse orientalism), but one cannot ignore it.

Orientalism is more than just racism. It is a complex of well-organised perceptions and judgments about the "Other" that the Occident has created about the Orient and imposed on the Orient. It started during the colonial period and still continues. Using the problem of the two stories, which we are using as a hermeneutical key, orientalism devalues and even negates the second story. It assumes that the so-called "Other" cannot speak for itself and therefore has to be represented; and consequently the "Other" is insidiously represented in images and terms that the Occident has fashioned for it.

In dealing with our colonial heritage, the move from viewing it as an amorphous and undefined annoyance to tackling it as a more specific enterprise became possible with the ground breaking work of the Palestinian scholar Edward W. Said (1935–2003). Though his book *Orientalism*[1] specifically addresses the Islamic Orient of the British and French Empires, i.e. West Asia and North Africa, what he has to say about the operation of orientalism in general has a bearing on the whole of Asia. Said followed up his earlier book with *Culture And Imperialism* "to expand the arguments of the earlier book to describe a more general pattern of relationships between the modern metropolitan West and its overseas territories."[2] Postcolonialism as a critical response to orientalism from Third World intellectuals in western academies took off principally from his writings. Several theologians and biblical scholars of Third World origin in western academies also use postcolonial criticism. Its practice is now appearing, albeit sporadically and perhaps even reluctantly, in theological studies done in Asia.

The main purpose of this chapter is twofold. One is to sketch the contribution of Said for understanding the character and perils of orientalism, which is what buttresses colonialism. The other is to address the reasons for the reluctance of scholars in Asia to take on board the insights of postcolonialism; and then explore ways in which those who address the reality of empire, so to speak, from within the "belly of the beast" and those in Asia who have to contend directly with "the beast" itself could engage in a fruitful conversation.

Given these rather two specific intentions, the choice of writings would be both selective and limited, and would avoid major excursions into the vast array of theories and practices of postcolonialism that followed from the work of Said.

I will *first* evaluate the contribution of Edward Said who says that his experience in the West as a displaced Arab Palestinian provided him with the needed perspective to elaborate on "Orientalism" and later, by implication, on the broader subject of "Culture and Empire". As one in "the belly of the beast," he writes

> My own experiences of these matters are in part what made me write this book [*Orientalism*]. The life of an Arab Palestinian in the West, particularly in America, is disheartening. There exists here an almost unanimous consensus that politically he does not exist, and when it is allowed that he does, it is either as a nuisance or as an Oriental.[3]

What Said has to say is important not only for understanding emphases in postcolonialism and postcolonial theological writings that are beholden to Said's work, but also for suggesting the ingredients for a fruitful conversation between Asian theologians in the East and the West as they attempt to shake off the colonial imprints on their theological responses to Asian realities.

Second, I will assess the strengths and limitations of postcolonialism in general using Arif Dirlik's critical essays in *The Postcolonial Aura: Third World Criticism in the Age of Global Capitalism*,[4] especially the essay that carries the title of the book, and Robert J. C. Young's *Postcolonialism: An Historical Introduction*.[5] Though not a postcolonial critic himself, Arif Dirlik (originally from Turkey) shares the experience of most postcolonial critics—Third World intellectuals in First World academe—and is thus better placed to review the writings of

his colleagues, which he does primarily as a historian. He was professor of history at Duke University and the University of Oregon.
Besides his general interest in history, Dirlik has published exten-
sively on the historiography of China, the formation of the Chinese
Communist Party, the history of Chinese anarchism, and post-colonial globalism. Robert Young, now in the USA, was previously Professor of English and Critical Theory at the University of Oxford.
Acclaimed as the foremost postcolonial theorist in Britain, Young's
writing on postcolonialism is undergirded by his experience of the
gratuitous violence of colonialism during the Algerian war of independence. He says that in writing his book he was haunted by
memories of his childhood in Algeria through two black and white
photographs of Algerians: "Both interpellate me with the transgen-
dering force of colonial power, and the brute reality of its realiza-
tion."[6] In making this choice I do not reject or undervalue other
writings on postcolonialism. Given the fact that, as its practitioners
would readily admit, postcolonialism including its theological variety
is a "salmagundi"[7]—a varied collection of critical responses to the
effects of colonialism as encountered in a post-colonial age—I have
chosen these two scholars to approach postcolonialism in an organised and rather linear way. There is also another reason for making
this choice. Given the opaqueness of the prose of much of postcolonialist writings and the seemingly endless intellectual obfuscation that
its proponents seem to indulge in (I would exempt most postcolonial
theologians), these two writers help us to understand in as clear a way
as possible both the strengths and limitations of postcolonialism.

THE CONTRIBUTION OF EDWARD SAID TO THE
FASHIONING OF POSTCOLONIAL CRITICAL THINKING

While the attitude implied in orientalism may have originated with
travellers to Asia and imperial administrators, as a discipline it belongs
to the academy. As Said puts it,

> Orientalism is a style of thought based upon an ontological and episte-
> mological distinction made between "the Orient" and (most of the time)
> "the Occident". Thus a very large mass of writers . . . have accepted the
> basic distinction between East and West as the starting point for elab-
> orate theories, epics, novels, social descriptions, and political accounts
> concerning the Orient, its people, customs, "mind," destiny, and so on.[8]

Using an aspect of Michel Foucault's notion of "discourse" as the articulation of an unequal power relationship, Said argues, "My contention is that without examining Orientalism as a discourse one cannot possibly understand the enormous systematic discipline by which European culture was able to manage—even produce—the Orient politically, sociologically, militarily, ideologically, scientifically, and imaginatively during the post-Enlightenment period." Consequently, "the Orient was not (and is not) a free subject of thought or action."[9]

The Occident's creation of the Orient was not just pure imagination. There is an Orient, which however has not been given the chance, most times, to speak for itself. Reflecting the opinion of Karl Marx ("They cannot represent themselves; they must be represented.") as typical of orientalist thinking, Said says, "The relationship between Occident and Orient is a relationship of power, of domination, of varying degrees of a complex hegemony, and is quite accurately indicated in the title of K. M. Panikkar's classic *Asia and Western Dominance*."[10]

Hence, it would be naïve to assume that orientalism is no more than a figment of Occidental imagination, which would disappear once it is exposed as a structure of lies. Rather, "what we must respect and try to grasp is the sheer knitted-together strength of Orientalist discourse, its very close ties to the enabling socio-economic and political institutions, and its redoubtable durability."[11]

After identifying orientalism as a discourse à la Foucault, Said uses Antonio Gramsci's description of hegemony to continue his argument. Gramsci differentiates between civil and political societies in which the former is made up of voluntary affiliations (families, schools, trade unions) and the latter of state institutions (the army, the police, the central bureaucracy) whose role in the polity is direct domination. In civil society culture operates largely through common consent, not coercion, to bring together ideas and values. In political society certain cultural forms predominate over others and provide cultural leadership, which Gramsci labels "hegemony". In cultural hegemony a ruling class imposes its worldview made up of its preferred beliefs, values and mores on a culturally diverse society arguing that what it is doing is beneficial for all instead of admitting that it privileges the ruling class. Cultural hegemony is an artificial albeit powerful social construct. Said argues, "It is hegemony, or rather the result of hegemony at work [in the industrial West], that gives Orientalism the durability and strength I have been speaking about so far." It provides the basis for dividing the "us" (European, American) from "them" (the others) and specifying the relationship between the two as a vis-à-vis, "us" over against "them". Intrinsic to European culture is the indwelling of the idea of the Orient in perceptions and articulations of the Occident, and through which the superiority of the European is asserted: "It can be argued that the major component in European culture is precisely what made that culture hegemonic both in and outside Europe: the idea of European identity as a superior one in comparison with all the non-European peoples and cultures. There is in addition the hegemony of European ideas about the Orient, themselves reiterating European superiority over Oriental backwardness, usually overriding the possibility that a more independent, or more sceptical, thinker might have had different views on the matter."[12] During the post-Enlightenment and colonial period until now, this positional superiority has not been surrendered; and it governs almost all relationships between the Occident and the Orient whether it is through soldier, missionary, trader or writer. Consequently, this positional superiority undergirds the knowledge that is manufactured through these relationships. In other words, for instance, with some notable exceptions, one is European first and missionary second.

From culture to politics: "My idea is that European and then American interest in the Orient was political according to some of the obvious historical accounts . . . but it was culture that created that interest, that acted dynamically along with brute political, economic and military rationales to make the Orient the varied and complicated place that it obviously was in the field I call Orientalism."[13] Or, as Robert Young, commenting on Said's work puts it: "What Said shows is that the will to knowledge, and to produce its truth, is also a will to power. Academic knowledge is also a part of the apparatus of western power. . . . It was the fundamental argument repositioning academic knowledge from its claims to objectivity and autonomy that was at the basis of the impact that *Orientalism* achieved in the academy."[14]

The force of Said's argument resides in the detailed and meticulous work he has done to expose manifestations of orientalism in the written accounts of the Occident's relations with a particular geographical area. Analysis precedes and informs his basic position that culture does not simply reflect political attitudes, in this case orientalism, but in fact actually shapes them.

While Said himself did not propose a form of postcolonial theory and criticism, several intellectuals from the former colonies now in western academes have taken up both his invitation—"I have consoled myself with believing that this book is one instalment of several, and hope there are scholars and critics who might want to write others"[15]—and his warning—"My hope is to illustrate the formidable structure of cultural domination and, specifically for formerly colonized peoples, *the dangers and temptations of employing this structure upon themselves or upon others.*"[16]

Culture and Imperialism is a collection of lectures Said delivered after completing *Orientalism*. In the introduction, apparently written after the completion of the book,[17] Said presents his main findings, which are amplified in the body of the book. On a broader geographical canvas he is able not only "to illustrate the formidable structure of [imperial] cultural domination" that was the subject of *Orientalism*, but also to show cultural resistances to such domination, which by and large informed the struggles for independence in the colonised countries. "Never was it the case that the imperial encounter pitted an active Western intruder against a supine or inert non-Western native, there was always some form of active resistance, and in the overwhelming majority of cases, the resistance finally won out."[18]

What Said has to say about culture and imperialism is not simply locked into what happened at a particular historical period but is also pertinent for our time. While colonialism as such, that is the occupation of foreign lands, is by and large a thing of the past, imperialism is a perduring reality. It finds expression through the imperial pretentions of the USA and its allies as well as in the thinking and behaviour of Russia. Imperialism is also evident in the emerging Asian superpowers, such as China, or in the many dictatorships that afflict several Asian countries, which prescribe for the ruled what they should think and how they should behave, and suppresses opposing writings and writers. It is this fact that gives postcolonial writings, which followed from Said, their relevance for today.

While what "imperialism" denotes may not need much explanation, "culture" is too broad a concept and needs some refining when speaking of culture and imperialism. By "culture", Said means two things. "First of all it means all those practices, like the arts of description, communication and representation, that have relative autonomy from the economic, social and political realms and that often exist in aesthetic forms. . . ." Since his main focus is on the modern western empires of the nineteenth and twentieth centuries, he chooses the novel, among other aesthetic forms, as "immensely important in the formation of imperial attitudes, references and experiences." Although the main battle in colonialism as an expression of imperialism is on who owns the land, contesting claims were first of all decided in narrative. Said holds that the power to narrate and even to block out other narratives is a key element in the relationship between culture and imperialism.

> Most important, the grand narratives of emancipation and enlightenment mobilized people in the colonial world to rise up and throw off imperial subjection; in the process many Europeans and Americans were also stirred by these stories and their protagonists, and they too fought for new narratives of equality and human community.[19]

Second, "culture is a concept that includes a refining and elevating element, each society's reservoir of the best that has been known and thought." Expressions of culture are in many ways palliatives inuring us from "modern, aggressive mercantile, and brutalizing urban existence." But in time culture becomes a source of identity when associated with the nation or state, and a "combative one" at that. In the realm of imperial politics and writing culture serves not only to elevate the imperialist but also to relegate the other to a subservient or inferior race with crude epithets such as "niggers" or "kaffirs" as used in Afrikaans. In colonised countries where identity politics is rife, one's culture becomes on the one hand a means of opposing liberal philosophies such as multiculturalism and hybridity, and on the other producing religious and nationalistic jingoism that is rife in many, if not all, nations.

To illustrate the way in which culture functions in this second sense in the hands of imperialists, Said examines two great novels—Charles Dickens's *Great Expectations* (1861)[20] and Joseph Conrad's *Nostromo* (1904).[21] The principal theme of *Great Expectations* is the self-delusion of its principal character Pip who attempts to break into the rigid class system prevalent in Britain without either the necessary hard work or the aristocratic financial means required. Early in life Pip helps a condemned convict, Abel Magwitch, who after being transported to Australia anonymously pays back his benefactor with large sums of money. Since the lawyer who disburses the money says nothing about the source, Pip assumes that the source is an elderly gentlewoman, Miss Haversham. Old and ailing, Magwitch returns illegally to London, but is initially unwelcomed by Pit because the man had been removed from England and "reeks of delinquency". Though in the dénouement Pip and Magwitch are reconciled, at the heart of this novel is an acknowledgment of the social rigidity that defines Britain and the way in which it imperially views Australia, a penal colony. A form of social apartheid operates in which those who are sent there may make good but could not return because their experience is assumed to have permanently warped them. Australia's novelists, however, present another picture of life in Australia in which there is an optimistic transformation of social space in which a new egalitarianism removes social barriers. Said contends, "The prohibition placed on Magwitch's return is not only penal but imperial. Subjects can be taken to places like Australia, but they cannot be allowed a return to metropolitan space, which, as all Dickens's fiction testifies, is meticulously charted, spoken for, inhabited by a hierarchy of metropolitan personages."

Nostromo is located in a Central American republic, which is independent unlike the British colonies in Africa or Asia. However, these republics appear ungovernable. Governing them, opined the great nineteenth century general Simón Bolivar, who defeated the Spanish Imperial government to gain independence for these republics, is like ploughing the sea. Yet, America is enticed into this setting because of its mineral resources and exhibits another aspect of imperial culture. The San Francisco financier, who backs the British owner of the San Tomé mine, is clear that they should not be drawn into any great trouble. "We can sit and watch." Yet, "someday we shall step in. We are bound to." The greatest country in the whole of God's universe, namely the United States of America, would authorise everything from industry and law to politics and religion. "We shall run the world's business whether the world likes it or not. The world cannot help it—and neither can we, I guess." The attitude Conrad portrays is proleptic of the American Empire and the role it arrogates for itself. Said comments, "The rhetoric of power all too easily produces an illusion of benevolence when deployed in an imperial setting. Yet it is a rhetoric whose damning characteristic is that it has been used before" by all preceding empires.

Said continues,

> For if it is true that Conrad ironically sees the imperialism of the San Tomé silver mine's British and American owners as doomed by its own pretentious and impossible ambitions, it is also true that he writes as a man whose *Western* view of the non-Western world is so ingrained as to blind him to other histories, other cultures, other aspirations. All Conrad can see is a world totally dominated by the Atlantic West, in which every opposition to the West only confirms the West's wicked power. What Conrad cannot see is an alternative to this cruel tautology. He could neither understand that India, Africa and South America also had lives and cultures with integrities not totally controlled by the gringo imperialist and reformers of this world, nor allow himself to believe that anti-imperialist independence movements were not all corrupt and in the pay of the puppet masters in London or Washington.[22]

The reconciliation of Pip with Magwitch in *Great Expectations* in no way disrupts the carefully chartered social space of imperial Britain. Neither does it acknowledge the validity of the social space being chartered in Australia as reflected in works such as *The Fatal Shore* (Robert Hughes) and *The Road to Botany Bay* (Paul Carter). In *Nostromo*, Joseph Conrad neither can see nor acknowledge alternative Latino cultures. While in both instances Said draws attention to alternative literature, he does not mention indigenous oral cultures— Aboriginal in Australia and Native American in Central and South America. Oral cultures do not figure in his analyses of the operation of imperial culture and the ways in which it either put down or decimated indigenous cultures. This fact is to be noted not as a deficiency, but as an implicit acknowledgment of a limitation in what he attempts to do and does not pretend to do.

THEMES OF RESISTANCE CULTURE

Said observes that the recovery of geographical territory, which is at the heart of decolonisation, was preceded by the charting of cultural territory. It was a period when the ideology of nationalism was shaped in which culture played a role to give structure to nations that were formed during the colonial period for a wider unity than ever

known before. Though a simple idyllic return to the past was not sufficient, the process nevertheless entailed "the rediscovery and repatri-
ation of what had been suppressed in the native's past by the process
of imperialism" to forge a new national identity.

One theme had to do with the recovery of the corporate self that
was debased in the culture and behaviour of the Empire. It is one
of the tragedies of resistance "that it must to a certain degree work
to recover forms already established or at least influenced or infiltrated by the culture of empire," which had constructed a corporate
self from which the newly emerging nations could not escape. The
way forward was to occupy and subvert imperial culture to achieve
recognition: "to rechart and then occupy the place in imperial cultural forms reserved for subordination, to occupy it self-consciously,
fighting for it on the very same territory once ruled by a consciousness that assumed the subordination of a designated inferior."[23] Said
names this process "reinsciption".

One of the examples Said gives is that of Africa, which western
powers viewed as blank space to be charted and recharted by explor-
ers and ethnographers in which the "native" hears the strident note
of control and authority. For the native, that note sounds like banishment from the heart and from the home. A telling example of
countering such banishment is Nguiwa Thiongo's *The River Between*,
in which he rewrites Conrad's *Heart of Darkness*. In Conrad's narrative, the river Congo is like a large uncoiled snake with its head
in the sea and the rest of it snaking over a vast unchartered land.
Nguiwa Thiongo infuses *life* into Conrad's river from the beginning:
"The river was called Honia, which meant cure, or bring-back-to-
life. Honia river never dried: it seemed to possess a strong will to
live, scorning droughts and weather changes. And it went on in the
very same way, never hurrying, never hesitating. People saw this and
were happy." Said says "In Ngui the white man recedes in importance—he is compressed into a single missionary figure emblemat-
ically called Stanley—although his influence is felt in the divisions
that separate the villages, the riverbanks and the people from one
another."[24] These are unresolved tensions that would continue to
challenge the nations of Africa. Said concludes:

> The post imperial writers of the Third World . . . bear their past within
> them—as scars of humiliating wounds, as instigation for different prac-
> tices, as potentially revised visions of the past tending toward a post-

colonial future, as urgently reinterpretable and redeployable experiences, in which the formerly silent native speaks and acts on territory reclaimed as part of a general movement of resistance, from the colonist.[25]

A related motif is the self-conscious messing with the literature that the colonist required the natives to read and absorb into their personalities. Said gives as an example the ways in which Shakespeare's *Tempest* was read and developed in the new American and Caribbean nations. After surveying some of these writings, Said asks "How does a culture seeking to become independent of imperialism imagine its own past?"

> One choice is to do it as Ariel . . . a willing servant of Prospero. Ariel does what he is told obligingly and, when he regains his freedom, he returns to his native element, a sort of bourgeois native untroubled by his collaboration with Prospero. A second choice is to do it like Caliban, aware of and accepting his mongrel past but not disabled for future development. A third choice is to be a Caliban who sheds his current servitude and physical disfigurements in the process of discovering his essential pre-colonial self. *This* Caliban is behind the nativist and radical nationalisms that produced concepts of *négritude*, Islamic fundamentalism, Arabism and the like.[26]

The dangers of the first and third choices, though inevitable in the process of decolonisation, are all too obvious. The first simply replicates white officers in a post-colonial setting. Only the colour of the skin is different. The third, though an initial step—the recognition and affirmation of one's subject self—could lead to a frozen rigidity: "The dangers of chauvinism and xenophobia (Africa for the Africans) are very real." Said contends that "it is best when Caliban sees his own history as an aspect of the history of all subjugated men and women, and comprehends the complex truth of his own social and historical situation."[27]

It is not sufficient for Caliban to assert a different identity. Rather, he needs to see that he has a history open to development, which is not self-centred but corporate. He views his history as part of the history of all subjugated people attempting to break into a new liberating future. This is a work of imagination. In brief, it is a cultural effort that takes into account several factors. First, the birth of a nation is not the end but the beginning that carries with it several unresolved tensions. Said refers to Salman Rushdie's *Midnight's Children* as "a brilliant work based on the liberating imagination of independence itself, with all its anomalies and contradictions working themselves out. The conscious effort to enter into the discourse of Europe and the West, to mix with it, transform it, to make it acknowledge marginalized or suppressed or forgotten histories is of particular interest in Rushdie's work."[28] Postcolonial discourse continues, even after nationalism ends having accomplished its task, to create and sustain a liberating culture. It eschews separatist nationalism and moves "toward a more integrative view of human community and human liberation." In this project, which embraces differences, the women's movement played an important role during the period of decolonisation. Said lists a number of women pioneers in several Third World countries who often in alliance with western movements for women's rights worked not only for the emancipation of women from unfair male practices such as *sati* and foot-binding but also for women's education.[29] Second is the acknowledgment and assertion of "hybridity". In the process of Caliban appropriating his mongrel identity, rejecting the demeaned status assigned to him by imperial culture and seeking a new liberating future, he finds that he is heir to many cultures comingling in him. As Said puts it, "The history of all cultures is the history of cultural borrowings. . . . Cultures are not impermeable, just as Western science borrowed from Arabs, they had borrowed from India and Greece. Culture is never just a matter of ownership . . . but rather of appropriations, common experiences, and interdependencies of all kinds among different cultures."[30] Elsewhere he refers to Homi Bhabha's complex work on hybridity, and Bhabha's insistence that all cultures are hybrid and are "encumbered or entangled or overlapping with what used to be regarded as extraneous elements."[31] Third is the role of language. Said accepts and encourages the use of national languages saying that "without the practice of a national culture—from slogans to pamphlets and newspapers, from folktales and heroes to epic poetry, novels and drama—the language is inert; national culture organizes and sustains communal memory."[32]

While what he says is apt where there are acknowledged common national languages such as Arabic, Bahasa Indonesia and Swahili, the matter becomes more complex in countries such as India and Sri Lanka where several languages (not just dialects) with their own cultures and histories tied to specific races vie for a place in the cultural construction of a nation. An initial attempt to have Hindi as the main national language in India had to be abandoned. The blanket imposition of Sinhala in Sri Lanka with the policy of "Sinhala only" was disastrous. How do Asian countries with several distinct languages work together? Some have found a way forward with the adaptation of English in forms that are not only different from imperial English but are models of resistance. Salman Rushdie uses "the chutnification of English" in his *Midnight's Children* to spice up the language. A Japanese ecumenical worker, Tosh Arai, described his quaint language as "ecumenical English", which is a hybrid. It is amusing to notice in public meetings the exasperation of those who have to endure the mauling of their mother tongue, which has now become in various forms the language of the colonised. Even more pathetic are the attempts of white folk to "correct" the language of indigènes at public meetings, which is another feeble colonial effort.

Time and again Said returns to his main point that the cultures of the decolonised are not static but in process. While narrow nationalist resistance served a purpose during the initial stages in the struggle against imperialism, there is now "a noticeable pull away from separatist nationalism to a more integrative view of human community and human liberation"[33] that draws from many cultures both East and West. Resistance to such development is often scuppered by various forms of identity politics, yet the struggle for "a more integrative view of human community" must go on. Said's hope is that "far from being at the end of history, we are in a position to do something about our own present history and future history, whether we live inside or outside the metropolitan world."[34]

POSTCOLONIALISM—A CRITICAL ASSESSMENT

My concern in this section is to bring postcolonialism as fashioned by Third World émigrés in the West into an interface with Asian reluctance or better "unease" with it; and to seek a better interaction than simply confrontation. The intention would be to realise Said's hope that instead of being at the end of history we are at its beginning and can do something about it whether one lives inside or outside the metropolitan world.

A good part of the difficulty in accomplishing the task Said has set before us is the varied senses in which the term "postcolonial" is used. Dirlik identifies three prominent uses of the term:

(a) As a literal description of conditions in formerly colonial societies, in which case the term has concrete referents as "postcolonial societies" or "postcolonial intellectuals" . . . (b) as a description of a global condition after the period of colonialism, in which case the usage is somewhat more abstract and less concrete in reference, comparable in its vagueness to the earlier term, Third World, for which it is intended as a substitute, (c) as a description of a discourse on the above conditions that is informed by the epistemological and psychic orientations that are products of those conditions.[35]

These usages of the term are many a time conflated without due regard to difference leading to confusion and perhaps even needless confrontation.

Beginning with postcolonial in the third sense, several of the critical stances taken in it predate its appearance. For instance, the aversion to meta-narratives is already found in post-structuralism and in various other forms of post-modernism. "Hybridity" as a cultural fact has always been admitted though the response to it has been varied. According to Robert Young, using Ashish Nandy's *The Intimate Enemy: Loss and Recovery of Self under Colonialism*, Gandhi was the first person to use hybridity as a political tool in his conflict with colonialism.[36] Postcolonial criticism draws its inspiration from the various freedom movements and nationalist struggles that coincided with the collapse of colonialism as an imperial ordering of the globe. Equally important are the various anti-colonial and anti-imperial ideologies, especially Marxism, which functioned in the various liberation movements.

Also, as Dirlik shows, postcolonialism as resistance against colonialism is as old as colonialism itself; and even in a country like China, which was never totally brought under colonial rule, there has been a mixture of western thought and eastern concepts to create an indigenous form of resistance to colonialism with a post-colonial intention. In other words, postcolonialism in this sense is to be seen as co-extensive with colonialism itself.[37]

Since postcolonialism as a critical discourse draws from several sources that predate it, and furthermore is pluriform, though there are common characteristics, it may be worth approaching the subject more historically. This is what Dirlik does. To the question, "When did it begin and where?" Dirlik responds, "When Third World intellectuals have arrived in First World academe." As Dirlik admits, this response is only partly facetious, because the rise of postcolonial criticism in the mid 1980s not only coincided with the movement of a number of intellectuals from the Third World to the First World, but it also served to articulate their Third-Worldness as something to be taken seriously in First World academies. In other words, postcolonial criticism is the transformation of a Third World identity into a postcolonial consciousness in a First World situation. Thus, as Gyan Prakash, a postcolonialist, states,

> The third world, far from being confined to its assigned space, has penetrated the inner sanctum of the first world in the process of being "third worlded"—arousing, inciting, and affiliating with the subordinated others in the first world. It has reached across boundaries and barriers to connect with the minority voices in the first world: socialists, radicals, feminists, minorities.[38]

Leaving aside for the time being the contestable assertion that postcolonialism has in fact connected with other minority voices in the first world, to use this "happening" as a starting point for understanding postcolonialism makes sense because otherwise postcolonial does not really refer to any definable period except in a general sort of way as the period after the collapse of the various western and Japanese empires. As a comment, the Indian political analyst, Ninan Koshy, wrote to me in an email in 2012 (now lost):

> I have always felt that politically the theory [postcolonialism] has serious limitations because in a way there is no period that can be called postcolonial. This is because neo-colonialism took over in many countries as soon as they became independent, then through globalization a form of colonialism appeared, and now the empire is out of the closet. Political writings use mainly post-independence for purposes of periodization.

In using the movement of Third World intellectuals into western academe to set out the characteristics of postcolonialism, Dirlik uses principally the writing of GyanPrakash, which he considers the clearest articulation of what is postcolonialism. In the words of Gyan-Prakash, these Third World voices "speak within and to discourses familiar to the West instead of originating from some autonomous essence."[39] It is this location that gives postcolonialism as an outlook and postcolonial criticism as its application its primary character.

Fundamental to postcolonial discourse is its strenuous resistance and criticism of Eurocentrism. Taking off from post-structuralism, postcolonialism rejects meta-narratives or master narratives. Principal of the meta-narratives it rejects is modernisation in its bourgeois as well as in its Marxist form. Bourgeois modernization represents the renovation and redeployment of colonialism as economic development. Marxism, while critical of the bourgeois form, also promulgates a teleology in terms of the narrative of the modes of production. Several postcolonialists accept Marxist social analysis as do most liberation theologians but reject its teleology. Postcolonialism not only rejects orientalism as the construction of the Other in the image dubbed on it by Europe, but also nationalism because in the process of challenging colonialism it has put forward a national essence in history. Dirlik quotes Gyan Prakash:

> One of the distinct effects of the recent emergence of postcolonial criticism has been to force a radical re-thinking and re-formulation of knowledge and social identities authored and authorized by colonialism and western domination. . . . This is not to say that colonialism and its legacies remained unquestioned until recently: nationalism and Marxism come immediately to mind as powerful challenges to colonialism. But both of these operated with master narratives and put Europe at its centre. Thus, when nationalism, reversing Orientalist thought, attributed agency and history to the subject nation, it also staked a claim to the order of Reason and Progress instituted by colonialism and when Marxists pilloried colonialism, their criticism was framed by a universalist mode-of-production narrative.[40]

Intrinsic to this stance, as Dirlik points out, is the repudiation of all "foundational historical writing." Dirlik quotes Prakash to explain a "foundational" view, which is "that history is ultimately founded in and representable through some identity—individual, class, or structure—which resists further decomposition into heterogeneity." Foundational historiography is then to be perceived as discursive articulations from various standpoints with various vested interests to constitute their objects of knowledge. The "Third World" is to be seen as a variety of shifting positions. This means, as Dirlik points out, "They [subject positions] are best comprehended historically in their heterogeneity than structurally in their 'fixity'." If any global consequence is to be seen it is simply the local subject positions projected on to a global scale.[41]

Allied to the repudiation of "foundational" historiography is post-colonialism's rejection of all binarisms or the currency of oppositional categories that imply centre-margin thinking. It sees this tendency as endemic to "foundational" historiography. Rejecting binarisms does not mean the absorption of the previous third world into the first world. Rather, it is the creation of a tangential reality of "inbetween-ness", "hybridity", and a host of other descriptions that on the one hand indicate the porosity of boundaries and on the other the post-colonial subject's refusal to be drawn into either Eurocentrism or Orientalism.[42]

The rather brief and perhaps not so adequate description of the contours of postcolonialism given above should suffice to introduce three of its palpable limitations, which are all related to the distance between postcolonial discourse and history or better its configuration of history. My intention in pointing out limitations is not to disparage postcolonial criticism as an articulation of postcolonialism, but rather to show what postcolonial criticism can do and cannot do; and then provide other perspectives to augment postcolonial critical practices.

The *first* limitation is that in using its relationships and articulations in the West as normative, the claims of postcolonialism to speak for all disadvantaged people globally may be a claim too far.

The practitioners of postcolonial criticism in biblical and theological studies have also claimed, as does Gyan Prakash quoted above, a universal validity for their approaches and reprimanded those who have not taken it seriously in their approaches. R. S. Sugirtharajah said in 1998, "So far, however, there has been relative neglect of one of the most challenging, critical and controversial theoretical categories of our time—postcolonialism."[43] In his later book, *Postcolonial Reconfigurations* (2003), he repeats what he said earlier.[44] In the *Dictionary of Third World Theologies* (2000), Wong Wai-Ching proposes postcolonialsm as the only vestment in which Asian theology and other Third World theologies would find their true voice even though in challenging western theological constructions they may have engaged themselves in a postcolonial task: "However, if one takes seriously the critiques raised by postcolonial theorists, Third World theologies have yet to benefit from postcolonial critics

by taking on a self-critical perspective toward their strong dependence on a Third World identity. This dependence has resulted in
their freezing themselves within a category of difference designed by
the West."[45] She advances the same argument in her book, *The Poor
Woman: A Critical Analysis of Asian Theology and Contemporary Chinese Fiction by Women*, in which she subjects a cursory review of the
work of Asian theologians to the tenets of postcolonialism and ends
with the conclusion that the most that can be said about Asian theology is that it is "another name for non-Western theology."[46] Writing
in 2005, Kwok Pui-Lan bemoans a lack of interest in postcolonialism:
"Even progressive theologians in the United States—feminist, liber-
ationists, and racial minorities among them—who have championed
the use of critical categories such as gender, class and race in their
works, have not sufficiently addressed theology's collusion with colonialism in their theoretical frameworks."[47]

Yet, the response to this invitation or challenge has been meagre.
With the exception of those in Hong Kong and South Korea and a
few scattered in other places, Asian theologians have been strangely
silent. The assumption that new ideas take time to percolate does not
commend itself in this case, because postcolonialism is addressed to
those in the academy and intellectuals are usually swift to seize on
what they deem to be a good idea.

One of the reasons for this neglect is that, like Wong Wai-Ching,
postcolonial critics speak unfavourably of other scholarly enterprises,
which does not encourage general acceptance of postcolonial criticism. For instance, in the midst of some excellent postcolonial critical
observations, Sugirtharajah dismisses almost out of hand theological
efforts of scholars who do not embrace postcolonialsm. The work
of scholars in the Jesus Seminar, to whom I am indebted for understanding how Jesus confronted the oppressive Roman Empire of his
time, he rejects: "The significance of Jesus that they come up with
lies in portraying him as an odd, discomforting and politically disinterested figure who is an embarrassment both to conservatives and
to radicals."[48] A scholar in the Jesus Seminar, Steven Patterson, said
to me, "Postcolonialists just shoot from the hip!" I would grant that
the writings of John Dominic Crossan and others in the Jesus Seminar are controversial, but they are not irrelevant in the modern quest
for the historical Jesus. While there is much to gain from the writings
of these scholars, I do not imply that one has to buy into all of their

opinions. Sugirtharajah is equally hard on the work of Indian theologians. He dismisses the theological expressions of the Dalits by targeting the colonial missionary enterprise: "Most Christians in India come from the depressed classes and are beneficiaries of the colonial civilizing mission. They only saw the kinder side of colonialism, through schools, medical work and development projects, hence the reluctance to raise awkward questions about the colonial enterprise."[49] What is ignored in this comment is the fact that in seizing on the liberating message of the gospel, the Dalits were able to assert a different self-identity enabling them to contest the social tyranny of the Brahmins who fashioned the iniquitous caste system. (More will be said on this matter in chapter 5.) For a different reason, the renowned Indian theologian M. M. Thomas also comes in for censure because he does not view British imperialism as an unmitigated evil. He sees it as an aspect of God's providence serving to correct traditional Indian life to put India on the path to progress and nationhood. While he concedes that Thomas may have a point, Sugirtharajah goes on to say, "People who imagine themselves to be agents of God's providence and conscious of God's call end up as self-righteous and become destructive of their fellow human beings."[50] While Sugirtharajah's argument that Indian theologians, by and large, have not adequately taken into account the depredations of colonialism is well-taken, for us then to drive his argument all the way and consider Indian theology as merely encrusted either in colonialism or naïve anti-colonialisms would be a mistake. An either-or position, which postcolonialsm itself would be inclined to reject, could lead to the unsavoury conclusion that the theologians who do not embrace postcolonial critical thinking are either deluded or stupid!

The other reason why postcolonial critical thinking has not caught on more widely is its ambivalent response to direct historical engagement. Since postcolonialism as a scholarly enterprise originated from Indians domiciled in the West, I decided to question a few colleagues in India. The most I was able to elicit from Felix Wilfred was, "It may be good for our people in the West, but here we have reservations." A somewhat cynical but not altogether facetious remark from another Indian theologian M. P. Joseph, quoting the opinion of an Indian Christian activist, was "When daily rice no longer represents the struggle for life, postcolonialism could be appealing."

Even racial minorities in the USA respond in a similar vein. When

I questioned the renowned Black Theologian James Cone, a personal friend, he responded in an email on 11 November 2014, "Postcolonialism sounds like post-racism, which gives academics a lot to talk about, but does not seem to arise organically out of the oppressed community fighting for life and justice."[51]

It is interesting that in his article, "Black theology and postcolonial discourse,"[52] Edward P. Antonio holds that James Cone is actually a postcolonialist. Antonio does this almost by rewriting the "rule book" of postcoloniality. While Gyan Prakash argues that the Third World voices in western academia "speak within and to discourses familiar to the West instead of originating from some autonomous essence," Antonio suggests that the roots of black theology as postcolonial discourse reside in its historical legacy: "through the role slave religion played in protesting, challenging resisting and subverting slavery and its colonial underpinnings long before its formalization into the academic discourse of theology."[53]

He gives a synoptic account of the legacy of black theology beginning with slave protests and rebellions which led to the articulation of black consciousness in black critical social theory represented by a long line of black thinkers, such as Alexander Crummell, Edward Blyden, Sojourner Truth, W. E. B. DuBois, Frantz Fanon, and many others.

> What I want to suggest here is that in different ways these thinkers represent a genealogical meeting place for black theology and postcolonial theory both in the sense in which I have characterized postcolonial discourse as moral protest and as an imagined future, as well as in the sense anticipating the actual, historical postcolonial movements of the nineteenth and twentieth centuries.[54]

Black critical social theory found expression in black movements such as Pan-Africanism, Negritude and the civil rights movements, which inspired a global vision of a world without colonial domination.

He ends his essay with a note on the thinking of James Cone as an example of black theology's participation in the postcolonial discourse of the twentieth century.

In this survey he argues that the *denigration* of other races of which slavery is a prime example is intrinsic to the despicable process of "othering". This process of denigration is at the core of colonial expansion and the reality of empire. Though slave rebellions and protests, which countered this process, are not necessarily postcolonial in the strictest sense, postcoloniality is embedded in them in that in wrestling with oppressive historical conditions they lean towards a utopia rid of slavery. Slaves recast the religion of the "masters" for it to become a religion of protest, which carried the promise of equality for all before God. He sees this yearning for an alternative social arrangement of equality and freedom developed in black critical social theory as an expression of postcolonial critical thinking. In black critical social theory the yearning for an utopia is grounded in history and is to be realised in history as an alternative arrangement disabling white supremist social and political arrangements.

> To portray black critical social theory and the acts of protest it represents as utopian is not to say that postcoloniality is unattainable . . . , and it is not to disconnect black resistance from history. Rather, the ideal of a world that has overcome colonialism is provoked and informed by the experience of wrestling with existing historical conditions. I am proposing that in this regard we think of postcoloniality as an imagined moral vision of social formation characterized by racial justice and peace. In other words, slave protests [the matrix of black critical social theory] were often driven by an imaginative utopian impulse that gestured toward postcoloniality and in so doing inscribed its moral and rhetorical possibility.[55]

Pan-Africanism in its various forms is witness to black critical social thought transcending geographical borders to take postcolonial discourse to a global level that not only advocates black solidarity but also encompasses all oppressed black communities who are searching for a postcolonial world of freedom and social equality.

James H. Cone, the progenitor of black theology, Antonio argues, moved black theology as postcolonial discourse to another level. In discussions at the Ecumenical Association of Third World Theologians (EATWOT), Cone desired that the bridge between black American history and African history be restored. Invoking Pan-Africanism as a model, at the 1977 meeting of EATWOT in Ghana, Cone called for a serious dialogue between African and black nationalism arguing that "there is some sense in which the Black World is one." Antonio notes that in subsequent meetings, Cone tried to advance Black unity "as a political metaphor for the global unity of all oppressed peoples." At the meeting of EATWOT at New Delhi (1981), Cone said:

All Third World theologies began as a reaction to the dominant theologies of Europe and North America. Whether one speaks of Latin America, African, Asian or Caribbean theologies—all of these recent theological developments in the churches and seminaries of Third World nations signal the rejection of the missionary theologies of their former colonizers.

Antonio remarks, "Thus by making African American religious protest against racism fit into a broader movement of global protest against racist colonialism, Cone locates black theology firmly in the context of postcolonial discourse both in the moral, rhetorical and utopian sense."

However, commonalities in the origin of Third World theologies did not easily lead to an affirmation of mutuality, so that black unity could be perceived as a political metaphor for the global unity of all oppressed peoples. Noting the abhorrence of black theology in the USA as understandable though deplorable, Cone experienced the same rejection in some quarters of EATWOT. With dismay he declared in 1986, "We are your brothers and sisters and feel hurt when you reject us. We are culturally, politically and economically Third World People living in the First World." Consequently,

> ... we cannot have genuine dialogue in EATWOT until we learn how to treat each other as equals with love and respect, until everybody's experience is valued as much as others. When this happens, we will be able to explore our commonalities and divergences with creativity, learning from each other.[56]

Instead of cutting and shaping black theology to fit into the prefabricated thought structure of postcolonialism, Antonio sees it as participating in a legitimate postcolonial discourse that anchors itself in history and fingers racism as the primary villain in the projection and building of empire. Incidentally, I think he also meets Cone's reservation about postcolonialism to which I referred earlier.

While black theology foregrounds the issue of race in the historical reality of empire in postcolonial discourse, American indigenous theology highlights another aspect of disabling power relationships. When I asked another friend, Tink Tinker, an indigenous American belonging to the Osage Nation, about the usefulness of postcolonial criticism in indigenous theology, he responded in an email to me on 8 November 2014,

> The [postcolonial] discourse may have properly begun with Said and then advanced by Spivak and Bhabha, but it was then commandeered by a class of White theorists (with roots in critical theory stuff) who have made it a *new trope to power*. It has largely become a discourse equal in its turgidity to the French critical theory gang and seems to function to advance the academic potency of Whiteness—against all protestations to the contrary. While there are flashes of real usefulness in all of them, they have largely created a language that is only accessible to initiates . . . Anyway, American Indian scholars with rare exception attack American history of violence much less opaquely.[57]

Apropos of the problem of power that Tinker raises is the counter-opinion of a Canadian postcolonial critic, Diana Brydon, whom Dirlik quotes: "While postcolonial theorists embrace hybridity and heterogeneity as the characteristic postcolonial mode, some native writers in Canada resist what they see as a violating appropriation to insist on their ownership of their stories and their exclusive claim to an authenticity that should not be ventriloquized or parodied." While Brydon has some sympathy for such a stance, she argues that tactically it may prove to be self-defeating "because they depend on a view of cultural authenticity that condemns them to a continued marginality and an eventual death." Dirlik comments, "In other words, be hybrid or die!"[58]

Brydon's attitude is also revealing of the tendency of most post-colonials to take for granted the present economic and political organization of the world. To be more specific, postcolonialism strangely ignores the positions of power its protagonists occupy. It therefore fails when the struggle for justice and liberation is historically more specific as in the black struggle against white supremacy that is structured into society and the struggle of indigenous Americans against the continued violence that white society perpetrates on them economically and politically. To condemn such historical struggles as unwarranted and unhelpful expressions of binarisms would in effect emasculate the struggles of those on the margin. Who or what is "the beast" is a legitimate question to ask in specific historical struggles for dignity and freedom.

I concede that disparate struggles for justice and freedom are in danger of suffocation through isolation. Yet, the road to a meaningful global coalition of marginalised voices is considerably more arduous than what postcolonial critics envisage. That this is the case became apparent in the several meetings of the Ecumenical Association of Third World Theologians as M. P. Joseph elucidates in his book, *Theologies of the Non-Person: The Formative Years of EATWOT.*[59] As Joseph indicates two particular events were at the heart of the formation of EATWOT. One was that third world theologians from one country visiting another could detect similarities in their respective contextual theologies, which reflected the concerns of the poor. The other was that third world theologians participating in western ecumenical discussions found themselves trapped in an agenda not of their own making. They strained themselves attempting to express their theological positions vis-à-vis western theological canons rather than in talking to each other. A different forum was needed.[60] While similarities in concerns brought third world theologians together in EATWOT, no particular perspective was allowed to dominate others. For a time Latin American liberation theology postured as the most amiable framework for the expression of all third world theologies. At the meeting at Wennappua, Sri Lanka (7–20 January, 1979), in which I participated, this framework was rejected in favour of a more open framework that would permit the expression of both commonalities and divergences. Within such a framework it was felt there could be a process of mutual learning in which divergences would enrich rather than vitiate commonalities in the search for freedom and justice in a global solidarity of those on the margins.[61]

Those who are concerned with the historical reality of empire as a post-colonial condition point to a *second* limitation of postcolonialism. Addressing the Congress of Asian Theologians at Chiang Mai in August 2003, Ninan Koshy said,

> Asian theologians may want to look at the term "postcolonialism" in this new imperial age. Third World theologians do emphasize that the term means not only a simple periodization after Western countries dominated militarily but also a methodological revisionism that enables a wholesale critique of Western structures of knowledge and power since the Enlightenment. It has been recognized that [as Wong Wai-Ching notes on page 169 in the *Dictionary of Third World Theologies*] "Postcolonial theory is most essential to Third World theological reflection if one understands it as a critical tool addressing primarily imperialism's general and continuing ideological roles in peoples and cultures of the Third World countries." But the question has to be raised whether the theory is adequate when imperialism is no longer general but concrete

as empire and the role is not just ideological but political, economic and overwhelmingly military.[62]

Dirlik refers to a conversation between Indian intellectuals and Gayatri Chakravorty Spivak, a Non Resident Indian intellectual who is a postcolonialist, which also reflects Koshy's reticence with regard to the use of postcolonialism. When Spivak said that the Indians had misunderstood what she said and that in fact she "had constituted them equally with the diasporic Indian as the postcolonial intellectual," they responded, "What we write and teach has political and other actual consequences for us that are in a sense different from the consequences, or lack of consequences, for you." As Dirlik notes, since as a discourse postcolonialism deals with representations and denies a foundational position to history, it does not, or even cannot, articulate a position vis-à-vis "global capitalism".[63]

As a discourse postcolonialism inhabits the domain of literature, and successfully deals with the colonised and colonising psyche, but shies clear of most major political engagements and consequences. To put it more bluntly, it is discourse that assumes, even advocates, but does not engage directly in praxis. Allied to this fact is the physical position of postcolonialists. While they deem political, social and geographical boundaries to be porous and thus inconsequential, they do not concede that this porosity favours some and not others. To illustrate, economic globalisation with its ideology of neo-liberalism announces "freedom", but this freedom is for international finance and markets and those who have gained by these. Labour is not free to move across geographical borders. Postcolonialists do not face this restriction as do most Third World intellectuals. (Those with Indian passports have one heck of a time trying to get visas just to visit either Europe or America!) Furthermore, postcolonialism does not readily admit that it gains from capitalism's scrambling of the globe. First and Third worlds now exist everywhere and postcolonialists gain in being part of the West's First World—a location they inhabit in relation to all Third World peoples both in their new societies and the societies from which they originated.

To face this restriction or even to be cognizant of it in one's life, not just thought, is to be aware of a new globalism with structures of injustice that are endemic to it. Now "global capitalism" has escalated politically and militarily, as Ninan Koshy notes, and is tangibly present as a new imperial order that is attempting to reorder the world with the slogan "war on terror".[64]

The *third* limitation, when not viewed purely negatively, is in fact the major contribution of postcolonialism. Limiting itself to literature in the field of cultural studies, it exhibits great dexterity in unmasking colonial and colonising intentions, which shape our thinking and actions. This location goes back to Said himself. As Young remarks, "The production of a critique of Orientalism even today functions as the act of ceremony of initiation by which newcomers to the field assert their claim to take up the position of a speaking subject within the discourse of postcoloniality."[65] For Said, orientalist writings as literature reflect a false value system and a lopsided world view that privileges the Occident at the expense of the Orient. As we saw above, Said understood such writings as "discourse", as an exercise in power, through which the Orient, as "the Other", was indispensable for the self-presentation of the Occident. Following him postcolonial critics set several texts from different historical periods under one rubric "Orientalist discourse" and analyse these with a set of factors that would surface the Orientalist "leanings" embedded in the texts. In other words, as Young puts it, "The colonial discourse analyst analyses the representation as a representation, while the historian generally analyses the representation in terms of what it represents."[66] The postcolonial critic is not primarily concerned to compare the representation with the referents with questions about accuracy of representation, which is the major concern of the historian who would want to amass and evaluate evidence, and then identify historical alternatives worth pursuing in the present. Rather, the primary concern of the discourse analyst is to analyse the forms of representation, how they are structured, and what assumptions they contain and what ideologies they project. As Young notes, "Colonial discourse analyses are analyses of representations rather than investigations that seek to deliver facts or appraise evidence."[67] Consequently, as remarked above in the second limitation of postcolonialism, the relationship between history as represented and the real becomes nebulous, and in fact the truth or falsehood analysed is deemed to be in the representation itself. Texts are wrenched from their historical contexts and referents, and treated synchronically "as if they existed in an unhistorical unchanging spatialized textual continuum."[68] To put the matter another way, historical writings have been subsumed under colonial discourse analysis and made a part of literature and the study of culture.

Once we get away from the notion that postcolonial criticism should be about reconstructing history and instead recognise its value in deconstructing texts that shape historical thinking and political engagement, its value is immense. Located in the First World as "Third-Worlded" subjects, postcolonialists *experience* first hand how imperialism operates and the sway that it has in the academy, which then finds expression in the political and military actions of the Occident. In contesting and unmasking colonial and colonising intentions, it does what Said expects of it, namely "to illustrate the formidable structure of cultural domination and, specifically for formerly colonized peoples, the dangers and temptations of employing this structure upon themselves or upon others." Postcolonial criticism also points to another danger, namely that in combating imperialism on the ground in various forms of historical engagement, there is the possibility of retreating into a narrow "subjecthood", whether it be nationalism as an ideology or some form of debilitating identity politics. In contrast, postcolonial criticism at its best reflects the generous vision of Said that "Caliban" in recovering and asserting his new-found identity sees that he has a history open to development, which is not self-centred but corporate. He views his history as part of the history of all subjugated people attempting to break into a new liberating future.

What is required between those who contend with imperialism from within the "belly of the beast" and those from outside who experience the imposition of empire on them is not confrontation but collaboration with neither side making *exclusive* claims to authenticity. It is a claim too far for postcolonialists to assume that the struggles of all minorities for justice and liberation are either already subsumed in postcolonialism or would not be valid or articulate unless they are subsumed in postcolonialism. Stressing its nebulous connection with history and the fact that it gains from capitalism's scrambling of the globe, for those directly engaged in confronting the beast in historical engagement to dismiss postcolonialism out of hand as irrelevant for their struggles would also be a mistake. In brief, the way forward may lie in taking on board informed criticism of postcolonialism and seeing it alongside the interests of the broader movement of resistance against the historical reality of empire that is either seducing

Asian nations into its orbit or finds expression in newly formed Asian empires. It could also be used profitably to expose the reactionary expressions of those who base nationhood on the narrow self-interests of some form of identity politics, which both denies and combats pluralism.

Moving on to the field of theology, while it is true that most theologians working with postcolonial criticism are either located in the first world or economically in the first world part of the third world, to make this fact the primary basis for evaluating their work would be unproductive, since our primary concern is to see how a fruitful conversation could take place between theologians in Asia and abroad. In other words, how do we institute if not restore a conversation? To accomplish this task, we need to position the two differently. Those doing their theology in basically first world settings are more directly up against theologies that either promote or are informed by colonial theological approaches. They engage colonial theologies at a critical time when within the various theological disciplines themselves there are questions and uncertainties about the positions that hitherto have been held as universally valid. To take but one example, in the field of biblical studies the claims of historical critical methods to get us behind the text to the original text in which authorial intention may be discovered are being seriously contested.[69] In this situation, postcolonial theological approaches are exposing colonial intentions both in so-called "received theology" and in their epistemology, and show what theology can do and should not pretend to do. Thus, as Sugirtharajah succinctly states:

> Theologians often assume the role of legislators, and expect that their hermeneutical treatises will change the world. The task of theologians is not to change the world but to understand it. Theology does not create revolution; it changes people's perceptions and makes them aware of the need for revolution. Its function is to make people see more, feel more and rekindle the fire of resistance.[70]

From this perspective postcolonial critical thinking also serves western academies. As a professor of biblical studies, Deborah Krause in the USA said to me with reference to the postcolonial writings of Asian theologians, "Besides presenting us with alternative approaches to biblical studies, it is refreshing also to have alternative readings of the text from which we could profit."

Since postcolonial criticism as an expression of postcolonialism does not promulgate a theory as such, in the next chapter we will view its expression in the theological arena mainly through the writings of a select number of Asian scholars. As we noticed earlier, though not an explicit postcolonial scholar, Ahn Byung-mu uses an approach that is similar to that of postcolonial critics. Archie Lee uses postcolonial criticism in a discriminating way in his reclamation of biblical texts as living Asian texts impact on them. In the next chapter we will evaluate the contributions of other Asian theologians who address Christian Scripture from a postcolonial perspective.

Notes

1. Edward W. Said, *Orientalism* (New York: Vintage, Random House, 1979), republished with an Afterword in 1994, and with a new Preface in 2003 by Penguin.

2. Edward W. Said, *Culture and Imperialism* (New York: Vintage Books, 1993), xi.

3. Said, *Orientalism*, 27.

4. Arif Dirlik, *The Post Colonial Aura: Third World Criticism in the Age of Global Capitalism* (Colorado & Oxford: Westview, 1997).

5. Robert J.C. Young, *Postcolonialism: An Historical Introduction* (Oxford: Blackwell, 2001).

6. Young, *Postcolonialism*, vii.

7. R.S. Sugirtharajah, *Asian Biblical Hermeneutics and Postcolonialism: Contesting the Interpretations* (New York: Orbis, 1998), 15.

8. Said, *Orientalism*, 2–3.

9. Ibid., 3.

10. Ibid., 5.

11. Ibid., 6.

12. Ibid., 7.

13. Ibid., 12

14. Young, *Postcolonialism*, 387.

15. Said, *Orientalism*, 24.

16. Ibid., 25. Emphasis added.

17. The use of lower case Roman numerals to paginate an introduction or a preface usually indicates that these were written after the completion of the main body of the book, which would be paginated using Arabic numerals.

18. Said, *Culture and Imperialism*, xii.

19. Ibid., xiii.

20. Ibid., xiv–xvi.

21. Ibid., xvii–xviii.

22. Ibid., xviii.

23. Ibid., 210.

24. Ibid., 211.

25. Ibid., 212.

26. Ibid., 214.

27. Loc. cit.

28. Ibid., 216.

29. Ibid., 218.

30. Ibid., 217.

31. Ibid., 317.

32. Ibid., 215.

33. Ibid., 216.

34. Ibid., 219.

35. Dirlik, "Post Colonial Aura," 54

36. Young, *Postcolonialism*, 345–47.

37. Dirlik, "Postcolonial Aura," 59.

38. Quoted by Dirlik in "Postcolonial Aura," 57.

39. Ibid., 57, 64.

40. Ibid., 55–56.

41. Ibid., 57.

42. Ibid., 57–58.

43. R.S. Sugirtharajah, *Asian Biblical Hermeneutics*, ix.

44. R.S. Sugirtharajah, *Postcolonial Reconfigurations: An Alternative Way of Reading the Bible* (St Louis: Chalice, 2003), 100.

45. Angela Wong Wai-Ching, "Postcolonialism" in *Dictionary of Third World Theologies*, ed. Virginia Fabella, M. M. and R. S. Sugirtharajah, (New York: Orbis, 2000), 169–70.

46. Angela Wong Wai-Ching, *The Poor Woman: A Critical Analysis of Asian Theology and Contemporary Chinese Fiction by Women* (New York: Peter Lang, 2002), 30.

47. Kwok Pui-Lan, *Post Colonial Imagination and Feminist Theology* (Louisville: John Knox, 2005), 7.

48. R.S. Sugirtharajah, *Postcolonial Reconfigurations*, 100.

49. Ibid., 101.

50. Ibid., 155.

51. See James H. Cone, *The Cross and the Lynching Tree* (New York: Orbis, 2014) chapter 1 for an illustration of what he means by a discourse arising organically from an oppressed community fighting for life and justice.

52. Edward P. Antonio, "Black Theology and Postcolonial Discourse," in *The Cambridge Companion to Black Theology*, ed. Dwight N. Hopkins and Edward P. Antonio (Cambridge: Cambridge University Press, 2012), 298–308.

53. Antonio, "Black Theology," 300.

54. Ibid., 304.

55. Ibid., 303.

56. Ibid., 305–6.

57. George E. "Tink" Tinker, *American Indian Liberation: A Theology of Sovereignty* (New York: Orbis, 2008) is a useful introduction to Indigenous Theology. See in particular his first chapter that deals with methodology from an American Indian perspective.

58. Dirlik, "Postcolonial Aura," 60.

59. M.P. Joseph, *Theologies of the Non-Person: The Formative Years of EATWOT* (London: Palgrave Macmillan, 2015).

60. Joseph, *Theologies of the Non-Person*, 1–5.

61. Ibid., 85, and 167–99.

62. Ninan Koshy, "Socio-Political and Economic Concerns in Building Communities," *CTC Bulletin* 20, no. 1 (April 2004): 1.

63. Dirlik, "Postcolonial Aura," 61.

64. See further Ninan Koshy, "The Global Empire," *Reformed World* 56, no. 4 (2006): 333–47.

65. Young, *Postcolonialism*, 384.

66. Ibid., 390.

67. Ibid., 391.

68. Ibid., 390.

69. See Edgar W. Conrad, *Reading Isaiah* (Minneapolis: Augsburg Fortress, 1991), 1–27; and his essay, "How the Bible was Colonized," in *Scripture, Community and Mission: Essays in Honor of D. Preman Niles*, ed. Philip L. Wickeri, (Singapore: Christian Conference of Asia and London: Council for World Mission, Second Printing, 2003), 94–107.

70. Sugirtharajah, *Postcolonial Reconfigurations*, 125.

4.

Postcolonial Biblical Criticism: Addressing Colonial Entanglements

Postcolonial biblical criticism questions the assumption that the Bible and translations of it are innocent of political, especially colonial, intentions; and raises queries along three different but related fronts. The first has to do with how the various powerful empires of the time—Egypt, Assyria, Babylonia, Persia, Greece (Macedonia), and Rome, which succeeded each other—impacted on the writing and shaping of texts. The second is to identify the residue of interpretation that the colonial enterprise has left on the continued reception and use of the Bible. Specific to this matter is the reifying of expressions of Christian triumphalism as an offshoot of colonialism that are embedded in translations of the Bible. The third is to see how the Bible could speak to a plurality of voices so that it could be relevant today in the search for alternatives of hope in the social and political arena. These queries are not just peculiar to postcolonial biblical criticism. Perspectives I have used in the previous chapters on counter-colonial approaches reflect responses to these queries. What postcolonial biblical criticism does is to bring these perspectives together in a more focused way.

This chapter will address in the main the second and third queries; and will be in three parts. The first part sketches the way in which postcolonial biblical criticism deals with colonial entanglements in Christian Scripture especially in its myriad translations from the original Hebrew, Aramaic, and Greek. It argues that the Bible is essentially literature and needs to be treated as such. It transposes into biblical criticism Edward Said's dictum that literature does not simply reflect reality but shapes our perception of reality. The second part exposes some of the prominent ways in which patriarchy, which is allied to colonialism but not necessarily coterminous with it, suppresses the minority voices of women in Christian Scripture and tradition; and shows how these submerged voices could be heard in their own right. The third part is an example of how a particular text of Scripture—in this case John 14:6—which is traditionally used to argue for the exclusive claims of Christianity, could be interpreted in a multi-religious context so that it could speak to a plurality of voices.

Though they engage themselves in a postcolonial task, not all the writers I cite in this chapter identify themselves technically as belonging to the guild of postcolonialists.

I. POSTCOLONIAL CRITICISM
AND BIBLICAL INTERPRETATION

R.S. Sugirtharajah, who has done the most to delineate the function of postcolonial biblical criticism says, "What postcolonial biblical criticism does is to focus on the whole issue of expansion, domination, and imperialism as dominant forces in defining both the biblical narratives and biblical interpretation."[1] He explains:

> Postcolonialism is essentially a style of enquiry. . . . It instigates and creates possibilities, and provides a platform for the widest possible convergence of critical forces, of multi-ethnic, multi-religious, and multicultural voices, to assert their denied rights and rattle the centre. . . . As postcolonialism is not a theory in the strict sense of the term, but a collection of critical voices, an apt description would be to term it criticism. Criticism is not an exact science, but an undertaking of social and political commitment which should not be reduced to or solidified into a dogma. It is always *oppositional*.[2]

Sugirtharajah's brief introduction to the main purpose of the third chapter of his book succinctly describes the major intention of this discipline: "The overbearing thrust of this chapter is that postcolonial biblical criticism as such does not render meanings or answers but provides the ground rules for arriving at potential meanings."[3] In pursuit of this task, he applies insights from Said directly to a study of Christian Scripture as literature without getting enmeshed in general postcolonial discussions.

He does three things: First, he tracks the use of the Bible in the colonial enterprise and exposes colonial intentions both in the Bible and in interpretations of it. Second, he points to dissident voices in the third-world that proffered alternative readings, which challenged traditional western and indigenous interpretations that either reinforced or were impervious to the colonial strains in the Bible. Third, he suggests possible alternative methods for reading the Bible. It is not possible in a brief chapter to cover the whole gamut of his extensive writings. I will concentrate mainly on what he has to say on the use of the Bible, especially the King James Version, in the colonial enterprise, and how this version has impacted on the ways in which the Bible is received and interpreted today.

THE BIBLE AND WESTERN COLONIALISM

As Sugirtharajah rightly observes, before 1500 CE in Asia the Bible was a religious text alongside other religious texts. In large measure it was found in liturgical expressions and in iconic depictions.[4] The form of Christianity that flourished in spates at that time was mostly Nestorian, which had no political or military backing from any central western authority. It depended much on the disposition of Asian rulers for its acceptance and periodic survival. Matters changed after CE 1500 with the incursion of Portuguese Jesuit missions followed by Spanish and British missions, which had the blessing if not the overt backing of imperial authorities to introduce and maintain some form of Christendom or Christian dominion.[5]

Initially, the Bible as such did not enter the fray of the colonial enterprise. There were two main reasons for this. One was that the Bible was considered far too sacred a book to be entrusted to ordinary folk. While Hebrew, Greek and Latin (the Vulgate) were considered the appropriate languages for the Bible, translations into vernacular languages were deemed unseemly. Typical of this attitude was the opinion of a British prelate in the time of Henry VIII whom Sugirtharajah quotes, "The Bible is old; truth is old; God is old; and so is Latin, whereas English is new-fangled."[6] Even after Tyndale's translation was printed in 1525, there was a paucity of Bibles in English.

Implicit in not making the Bible available more widely was a second reason, which was more explicit in the Catholic assertion that translation is not sufficient maybe even dangerous without correct interpretation. Only the Pope and his bishops were authorised to do that. Consequently, the pastoral application of selected biblical texts in liturgies, catechisms and homilies were considered to be more important than the inherent authority of the texts themselves. More often than not biblical texts were used to reflect the doctrinal positions of the Church. The Council of Trent (1545–1563), which met largely to counter the Protestant Reformation, established the Latin Vulgate as the only authentic version of the Bible and forbade any translation contesting the Protestant fad of reading the Bible in vernacular languages. Sugirtharajah says in summary:

> The dominant perception was that, for the laity to grow in spirituality and personal holiness, direct access to the Bible was not necessary. The role of the laity was simply to listen to the Word expounded for them by the clergy. Thus the Bible was subjected to a rigorous control. The Council also insisted that the written tradition received by the Church must be held in equal reverence to the Holy Writ. The Bible was thus made an adjunct and a complement to Church tradition and teaching.[7]

Sugirtharajah contends that the real breakthrough in the Bible being freely available in vernacular languages was the work of the British and Foreign Bible Society, whose sole aim was to encourage a wider dispersion of the Bible. It was a Protestant effort. He quotes from George Browne's history of the society (1859):

> The Society is founded on the principle of reverence for the Holy Scriptures of the Old and New Testaments, as containing a revelation from God to men—a heavenly message addressed to all, and of supreme importance to every one of the human family. . . . Hence the Society aims to make these Holy Writings known in every nation and in every tongue, and, as far as may be, to render them the actual possession of every individual on the face of the whole earth.[8]

The society should be congratulated for breaking the nexus between a designated authority, claiming sole responsibility for interpreting the Bible, and the common reader. While conceding this point, one must also recognise the fact that despite its claim to be theologically neutral, since its work was pan-denominational, the aim of the society was patently political. It was to make the Bible available in translation to serve as an antidote to the idolatrous beliefs and practices of the "Natives", thereby disparaging their religion and culture, and as a way of inculcating the noble precepts and attitudes embedded in the Bible that made of Britain a great nation free of political upheavals. Consequently, this conviction found expression not only in the phenomenal growth of the society's auxiliaries both in Britain and abroad, but also in the thousands of languages into which the society translated the Bible.[9] This double intention, missionary and colonial, is evident in what the British governor of Madras said in 1847. Despite popular protests, Sugirtharajah notes, the governor argued,

> I can see no sufficient reason for objecting to the Bible being available in our public schools under the rule laid down by the council [of education]. It is the only means I know of giving to the Natives a practical knowledge of the sciences from whence arise all those high qualities which they admire so much in the character of those whom providence had placed to rule over them.[10]

TRANSLATORS AND INTERPRETERS

In critically examining a particular episode in translating the Bible and making it available to the general reader, Sugirtharajah surfaces a multi-faceted problem that is innate to this process. One could easily forget when reading the many translations available just in English that the latest book in the Bible is nearly two thousand years old. The matter of translating it and making it contemporary inevitably involves choice of words as well as interpretation. At this point the translator's ideological bent comes into play. I briefly give three examples.

In translating the New Testament and portions of the Old Testament from the original Greek and Hebrew, William Tyndale was inspired by Martin Luther's translation of the Bible into German, which had an impact on his own translation. Tyndale's Protestant bias was evident in the words he chose. He used "overseer" for "bishop", "elder" for "priest", and "love" rather than "charity". More controversially he translated the Greek *ekklesia* (literally "called out to assemble") as "congregation" rather than "church". He argued that his choice of words, which reflected the original Greek, did not support traditional Roman Catholic teaching, which was the official religion in his time. Enraged at his anti-Catholic bias, the authorities condemned him as a heretic and executed him in 1536.[11]

The so-called Geneva Bible, which followed Tyndale's bible, came from some eight hundred rich "dissenters" who fled to Geneva to escape the tyrannical reign of Mary Tudor (1553–1558). She abrogated the religious reform of her father (Henry VIII), who had separated the Church of England from the Roman Catholic Church; and she repudiated the religious leaning of her brother, Edward VI, whom she succeeded. During Edward's short reign (1547–1553) the country became openly Protestant; and a group of bishops produced the first Book of Common Prayer in English (1549), which supplanted the Latin liturgy and also expunged from the English text explicit Catholic rites. When Mary returned church and country to the Roman Catholic fold, she ferociously attacked her opponents. Some two hundred and eighty "dissenters" were burned at the stake, later earning her the sobriquet "Bloody Mary".[12]

Among those who fled to Protestant Geneva were some fine classical scholars who undertook translations of the New Testament from the original Greek and the Old Testament from the original Hebrew and Aramaic. These were the first to introduce chapter and verse divisions to make cross referencing of texts easier. Marginal interpretative notes were provided by eminent Protestant theologians, John Calvin, John Knox, Miles Coverdale among others. The marginal notes were of two kinds. One was to explain difficult words or original meanings. With a clear Protestant bias, the other made theological comments interpreting the text. These not only implied but also explicitly stated that Scripture enjoined disobedience to tyrannical monarchs and did not support church hierarchy. Also that one should confess one's sins only to God and not to bishops. The translation utilised a good percentage of the language of Tyndale, and continued its egalitarian character. It was a popular translation and was reprinted several times from 1560 onwards. Despite the emergence of the KJV in 1611, the Geneva Bible held sway for almost three quarters of a century. The last printing was in 1644. It was the Bible used by Shakespeare, John Bunyan and Cromwell's armies and was the bible of the Protestant pilgrims who went to America. As Bruce

M. Metzger says in the conclusion to his informative article on the Geneva Bible: "In short, it was chiefly owing to the dissemination of copies of the Geneva version of 1560 that a sturdy and articulate Protestantism was created in Britain, a Protestantism which made a permanent impact upon Anglo-American culture."[13]

When in 1603 James VI of Scotland, a descendent of Henry VII, succeeded Queen Elizabeth I as James I of England, he brought together two separate kingdoms. While he was King of Scotland he had to contend with Puritans who espoused extreme views savouring of republicanism. His skirmishes with Puritans influenced his religious policies when he became James I of England. In January 1604, he invited a group of churchmen to his palace at Hampton Court for a conference to deal principally with issues raised by Puritans in England who met him on his way from Edinburgh to London. Although loath to give too much prominence to the Puritans, he realised that it would be politically unwise not to include them at this conference. The matter of a new translation of the Bible arose almost by accident when John Reynolds, a prominent puritan who was president of Corpus Christi College, Oxford, persuaded the King to agree to a new translation of the Bible because those which were allowed in the reign of King Henry VIII and Edward VI were corrupt and not answerable to the truth of the original. James seized on this proposal with pleasure as a means of dealing with the Geneva Bible which he detested, not so much with the translation itself as the interpretative marginal notes.[14] He commissioned[15] some 47 scholars from the Church of England, divided into three "companies" (Oxford, Cambridge and Westminster) to undertake a new translation, but following as far as possible the Bishops' Bible where the original languages permitted (rule 1).[16] The new translation should reflect in its wording the ecclesiology and episcopal structure of the Church of England (rule 3). The integrity of the episcopacy would also ensure James's place as head of church and state, reflecting his oft repeated slogan "No bishop, no king". His authority to instruct came from his kingly authority ordained by God. Particularly revealing in this regard is his address to parliament in 1610, a year before the appearance of the new translation:

> The state of Monarchy is the supremest thing upon earth; for kings are not only God's lieutenants upon earth and sit upon God's throne, but even by God himself they are called gods. There be

three principal similarities that illustrate the state of Monarchy: one taken out of the word of God and the two other out of the grounds of policy and philosophy. In the Scriptures kings are called gods, and so their power after a certain relation compared to the Divine power. Kings are also compared to the fathers of families, for a king is truly *parens patriae*, the politic father of his people. And lastly, kings are compared to the head of this microcosm of the body of man.[17]

The new translation was not to have marginal explanatory comments like those in the Geneva Bible that irked the king. "No marginal notes at all to be affixed, but only for the explanation of the Hebrew or Greek words, which cannot, with some circumlocution, so briefly and fitly be expressed in the text" (rule 6). The translation began in 1605 and was finished in 1611. In the Book of Common Prayer (1662), the Authorised Version also known as the King James Version (KJV) replaced older authorised versions such as the Great Bible (1535) commissioned by Henry VIII, and the Bishops' Bible. By the first half of the eighteenth century, the KJV had become the only translation used in the Anglican and Protestant Churches.[18]

These three condensed accounts of the history of translations are intended to show not only how the biases of translators influenced translations, but also the positive or negative influence that the monarch had on the disposition of the translators. Also to be noted is the subsidiary but important fact that "proper interpretation", which was previously controlled by the central authority of the Church, was now a prerogative of the translator/s and subject to their particular viewpoint.

THE USE OF THE KING JAMES VERSION
IN THE BRITISH COLONIAL ENTERPRISE

In his well documented article, "The Master Copy: Postcolonial Notes on the King James Bible,"[19] Sugirtharajah argues that from its very inception, colonial intentions were all too evident. For instance, it is significant that the term "company" used for the three groups of translators in Oxford, Cambridge and Westminster headed by "directors" should mimic in its usage the language of mercantile companies that were about bringing goods from other countries. Trade then paved the way for colonising these countries. According to

Sugirtharajah, when "texts" are substituted for "lands", one sees the operation of the "rhetoric of appropriation", which works with the notion that the natural resources of the colonised belong to all and not just to the indigenous people from whom these are expropriated. In brief, he contends, the assumption is that "the British have every right to benefit from the cultural and religious riches of another people." Another important way in which he sees the "rhetoric of appropriation" working is when the original writers are disparaged. These, it is argued, do not really know how to appreciate and utilise the treasures that they have. Consequently, Christ's disciples were labelled an ignorant lot and their scholarship was despicable: "Mark for muddling Isaiah with Malachi, Matthew for . . . attributing the words of Jeremiah to Zephaniah," and so on. The Greek of the New Testament was also deemed to be "coarse and clumsy". Consequently, only in the hands of the English translators who applied stringent rules was the Bible redeemed to be the noble book that it should be.[20]

Intrinsic to making the Bible the noble book of the English-speaking people was the emphasis on nation and nationhood. Basing his judgment on Liah Greenfeld's treatise on nationalism,[21] Sugirtharajah notes an unusually high usage of the term "nation". There are some four hundred fifty-four occurrences of the word "nation" in the KJV compared to a hundred occurrences of *natio* in the Vulgate. The Hebrew terms denoting "people" in its various forms are consistently translated as "nation", where as in the Vulgate they are rendered as *populus*. The Greek terms *ethnos* and *genos* are regularly translated as "nation", while the Vulgate uses not only *natio* but also other terms such as *populus*, *genus* and *gens*. Quoting Liah Greenfeld, Sugirtharajah says that the term "nation" carries multiple meanings; and importantly in the KJV the term is used "to designate a tribe connected by ties of kinship and language, and race." In transforming and making the Bible, read "King James Version", the prized possession of the English with its emphasis on nationhood was but a short step to supporting the ambition of being a chosen nation, a new Cyrus, to liberate benighted people, and build the largest empire the world has ever known. No other translation of any other people took as central a place in defining their national identity as the KJV did in Britain.[22]

In disseminating the Bible to the colonies, the Bible Society used the KJV as a template for all vernacular translations and even suppressed earlier translations. Using as an example what the Bible Society did with regard to the Tamil translation, Sugirtharajah says,

> The resolution of March 5, 1841, of the Madras Auxiliary Bible Society states that there should be a fixed standard of translation and that such a standard is possessed in the authorized English version. The resolution went on to propose that because the translators lacked tools and had no access to books, and had not kept abreast of the latest critical ideas, they should adhere to the sense adopted in the English version rather than justify any appeal to the Textus Receptus of the Hebrew and Greek originals.[23]

Other Indian translations were also required to adhere to the same principles so that what the Authorised Version had accomplished in English would also be replicated in the Indian vernaculars and become the prized possession of the Indian Church.

The imposition of the KJV with its monarchical/colonial intentions either directly in English or through its vernacular clones did not always go unchallenged. Sugirtharajah gives several examples. During the Taiping Revolution (1850–1864), its leader Hong Xiuquan to the horror of the missionaries brazenly annotated the Chinese version of the KJV even stating that he was the divine son, the younger brother of Jesus, who had come to lead the revolt both against the Manchu rulers and foreign invaders and establish a "Heavenly Kingdom". J. C. Kumarappa, a Christian who openly joined Gandhi's freedom movement, was imprisoned with only a copy of the KJV to read. Instead of being seduced by the bible of the colonialists, he began to mess with the text. He annotated it making the annotations part of the text. He extended the Pauline passage that in Christ there is neither Jew nor Greek (Gal 3:28) to read "neither Hindu nor Muslim, neither Zoroastrian nor Christian." More famously he recast the words of Jesus in Matthew 25, to read: "I was beaten with laths and ye came not to dress my wounds, I fell down unconscious and ye gave me no water to refresh me. I was stripped naked and was indecently handled, but ye raised not your voice in protest." Kumarappa's intentions were clear. It is not with the arrogant British with their brutality but with the suffering satyagrahi (follower of Gandhi's principles of non-violent resistance) that Jesus identifies himself. In his hands, a colonial text was transformed to become a text of helpless sufferers on the margin.[24]

MODERN TRANSLATIONS

It is debatable whether subsequent English translations have fared any better and moved beyond the monarchical/colonial intentions encrypted in the KJV. Modern translations seem to have a different intention that skirts the problem. Today we have a plethora of bible translations. With a few exceptions, all of them carry the adjective "new" in their titles. Even those that do not are clear that their version is intended for the modern reader. All of these attempt to bridge the gap between the writings of an ancient people and the contemporary reader. Their basic intention is to make an ancient book modern. Inevitably, translation involves interpretation to suit the intended and varied readership. So, there is no longer a single bible but a number of bibles; and each version carries the theological bias of the translator/s and its intended readership.

Taking as an example the New Revised Standard Version (NRSV), Bruce M. Metzger, who chaired the translation committee, admits in his "Letter to the Reader"[25] that the NRSV is a direct descendent of the KJV, which he says has been called "the noblest monument of English prose" and has "entered . . . into the making of the personal character and the public institutions of the English speaking people." No change in intention here.

Yet, he says, it has defects that need to be rectified. By the middle of the nineteenth century the development in biblical studies and the discovery of manuscripts more ancient than those on which the KJV was based made it clear that a new translation was the best way forward.

In making the revision or new translation, the Division of Education and Ministry of the National Council of Churches of Christ, USA, the authorising body, instructed the translators "to continue in the tradition of the King James Bible, but to introduce such changes as are warranted on the basis of accuracy, clarity, euphony, and current English usage." So, working within the constraints of the original text, and taking into account injuries to the text in transmission, such as scribal errors in copying, the translators followed the maxim, "As literal as possible, as free as necessary." Metzger says that the NRSV is mainly a literal translation, and paraphrastic renderings have been kept to a minimum. He admits, however, "because no translation of the Bible is perfect or acceptable to all groups of readers . . . renderings of the Bible have proliferated."

In deviating from the text of the KJV, the translators were required to take into consideration the expectations of the modern reader. Older expressions and words such as "thou" were abandoned and so too the use of the gender specific masculine pronoun to signify generically both men and women. While there may not be reason to quarrel with these changes from the KJV, a more contentious issue is the use of the term "Lord" given in capitals. As Metzger correctly explains, in "pointing" (spelling) the Hebrew consonants YHWH with the vowels for 'adonai (Hebrew for "Lord"), the scribes alerted the reader to the sacredness of God's name, which is not to be pronounced. Instead, the alternative 'adonai should be read. In the New Testament, the Greek term kyrios is used as a title for Jesus, and rendered "Lord". While the technical explanations for capitalising "Lord" maybe correct, they bypass the fact that the term would sound both oppressive and offensive to those whom colonialism has brutalised. If the use of the masculine pronoun generically to denote both men and women is unacceptable what about the equally unacceptable use of "Lord" to denote divine human relationships?![26] The demands for political correctness could be endless.

The choice before us is clear. Either we reject the Bible and translations of it that in one way or another follow the KJV as nothing but poisoned chalices, which would both displease and disappoint Asian Christians. Or better, use insights from postcolonial criticism in our reading and interpretations of the biblical text to counter or deflect colonial perceptions. In brief, the task is to save the Bible from itself!

DECOLONISING THE BIBLE

There are two problems, which side by side, contribute to the Bible being used as an instrument of colonialism. One is that it is always used in translation so that a particular interpretation of the text rules. As we saw above, the egalitarian interpretations of the Geneva Bible following Tyndale's translation were rejected when the KJV with its monarchical/colonial slant gained prominence. In one way or another, it is the KJV that holds sway, while modern translations in making the Bible contemporary rarely if ever question the assumptions of the KJV.

The second and perhaps the more telling problem is that in using the Bible as an instrument to justify colonial depredations, the colonial imprints in the Bible have gained prominence and have contributed to the reading of the Bible as a colonial document that favours Christian triumphalism and denigrates other religions, cultures and peoples. I give two examples out of many that call for a critical reading of the Bible, whatever the translation, to circumvent this problem.

IS CONQUEST A BIBLE THING?

Sugirtharajah is convinced that it is so, and fingers this biblical motif as the primary villain in the Bible being used to justify the invasion and occupation of foreign lands as did Israel in invading and occupying Canaan, a land that did not belong to it. As an example of the use of this motif, Sugirtharajah cites the opinion of Robert Carroll, an Irishman, on Oliver Cromwell's 1649 campaign in Ireland:

> In the massacres of the Irish towns of Drogheda and Wexford, Cromwell played the biblical Joshua against the Irish as imagined Canaanites. Cromwell invited the Irish towns to surrender and annihilated the occupants when they refused to give themselves up to the invading English forces.[27]

Carroll reflects and embellishes the popular Irish notion that Cromwell an Englishman treated the Irish with disdain and thought nothing of invading and occupying their land and annihilating the occupants if necessary.

However, Tom Reilly, a descendent of a long standing Drogheda family has a different estimation of Cromwell's campaign in Ireland.[28] He says that he too was brought up on the popular Irish notion that Cromwell laid siege to Drogheda and made an example of the town when he captured and slaughtered the entire population. He cites an Irish textbook for eleven-year-olds published in 2004, which says, "Cromwell captured Drogheda. About 3,000 men, women and children were killed." Another textbook published in 2008 reads, "He [Cromwell] first laid siege to Drogheda. He was determined to make an example of the town. When he captured it he slaughtered the entire population." Appalled at such butchery, and that too from a man known for his religious devoutness and lofty moral principles, Reilly decided to investigate these accusations. When he consulted Drogheda's municipal records of 1649, a document missed by almost all Cromwellian scholars, he "read about the activities of hundreds of Drogheda people who went about their daily business in the days immediately after Cromwell's visit." So, an entire population was not annihilated. Reilly's considered opinion is that Cromwell's campaign was primarily against the royalists ensconced in Irish forts who were opposed to the parliamentarians. These were indeed destroyed when they refused to surrender to Cromwell's forces. In the crossfire between the forces several civilians may have died but there is no clear evidence that Cromwell was intent on annihilating the Irish and occupying their land. In the sack of Wexford many of its inhabitants were killed, but the town had no garrison and those killed were civilian volunteers in military posture.[29] While the evidence of history may not quite favour Carroll's opinion given above, seven centuries of ruthless British control over Ireland, beginning with the invading Normans in the twelfth century, hardens the perception that Cromwell's campaign in Ireland was a continuing expression of a conquest mind-set.

If caution is needed, whatever the historical facts, in juxtaposing Cromwell's campaign in Ireland with the biblical motif of conquest, it is present though hidden in the stated intentions of Christopher Columbus. Between his third and fourth voyages, with the help of a Carthusian monk, Columbus put together some two hundred prophecies drawn from the Bible and early church fathers with a preponderance of quotations from Isaiah whom he deemed to be not only a prophet but also an evangelist. The purpose of this collection was to convince King Ferdinand and Queen Isabella of Spain that the heathens were eagerly waiting for the good news and for their deliverance, so that the Spanish royalty would fund his forthcoming expedition. In the words of Columbus, "I have already said that for the voyage to the Indies neither intelligence nor mathematics nor world maps were of any use to me; it was the fulfilment of Isaiah's prophecy."[30] There is ample evidence that Columbus was a very religious man. Then, was the book of prophecies presented to Spain's royalty simply a ploy or was it a genuine expression of Columbus's sense of a God-given destiny? Debate on his motives continues to rage especially with 1992 commemorating the five-hundredth year of his so-called discovery of the new world.[31] Whatever his motives,

Columbus's evangelistic zeal resulted in the decimation and/or racial absorption of the indigenous population of the "Indies", and the conquest and plunder of a land and people. In their article, "Thief, Slave Trader, Murderer: Christopher Columbus and Caribbean Population Decline,"[32] Tink Tinker and Mark Freeland, both Native Americans, present with evidence the darker side of Columbus's excursions. In "God the Conqueror," Robert Allen Warrior, a Native American of the Osage nation reads the Exodus story as would a "Canaanite", the original inhabitants of the land "who should be at the centre of Christian theological reflection and political action."[33]

My main intention in choosing these two examples of "conquest" drawn from Sugirtharajah with my comments is not so much to question the religious motives or morality of either Cromwell or Columbus, about which there is continuing debate, but rather to show how in imperial/colonial enterprises colonial strains in the Bible become prominent. On the one hand, a conquest mentality justifies the depredations of the colonialist and projects a false opinion of racial superiority and, on the other, it denies the humanity of the conquered, who are depicted as irrational, insincere and unreliable.[34] The plea is that counter readings of Biblical narratives should also be taken into account in biblical interpretation.

ARE OTHER GODS MERE IDOLS?

In choosing prophecies from Isaiah to set himself up as God's chosen one to spread the good news of Christianity and convert the heathens, Columbus chose passages mostly from chapters 40 to 66, which heavily reflect changes that took place in the Jewish faith during and after the exile. In stark contrast to the brutal policies of the Babylonian empire, the Persian emperor Cyrus, who defeated the Babylonians and took over their empire besides other empires, instituted a foreign policy that was both humane and wise. Conquered people were permitted to return to their lands, and the whole empire was controlled through a system of satrapies. (A satrap was a local governor or viceroy who was responsible for a region and collected the taxes for the empire.) The Jews who returned from Persia to Jerusalem in 521 BCE were convinced that it was their god, Yahweh, who had chosen Cyrus to deliver them (Isa 45:1); and that Yahweh was the only true god. A good example is Isaiah 44:6–8 with its insistence "I am the first and I am the last", probably a play on God's name (cf. Exod 3:16), and ending with the question "Is there any god beside me?" Isaiah 44:9–20, a prose excursus following the poetic first section, ridicules other gods as mere idols, which are the work of human hands. The lofty poetry of Isaiah 40–66 was intended to encourage a dispirited people who had been broken with loss of land and temple. However, in giving prominence to the exclusive claim of Yahweh as the only true god, who had chosen them, the returning exiles were not only encouraged to rebuild the walls of Jerusalem and the temple at Jerusalem, but were also persuaded to exclude the old Jewish inhabitants of the land who were left behind during the exile. These were variously called Samaritans or derisively as "the people of the earth/land" (Hebrew *'am-ha'aretz*), who are an ignorant lot. These had married into other nationalities and were deemed to have sullied the pure Jewish faith with extraneous polytheistic elements.[35]

The belief in a male monotheistic god, carried over into Christianity from post-exilic Judaism, infiltrated western missionary endeavours, and created a posture of Christianity being over against other religions; and consequently people of other faiths are deprecated. As Sugirtharajah puts it,

> Biblical monotheism enforced choice. Non-biblical religions are portrayed as the pagan "other" of Christianity, propagating superstitious cults rather than a legitimate belief system. More pertinently, monotheistic ideals fail people who are part of a polytheistic world and are self-consciously pluralistic and constantly juggle multiple identities. Adherence to a monotheistic god meant erasing the various gods and goddesses of Asia.[36]

CONTRAPUNTAL READING:
RELEASING SUBMERGED VOICES

In the two examples I have given above of how colonial themes could be enhanced in the reading and use of the Bible, I have also drawn attention to largely ignored minority critical voices. The purpose of postcolonial biblical criticism on the one hand is to point to and critique colonial themes that are used to parade western Christian superiority, and on the other to rescue minority voices often silenced in the text.

An invaluable tool in this critical enterprise is the contrapuntal reading of texts, which Edward Said popularised. An accomplished performer (pianist) of western music, Said borrowed contrapuntal reading as a metaphor from music, to release silenced and minority voices to be heard in their own right. In contrapuntal music, "various themes play off one another, with only a provisional privilege being given to any particular one, yet in the resulting polyphony there is concert and order." In using counterpoint as a metaphor for a reading strategy, Said says that English novels could and in fact should be read contrapuntally as "shaped perhaps even determined by the specific history of colonization, resistance, and finally native nationalism" at which "point alternative or new narratives emerge."[37]

When the technique of counterpoint is moved from music to literature, its task is to surface critical voices that challenge and counter the dominant text. Dissident voices in the text and countervailing biblical interpretations prompt us to assert that a text without a subtext is not worth reading.[38] Polyphony is not only desirable but also essential if Christian Scripture is to shape our perception of reality. In other words, if the Bible in a derived sense is to be taken as the word of God that witnesses to the Word who is God, then the richness of the text as a whole has to be taken into account. It is a method that would critique the dominant voices in Scripture and their deployment in the colonial enterprise and privilege the often ignored subdominant voices. Through such forms of biblical interpretation new narratives would emerge and in fact do emerge. In the next section we will see how this takes place in Asian feminist hermeneutics as a case in point.

II. ASIAN FEMINIST HERMENEUTICS— RESTORING SUBDUED VOICES

Asian feminist hermeneutics is a comparatively recent development in Asian theology. In her book, *Introducing Asian Feminist Theology*, Kwok Pui-Lan says, "Although in early periods Asian Christian women had reflected on their faith, a collective, conscious attempt to do Asian feminist *liberation* theology did not begin until the late 1970s."[39] As Kwok notes, feminist liberation theology in Asia has not attempted to create another adjective for its theological enterprise as for instance womanist theology by African-American women and *mujerista* theology by Hispanic women.[40] These two theologies address a structural problem that has to do with dysfunctional gender relationships both within and outside their communities. In Asia, the problem is not just structural but is also ontological. The dominant male class and caste based religious philosophies of Hinduism, Confucianism and Shintoism have inscribed the place for women in their systems. The need to address the subservience of women in these systems, and the pan Asian struggle of women to overcome religious, cultural and social discrimination under patriarchal systems has prompted progressive women theologians to retain the term "feminist theology" for their several projects.

To see how patriarchy operates in dominant male class and caste based religious ideologies in Asia, I take the Laws of Manu as an example. It is a brahminic hybrid moral-religious codification for social and religious life formulated probably sometime around 500 BCE. Manu is clear that independence is not desirable for women. "A girl, a young woman, or even an old woman should not do anything independently, even in her own home. In childhood a woman should be under her father's control, in youth under her husband's, and when her husband is dead under her son's. She should not have independence" (5.147–49; 9.3). Implied in this stipulation is the assumed sexual danger a woman poses. Her sexual appetite needs to be curbed, so she has to be controlled. Moving on, should her husband die, she should not remarry but remain chaste for which she would be amply rewarded in the hereafter and be reunited with her husband. Wendy Doniger, from whom the quotation about Manu is taken, goes on to say, "Manu's fear that the widow might sleep with another man was an important strand in the later argument that the best way to ensure that the widow never slept with any other man but her husband was to make sure that she died with him."[41] That is *sati*. Though, as Doniger points out, other *shastras* (precepts, legal and religious codes) give the woman greater independence, so that she could even control the family's finances, it is the stark misogyny of Manu that seems to prevail: "Manu is the flag bearer of the Hindu oppression of women," says Doniger, "but the *shastras* are just as diverse here as on other points."[42]

In seeking to liberate Asian women from the evils of their culture or religion, such as foot binding in China and *sati* in India, colonial Christianity simply replaced one patriarchal attitude to women with another. These Asian religious and cultural aberrations have been fingered as examples of depravity in other religious cultures, and have been excuses to impose the "superior" male monotheistic religion of Christianity in Asia. A western colonial/male religion that sets aside indigenous religious and social practices decides what is best for Asian women. The process of "othering" continues, and is infused with colonial intentions.[43]

In her article "Unbinding Our Feet,"[44] Kwok Pui-Lan shows how colonial Christianity used its opposition to the practice of foot binding to strengthen its colonial grip on China and continued the silencing of women's voices.

Unequal British treaties in China in the mid-nineteenth century permitted the establishment of local Christian missions and churches. These were often described using military terminology. For example, the detailed and meticulous 1922 survey of churches and missionary personnel was entitled, *The Christian Occupation of China: General Survey of the Numerical Strength and Geographical Distribution of Christian Forces in China*. Commenting on the explicit military terminology, Kwok asserts,

> If military troops were deployed to serve imperialistic interests in those days, the "Christian forces" were commissioned under much nobler causes. One such cause was to save brown women from brown men, which some have called "colonialist feminism." . . . Saving brown women functions as a colonial ideology helping to camouflage the violence and brutality of colonialism by sugarcoating it as a form of social mission.[45]

She says that this attitude is so deep-seated in white women's consciousness that it surfaces in western feminist religious discourse such as in Mary Daly's *Gyn/Ecology: The Metaethics of Radical Feminism*. This uncritical approach permits Daly to claim a false catholicity for western feminism in which she states: "Those who claim to see racism and/or imperialism in my indictment of these atrocities [sati, footbinding, and genital mutilation] can do so only by blinding themselves to the fact that the oppression of women knows no ethnic, national, or religious bounds."[46]

It is not that Kwok and Asian feminist theologians are against collaborating with western feminists; in fact they welcome collaboration. Their concern in such collaboration is best described in

Katharine Doob Sakenfeld's presidential address, "Whose Text Is It?" to the meeting of the Society of Biblical Literature in 2007. While stressing the need to include the voices of women that have thus far been peripheral to the discipline of biblical studies, she argues that such welcoming should not obscure fault lines that exist between feminists who read the text from a western (Christian) feminist perspective and the perspectives of those who belong to different cultures who carry with them their conversations with other religious traditions. In the meeting between several feminist perspectives the tension between coloniser (West) and colonised (Third World) could also appear.[47] These tensions need to be taken into account if there is to be meaningful collaboration.

To encourage constructive dialogue or collaboration across fault lines, Kwok re-examines the specific practices of *sati* and footbinding from an Asian perspective to expose colonial intentions. It is not that *sati* and footbinding have to be abolished, but it is the way in which they are done that causes alarm.

On the matter of *sati*, Kwok quotes the opinion of the Indian feminist historian and cultural critic Lata Mani who says that when the British gradually expanded their control from Bengal to much of the Indian subcontinent, the British opposition to *sati* was not based on some kind of Christian benevolence. Rather, the debate during this period was on the feasibility of enacting a law that could easily inflame popular unrest and destabilise Britain's colonial control over India. To appease the Hindu population the authorities went to great lengths to show that in abolishing *sati* they were simply resuscitating ancient Hindu beliefs.[48] Kwok concludes, "Through an Orientalist study of scriptures, a Hindu past was reconstituted as a lost ideal, which contrasted sharply with the present degeneration of India."[49] This process did nothing to subvert the Hindu male oppression of women. Neither did it deal with the marginalising of women and the suffering of widows. One male structure, in this case a colonial one, simply replaced another male structure with a spurious reference to ancient Hinduism.

In her *Feminist Hermeneutics*, Pushpa Joseph, a Catholic Franciscan nun from India, shows the danger of this questionable approach to what Orientalists term "ancient Hinduism". In her discussion of the "Myth of the Glorious Vedic Womanhood" and the "Myth of the Aryan Woman",[50] she argues that Orientalists, many a time with the connivance of fundamentalist Hindu activists, have constructed myths. A myth is neither a lie nor a confession. Rather, it is an inflection, or rhetorical device, that sends out a message.[51] These two myths either de-sex a woman and turn her into an object of worship thus spiritualising womanhood or they simply stress her usefulness as a source of reproduction. "A woman's procreative role was originally a source of power. However, it has been rendered powerless through its subjection to male domination." The task for the feminist, she argues, is to retrieve motherhood as a source of liberation, so that women can have the power needed to exercise their rightful participatory role in public life from which they are now excluded.[52]

Staying with the rite of *sati*, a fruitful and liberating conversation within Hinduism is possible when, as Doniger points out and we have noted above, counter-*shastras* that clearly contradict Manu's misogyny and give women a more constructive role in religion and society are taken into account. Here then is a meeting point for Christian feminists with Hindu feminists who also at great peril to themselves challenge the chauvinism of ultraorthodox and fundamentalist Hindus who continue to define and control the motility of women in religion and society.

Returning to the matter of footbinding, Kwok notes several deficiencies in western missionary perceptions. For one thing, the practice was not so wide-spread and timeless as missionaries made it out to be. Kwok notes the particular periods in Chinese history when this practice was prevalent. For another, no Chinese woman's voice was consulted, because a missionary determination had already been made that the culture was backward. In the mid-nineteenth century there were anti-footbinding movements in China particularly from Chinese Christian women.[53] With reference to the missionary refusal to hear the voice of Chinese women, Kwok quotes the experience of Sophia H. Chen, a non-Christian Chinese literati, who happened to attend a lecture in the USA of a woman missionary who had just returned from China. Before giving the lecture, the missionary took a piece of chalk and put a small white mark on the blackboard, and said that the white mark represented the enlightened missionary presence in China while the rest was all black. Disgusted with such misrepresentations and caricatures of an ancient culture, Chen writes, "The mentality of the missionaries who came to China was not prepared to meet a culture that could rival the one they had been used to; they only looked for the dark and the savage, such as they had looked for and found in dark Africa."[54]

An even more troublesome issue in the matter of footbinding is the "voice" of the women whose feet were mutilated. Was this practice undertaken because the women concerned desired small feet to be more attractive to men or was it done so that their physical motility could be controlled? It is a question similar to the one that concerns the experience of widows who were subjected to the rite of *sati*. As Doniger notes, in her section on "Did she jump or was she pushed?" that the voices of those who willingly offered themselves to die on the funeral pyre of their husbands are not known. These, in a sense, speak, but cannot be heard. We only have the muted voices of those who managed or did not manage to escape this religiously sanctified murder—muted because reasons are attributed to them. Others speak for them.[55]

Commenting on the opinion of Gayatri Chakravorty Spivak, who wrote of "white men saving brown women from brown men", Kwok notes, "As passive victims, brown women were not allowed to speak. . . . The subaltern woman has been written, represented, argued about, and even legislated for, but she is allowed no discursive position from which to speak. By speech, Spivak has in mind access to symbolic and political power." If the subaltern can speak, the subaltern is not a subaltern anymore. Under mounting criticism that she has cast the subaltern woman forever as a silent object, within the totalising discourse of western and patriarchal domination, Spivak altered her position to say that the issue is not whether or not the subaltern woman can speak, but rather whether she can be *heard*.[56] Listening and hearing are important moods in all subaltern theology and especially in Asian feminist theology. When women are not heard or simply shunted off to do their own thing in a male determined conclave, their silence and non-cooperation become a political act of resistance.

It is not my intention in this short section to cover the whole gamut of what is Asian feminist theology, which would be an impossible task. Rather, my intention has been to identify the theme of silence and silencing in two different Asian cultures and show how patriarchy in collusion with colonialism especially in the form of Orientalist discourse has not only distorted the voices of Asian women but also strengthened structures of patriarchy that are endemic to Asian reality. I have tried not to homogenise the experience of Asian women by needlessly cutting across cultures. Equally, I have been mindful of what Wong Wai Ching has to say about casting Asian women as "either victims who suffered severely from inhuman systems of oppression or heroines who fought courageously to liberate themselves and challenged the hierarchical structures of Asian societies."[57] This she argues is an oversimplification.[58] In concentrating on the theme of silence and silencing, my intention is not to work on the victim/victimizer syndrome, but rather to open the space that Asian feminist theology is calling for in which the voices of women could be heard not just as pathetic victims but as those who are challenging unequal power relationships. It is this stress that Asian feminist and all feminist readings of the Bible attempt to take into account.

In pursuit of this task, feminist theologians have foregrounded the dominant patriarchal and androcentric language of the Bible. That this is the case Bruce Metzger admits in his "Letter to the Reader": "The mandate [to the translators] specified that, in reference to men and women, masculine oriented language should be eliminated as far as this can be done without altering passages that reflect the historical situation of ancient patriarchal culture."[59] Feminist biblical interpreters not only come up against the "ancient patriarchal culture" that the Bible reflects but also the fact that in the process of setting up the canon of the New Testament texts, writings attributed to women, such as the Gospel of Mary Magdalene, have been left out. A further complication is the fact that in viewing Jesus as the emancipator of women biblical texts have codified Jesus as anti-Jewish—a problem that Jewish feminist theologians have pointed out.[60] With the barriers that confront Asian feminist theologians, the tendency, perhaps even temptation, would be to continue on the line of deconstruction without embarking on positive moves to save the Bible from itself.

In her book, *Bread Not Stone*, Elisabeth Schüssler Fiorenza calls for a shift in reading strategy that has greatly influenced the approach of Asian feminist theologians. In her chapter on the hermeneutical centre of biblical interpretation, she says,

> The critical rereading of the Bible in a feminist key and from women's perspective is in the process of uncovering lost traditions and correcting mistranslations, of peeling away layers of androcentric scholarship, and rediscovering new dimensions of biblical symbols and theological

meanings. . . . The rediscovery . . . is made possible by two basic shifts in our perception of the world and reality and in our perception of the function of biblical texts and interpretations. Such paradigm shifts are on the one hand a shift from an androcentric to a feminist perception of the world and on the other hand a shift from an apologetic focus on biblical authority to a feminist articulation of contemporary women's experience and struggle against patriarchal oppression in biblical religion.[61]

In brief, Fiorenza's advice is that if what the text says is not emancipatory, it is not God's word but man's word. This approach to the biblical text is key if Asian Christian feminists are to challenge and dismantle the androcentric structures and thought of Asian churches which have housed themselves in prevailing Asian patriarchal cultures. This approach to the biblical text is also key for Asian Christian feminists who were working together with other Asian feminists engage in challenging Asian patriarchal structures and practices.

Besides following through with Fiorenza's suggestions that feminists should not let themselves be bound by the limits of the Canon and should seek countervailing voices, there are two principal projects among others that Asian feminists undertake in restoring and releasing subdued voices.

One is to address the Bible with constructive imagination, which Kwok Pui-Lan calls "postcolonial imagination". In her words, "To imagine means to discern that something is not fitting, to search for new images, and to arrive at new patters of meaning and interpretation." She continues,

I have attached more importance to the cracks, the fissures and the openings, which refuse to be shaped into any framework, and which are often consigned to the periphery. These disparate elements that staunchly refuse to follow the set pattern, the established episteme, the overall design that the mind so powerfully wants to shape, interest me because they have the potential to point to another path, to signal radically new possibilities.[62]

She identifies three facets to constructive imagination. One facet is historical imagination. "The project is to accord or restore to women the status of a 'historical subject'." It is to continue what Elisabeth Schüssler Fiorenza set in motion. Fiorenza argues that history is not simply a record of the past but a "perspectival discourse that seeks to articulate a living memory for the present and the future."[63]

The second facet is dialogical imagination.

It describes the process of creative hermeneutics in Asia. It attempts to convey the complexities, the multidimensional linkages, and the different levels of meaning that underlie our present task of relating the Bible to Asia. This task is dialogical, for it involves on going conversation among different religious and cultural traditions.[64]

The third facet is diasporic imagination, which takes into account the scattered and hybridised reality of modern life.

In releasing subdued voices or better identifying subdued voices, Kwok uses the method of diasporic imagination in her section on "finding Ruth a home".[65] In traditional interpretations of the text, Ruth moves from Moab to Israel and is absorbed into a Judaist culture, which becomes her home and she becomes part of that cultural lineage. Various communities from their several vantage points address the metaphor of home in contexts as diverse as kinship, patriarchal household, and hospitality to the strangers.

However, when the text is read against the present global scene of war, violence, ethnic strife and other upheavals, which drive many people into homelessness, migrancy and diaspora, "home is not a fixed and stable location but a travelling adventure, which entails seeking refuge in strange lands, bargaining for survival and negotiating for existence." This current global situation dislodges the understanding of home from its cozy connotations, and moves it into a new semantic field. Kwok then uses "finding Ruth a home" as a metaphor and heuristic device to interrogate current biblical approaches.[66] She recognises the fact that modern interpretative strategies are not so much concerned with authorial intentions and the past historical context of the text. Rather, their intention from the vantage of the community that interprets is to ask what the text is saying to the present.

In examining these approaches, her concern is not just to highlight what each is saying, but also "to investigate what is suppressed or ignored in order to allow a certain interpretation to be inscribed as a coherent or authoritative narrative." For her it is a project in deconstruction. She uses the approach of Spivak to see "the way in which narratives compete with each other, which one rises and which one falls, who is silent, and the itinerary of the silencing rather than the retrieval."[67]

Today the Bible is viewed not just as a religious text but as a cultural text that has shaped attitudes in the West. It is in the public domain. "Its interpreters are not limited to those within the faith community . . . but are likely to include cultural and postcolonial critics coming from many disciplines. . . . Their research interests are not so much motivated by the search for religious truth as for cultural and political meanings endorsed by the Bible."[68]

In this context, she identifies the Jewish writer Regina Schwartz who when presenting the theme of conquest in the formation of Israel as a chosen people was startled when a student asked, "What about the Canaanites?" Looking to the outside from within with themes of "covenant", "chosen people", and "promised land" evident in the colonising psyche of the West and the displacement of Arabs in Palestine by Israel, she is led to admit that in the matter of identity formation, implicit in Ruth, the act of distinguishing and separating from others entails violence. She is led to debunk identities of kinship, chosen people and monotheism. Laura Donaldson, a Native American, looks from outside into the biblical text and shows that there was the death of native cultures when it was introduced to Native peoples. Yet, through the long history of victimisation, Native peoples have read the Bible on their own terms from a "Moabite perspective" to surface "a meaning that resists imperial exegesis and contributes to the empowerment of aboriginal people everywhere."[69]

Pushpa Joseph illustrates the second project which Asian feminists undertake. It is to reread and recast the text so that the one who is silent or silenced takes centre ground. Having lived with and being involved in the struggles of battered women and those who have been forced to sell their bodies, the so-called "spoilt women", Joseph reads the Samaritan woman's meeting with Jesus from their perspective. She calls her rereading of the text a reverie which is an act of creative imagination that places marginalised women at the centre of the story. In the recasting of the story, a low caste woman who had been seduced and raped by high caste men meets a Jewish man who says he is thirsty and asks for a drink of water. In fear that this is another trap she attempts to flee but trips and falls, upsets the jar of water, and is drenched. She hears the voice again asking for a drink of water. There is water all over her, but where is the source? She screams at the man to leave her alone because she is only a spoilt woman from a low caste. She hears the voice again saying, "From your heart shall flow living water." From this affirmation she realises that she is no longer a spoilt woman. She is reconstituted as a person, who realises that she has been a victim of an unjust system. She then proceeds to talk to other women who were in the same plight. "I spoke to them of my new found freedom. Slowly women started to believe. Believe in the fullness of life that welled up within them."[70]

Projects restoring subdued voices in the first instance are acts of resistance or deconstruction. They strip away the patriarchal attitudes and androcentric language of the text and traditional male interpretations of it. Then they recast the text in ways that are emancipatory echoing the words of Fiorenza that if the Bible is to be read as the word of God, it has to be bread or rice and not stone.

III. RELEASING THE BIBLE IN A RELIGIOUSLY PLURAL WORLD

In using the problem of the two stories as a hermeneutical device for relating the Christian story (the Bible and Christian traditions) as text A with the world of other religions and their stories as text B, we noticed in previous chapters that the two do not necessarily dovetail into each other, because each has a different focal image for reading reality. In Christianity the Ultimate is viewed as personal, while for example in Hinduism and Buddhism the Ultimate is understood as transpersonal. Yet, differences need not lead to a collision, but rather to a mutual learning from each other. In this section we take the discussion a step further and address limitations inherent in Christian perceptions that block meaningful encounters between the stories or texts.

In this quest, I follow in large measure the article of S. Wesley Ariarajah, "Interpreting John 14.6 in a Religiously Plural Society."[71] Having devoted a life-time of ministry to inter-religious dialogue, he says that time and again his presentations are scuppered, or nearly so, with a voice from the audience saying, "But Jesus said 'I am the way, and the truth, and the life. No one comes to the Father except through me'." When accent is placed on the second part of this saying, it blocks any meaningful conversation in a multi-faith setting. How do we move on and release the Bible, with this text as an example, so it is a life-giving word and not a limiting stipulation?

The Gospel according to John is replete with a number of "I am"

sayings of Jesus. Ariarajah correctly observes that these "I am" sayings are expositions on the name of God, "I am who I am" (Exod
3:14).[72] They continue with the incarnational theme struck in the
Prologue of John's Gospel: " . . . and the Word became flesh and
dwelt among us and we beheld his glory." And it is addressed to those
who believed in "his name" and became children of God. As com-
mentaries on the disclosure of God's name as the Word of God, the
several "I am" sayings do not cancel each other out, but following
Jewish interpretive practice add layers of meaning, which enrich the
text. Plurality is welcome. It is not a distraction.

With this in mind, to interpret 14.6 in a way that is life-giving,
one has to appreciate the style that biblical writers often employ to
communicate their messages. As C.S. Song demonstrates in his book,
In the Beginning Were Stories Not Texts,[73] the issue for ancient writers was not a matter of historical veracity, but rather whether what
was being communicated was truthful. "Does it jive with our experience?" For instance, in Genesis 3 there are extensive conversations
between the Serpent, Eve, Adam and God. Ariarajah asks, "Who was
there at the beginning to record this conversation? Historical accuracy of events or conversations is a modern problem. Ancient people
looked for *meaning*."[74]

Besides style one has to note the basic intention of the Gospel writers. These are confessional documents which use history and story
as a matrix for communicating their messages. They were written to
communicate faith to the faithful so that their faith would hold firm
at stressful times. In using historical material to communicate their
messages, Gospel writers used historical episodes in different ways.
For instance, the account about Jesus cleansing the Jerusalem temple comes at the beginning of John's gospel account, while in the
synoptic gospel accounts it comes towards the end. To take a different example, during Christmas the narratives about the birth of
Jesus from Matthew and Luke are mashed together so that the shepherds and the wisemen make a common entrance. However, the two
accounts carry different messages. In Matthew all the main characters are male. Gabriel appears to Joseph, not to Mary as in Luke. The
wisemen, only in Matthew's account, are unwitting instruments in
Herod's murderous campaign to eliminate threats to his reign. Joseph
is forced to flee with his wife and child to Egypt. Will this child survive? Will the people to whom this gospel is addressed survive in a

brutal world in which Herod who rules with Roman authority is in control? A note of *anxiety* prevails. The account in Luke breathes a different air. The protagonists in the main are women and lowly people such as the shepherds. The prevailing mood is one of *joy*, especially with the singing of Mary (Magnificat), Elizabeh, and Simeon (*Nunc Dimittis*) at the birth of the Messiah, who is to give life to the least.[75]

Given the penchant for using history to communicate a message, the question whether Jesus actually said what he is supposed to have said in John 14:6 needs to be viewed in a way where factuality is not the controlling lens. For one thing, knowing that writers of the books in the New Testament knew nothing of other religions, to use them as weapons to castigate so-called unbelievers is both anachronistic and unfair. For another thing, as Ariarajah observes, the claim to be the "only way" is also observable in other "I am" sayings. In John 10, Jesus claims to be the only way—the true entrance—so that those who attempt a different mode of entry are thieves and robbers. In these cases, Ariarajah argues that it is one thing for a minority community surrounded by a truculent Roman and pagan world to claim a certain exclusiveness and quite another thing for a community that had the blessing of Rome, as in the time of Emperor Constantine, to claim the same exclusiveness.[76] The mood then changes from self-preservation to attack.

A further point that Ariarajah makes is worth noting. He follows the Latin American liberation theologian Juan Luis Segundo to say that each biblical text is accompanied by three "deaths". "The writer, the people to whom it was written, and the context that it sought to address are no more."[77] Consequently, any contemporary reading of the text introduces a particular present-day context which colours one's reading. (Even historical criticism which looks for authorial intentions cannot claim to be objective.) In this situation, it would be more honest to declare one's standpoint or the context from which one is reading the text. The hermeneutical cycle, which Latin American theology popularised, speaks of context reading text and text reading context. For Ariarajah, as it is for most progressive Asian theologians, the context is the world of many religions within which the Bible has to find its release, and from within which it must speak.

From this standpoint it is fruitless to pit snippets from the New Testament against each other to argue a point. Over against John

14:6 one could quote Matthew 7:21: "Not everyone who says to me Lord, Lord, will enter the kingdom of heaven, but only the one who does the will of my Father in heaven." Ariarajah's plea is that we listen to the total message of the writer setting it in the context of many faiths in which dialogue not religious confrontation is the mode of communication.

At the end of this book I will return to the implications of this position for a broader ecumenism than simply inter-confessional relations, and for a recasting of Christian theology.

Notes

1. R.S. Sugirtharajah, *Postcolonial Criticism and Biblical Interpretation* (Oxford: Oxford University Press, 2002), 25.

2. *Postcolonial Criticism*, 13–14. Emphasis added.

3. Ibid., 5.

4. R.S. Sugirtharajah, *The Bible and the Third World: Precolonial, Colonial and Postcolonial Encounters* (Cambridge: Cambridge University Press, 2001), 13–41.

5. See D. Preman Niles, *The Lotus and the Sun: Asian Theological Engagement with Plurality and Power* (Canberra: Barton, 2013), 203–48 for a fuller discussion.

6. Sugirtharajah, *The Bible and the Third World*, 47.

7. Ibid., 49.

8. Ibid., 53.

9. Ibid., 55–57.

10. Ibid., 53.

11. For a detailed account of the life and work of William Tyndale, see especially David Daniell, *William Tyndale: A Biography* (Yale: Yale University Press, 1994).

12. See Judith John, *Dark History of the Tudors* (London: Amber, 2014), 102–27 (Edward VI), and 129–57 (Mary).

13. Bruce M. Metzger, "The Geneva Bible of 1560," *Theology Today* 17, no. 3 (1960): 339–52.

14. Patrick Collinson, "The Jacobean Religious Settlement: The Hampton Court Conference," in *Before the English Civil War*, ed. Howard Tomlinson

(London: Macmillan, 1983), 27–51.

15. "King James' Instructions to the Translators," taken from Jack P. Lewis, *The English Bible from the KJV to NIV: A History and Evaluation* (Grand Rapids, MI: Baker, 1991) and Gustavus S. Paine, *The Men Behind the KJV* (Grand Rapids, MI: Baker, 1988). See both these works and Patrick Collinson, "The Jacobean Religious Settlement," for greater details on what I have said in the main text.

16. The Bishops' Bible was the work of a group of High-Church Anglican bishops headed by the then Archbishop of Canterbury in 1568 and revised in 1572 to counter the Geneva Bible.

17. This speech was made by James I before Parliament at Whitehall, 21 March, 1610. James I, *Works* (1616), 528–31.

18. For a well-documented and extremely readable account of the genesis and sway of the KJV in Britain and its influence on other translations, see Derek Wilson, *The People's Bible: The Remarkable History of the King James Version* (Oxford: Lion Hudson plc., 2010).

19. R.S. Sugirtharajah, "The Master Copy: Postcolonial Notes on the King James Bible," in *The King James Version at 400*, ed. David G. Burke, et al. (Atlanta: Society of Biblical Literature, 2013), 499–518.

20. Sugirtharajah, "Master Copy," 502–4.

21. Liah Greenfeld, *Nationalism: Five Roads to Modernity* (Cambridge: Harvard University Press, 1992), 52–53.

22. Sugirtharajah, "Master Copy," 512.

23. Ibid., 505.

24. Ibid., 510–12. For greater detail see R.S. Sugirtharajah, *The Bible and Asia: From the Pre-Christian Era to the Postcolonial Age* (Cambridge: Harvard University Press, 2013), 107–17.

25. Bruce M. Metzger, "Letter to the Reader," in *Holy Bible: The New Revised Standard Version with Apocrypha* (Nashville: Thomas Nelson, 1989), i–v.

26. See further R.S. Sugirtharajah, *Postcolonial Criticism and Biblical Interpretation*, 168–69.

27. R.S. Sugirtharajah, *Exploring Postcolonial Biblical Criticism: History, Method, Practice* (Oxford: Wiley-Blackwell, 2012), 32.

28. Tom Reilly, "Cromwell: The Irish Question," *History Today* 62, no. 9, (September 2012).

29. For a careful and detailed sifting of the evidence available, see Tom Reilly, *Cromwell: An Honourable Enemy* (County Kerry, Ireland: Brandon, 1999)

especially chapters two and three (Drogheda) and chapter four (Wexford).

30. Sugirtharajah, *Exploring Postcolonial Biblical Criticism*, 32–33.

31. For a convenient retelling of the Columbus story, see Washington Irving, *The Life and Voyages of Christopher Columbus* (Hertfordshire: Wordsworth Editions Ltd, 2008). See also Bryan F. Le Beau, "Christopher Columbus and the Matter of Religion," *Kripke* (Center for the Study of Religion and Society) 4, no. 1 (October 1992): 1, for a brief evaluation of the relationship of Columbus to religion.

32. Tink Tinker and Mark Freeland, "Thief, Slave Trader, Murderer: Christopher Columbus and Caribbean Population Decline," *WicazoSa Review* 23, no. 1, (Spring 2008): 25–50.

33. Robert Allen Warrior, "A Native American Perspective: Canaanites, Cowboys, and Indians," in *Voices from the Margin*, 3rd ed., R. S. Sugirtharajah, editor (New York: Orbis, 2006), 235–41.

34. Sugirtharajah, *Postcolonial Criticism and Biblical Interpretation*, 75.

35. See 2 Kings 17:24–41; Ezra 4:1–4; Nehemiah 6:1–14.

36. Sugirtharajah, *Exploring Postcolonial*, 38.

37. Edward W. Said, *Culture and Imperialism* (New York: Vintage, 1993), 51.

38. Sugirtharajah, "Master Copy," 515. His words, which I have altered, are "a book that does not contain its counterbook is not worth preserving."

39. Kwok Pui-Lan, *Introducing Asian Feminist Theology* (Cleveland, OH: Pilgrim, 2000), 26. Emphasis added.

40. Kwok, *Asian Feminist Theology*, 9.

41. Wendy Doniger, *The Hindus: An Alternative History*, paperback edition (Oxford: Oxford University Press, 2010), 325–26.

42. Doniger, *Hindus*, 327.

43. Kwok Pui-Lan, *Postcolonial Imagination and Feminist Theology* (Louisville, Kentucky: Westminster John Knox, 2005), 17.

44. Kwok Pui-Lan, "Unbinding Our Feet: Saving Brown Women and Feminist Religious Discourse" in *Postcolonialism, Feminism, and Religious Discourse*, ed. Laura E. Donaldson and Kwok Pui-Lan (New York & London: Routledge, 2002), 62–81.

45. Kwok, "Unbinding Our Feet," 63.

46. Quoted by Kwok in ibid., 62.

47. Katharine Doob Sakenfeld, "Whose Text Is It?" *SBL* 127, no.1 (2008): 5–18.

48. Lata Mani, *Contentious Traditions: The Debate on Sati in Colonial India*

(Berkeley: University of California Press, 1993). It is worth noting that this book is not available (banned?) in South Asia.

49. Kwok, "Unbinding Our Feet," 65.

50. Pushpa Joseph, *Feminist Hermeneutics: A Contextual Reconstruction* (Darjeeling: Salesian College Publications, 2010), 30–38.

51. Joseph, *Feminist Hermeneutics*, 29–30.

52. Ibid., 37–38.

53. Kwok, "Unbinding Our Feet," 70–73.

54. Quoted by Kwok in ibid., 62.

55. Doniger, *Hindus*, 612–15.

56. Kwok, "Unbinding Our Feet," 67–68.

57. Angela Wong Wai-Ching, *The Poor Woman* (New York: Peter Lang, 2002), 45.

58. Ibid., 60–61.

59. Metzger, "Letter to Reader," iii.

60. Kwok, *Postcolonial Imagination*, 93–98.

61. Elisabeth Schüssler Fiorenza, *Bread Not Stone: The Challenge of Feminist Biblical Interpretation* (Boston: Beacon, 1984, 1995), 1–2.

62. Kwok, *Postcolonial Imagination*, 30.

63. Ibid., 31.

64. Ibid., 38.

65. Ibid., 100–121.

66. Ibid., 102.

67. Ibid., 103.

68. Ibid., 119.

69. Ibid., 114–19.

70. Joseph, *Feminist Hermeneutics*, 210–14.

71. S. Wesley Ariarajah, "Interpreting John 14.6 in a Religiously Plural Society," in *Voices from the Margin*, 3rd ed., ed. R. S. Sugirtharajah (New York: Orbis, 2006), 355–70.

72. Ariarajah, "Interpreting John," 359.

73. C. S. Song, *In the Beginning Were Stories Not Texts: Story Theology* (Cambridge: James Clarke & Co., 2012). See especially chapter 10, "The Bible, Stories, and Theology," 153–70.

74. Ariarajah, "Interpreting John," 361.

75. See Raymond E. Brown, S.S., *The Birth of the Messiah* (New York; Double-day, 1977) for fuller descriptions of the content and purpose of the infancy narratives in both Matthew and Luke.

76. Ariarajah, "Interpreting John," 365.

77. Ibid., 367.

5.

Subaltern Hermeneutics:
Counter Theological Approaches

Suh Nam-dong (1918–1984) of Korea was one of the founders of the Minjung Theology movement. He presents the genre of story-telling as a "counter theology". Independently, Arvind P. Nirmal (1936–1995) of India, who did much to promote Dalit Theology, also speaks of his theology as a "counter theology". It is doubtful whether the two ever met or even knew about each other. Though the approaches of both are different, they enhance each other and present subaltern hermeneutics as a distinctive form of theological discourse that both theologians assert should impact on all Asian theological discourses.

If postcolonial criticism attempts to free the first story from colonial entrapments so it could be serviceable in the doing of Asian theology, subaltern hermeneutics presents the radical challenge of the second story. To understand better the challenge that subaltern hermeneutics poses, I will draw from the biographies of both, and show how personal experiences led them to voice counter theologies.

SUH NAM-DONG—STORYTELLING AS A COUNTER THEOLOGY

I begin my introduction to Suh Nam-dong's approach with an incident related to me by Park San-jung, a Korean, who was on the staff of the WCC at the time. Suh Nam-dong was already a well-known systematic theologian in Korea. Because of his expertise in theological matters, he was invited to serve as a commissioner on the Faith and Order Commission of the World Council of Churches (WCC). At one of the commission's meetings, Hans Ruedi-Weber, who was WCC's Director for Biblical Studies, was invited to give a series of studies on various biblical themes. He decided to focus on the Resurrection as one of the themes.

Ruedi-Weber approached his colleague Park and asked him whether there was a Korean-take on the Resurrection; and Park suggested that he look at Kim Chi Ha's play, "The Gold-Crowned Jesus." Ruedi-Weber used material from this play in one of his presentations; and ended by saying, "If you want to know more about this play and its author you might want to ask Professor Suh Nam-dong who is with us as a member of the Commission." No one approached Suh, and it was in one sense fortunate, because as Suh later told Park, "I was embarrassed by Weber's announcement. I had neither heard of Kim Chi-ha nor knew anything about this play or his other writings." All writings from Korean dissidents, including those by Kim Chi-ha, were banned in Korea at that time.

On the way back to Seoul, Suh checked into a hotel in Tokyo; and he went out and bought writings in Korean and Japanese on the human rights and democracy struggles in Korea. He remained in his room and read day and night. After a week he phoned Oh Jae-shik, a fellow Korean, who at that time was responsible for Urban Industrial Mission located in Tokyo, and said to him, "I am now ready to meet with you." Urban Industrial Mission of the Christian Conference of Asia was committed to working with industrial workers and rural peasants to champion their struggles for human rights and dignity. There were long conversations between the two as Suh sought to understand the struggle for human rights and democracy in Korea. After a few days he returned to Seoul a "convert". I received this part of the story from Oh Jae-shik.

As he engaged himself in the struggles for democracy and human rights and became a spokesperson for the down-trodden *minjung*, he was dismissed from his professorship. He was imprisoned and tortured in the aftermath of the Kwangju uprising (May 18–27, 1980). Possibly because of what happened to him in prison, he fell ill and died shortly thereafter. In between release and death, he presented a paper on "Story-telling: A Counter-Theology"[1] and followed it up with another paper, "Cultural Theology, Political Theology and Minjung Theology,"[2] the latter being a criticism of Choan Seng Song's theology of transposition. Just as Ahn Byung-mu discovered the Jesus of history through the experiences of the *minjung* (*ochlos*) of Jesus's time, Suh discovered Jesus the story-teller through the centuries old folk-tales (*mindam*) of the *minjung*, which expressed their *han*.[3] He revolted against the formalising of theology through creed and doctrine in which he himself had indulged at one time.

Though the specific socio-political situation which Suh addressed is past, his theological position is not out-dated. It must remain to challenge all Asian theologians and especially those in Korea when the country as a whole has embraced the free market economy and the tenets of capitalism ("liberal democracy"). Churches and Christians have bettered themselves economically and socially and have mostly abandoned the plight, religion and culture of the *minjung*. Suh's challenge to his Korean theological colleagues of his time is still pertinent: "A limited study that only operates at the level of the supra-structure of ideas *without dealing with the material structure of historical revelation* will be an illusion or a ghost. That kind of theology will eventually be taken over by the ideology of the rulers, and prescribed as sleeping pills for the *minjung*."[4] And, by implication, for all oppressed people.

It is possible though not certain that Ahn Byung-mu and Suh Nam-dong influenced each other in using the genre of story-telling as a vehicle for doing theology. For both, it is the historical Jesus that is primary. In his essay, "The Transmitters of the Jesus-event," Ahn argues,

An important characteristic of minjung language is its story-style. This language is very different from the language used for proclamations or for apologetic arguments. The Jesus-event in Mark's gospel, including the passion narrative, consists of stories. . . . A sociological approach as to how stories, as minjung language, originate and function will provide a clue for a fresh understanding of the Jesus-story in the synoptic gospels.[5]

In this essay and elsewhere, as noted in chapter 1, Ahn contends that the kerygma, or the church's proclamation about the risen Christ, followed rather than preceded the Jesus-event. The story of the Jesus-event was carried mostly in the form of rumours.[6] From Ahn to Suh: if it is through the stories preserved in the synoptic gospels that one encounters the historical Jesus, then it is through the stories of the *minjung* that one encounters the God of history. In his words, echoing the position of Ahn Byung-mu, "We (the *minjung*) are the text and the Bible is the context."

Suh's basic position is that taking up the cause of the workers and suffering masses should not be a matter of condescension but should rather be one of identification. For a literati from the privileged class (*yangban*) as he was, the first step is to listen to the stories that come from the *minjung* in their own terms without attempting either hastily to theologise them or to use them as receptacles for one's prefabricated theological positions. It is in listening to these stories in their own terms that a counter-theology could emerge as did the stories about the Jesus-event as a counter theology that challenges presentations of the Kerygmatic Christ.

To understand what he means by the term "counter theology" I will narrate in brief two stories he uses to present the genre of story-telling as a counter theology.

The first story is about Ahn-gook, a handsome son of Kim Sook, a renowned scholar and high-ranking government official. Ahn-gook had a problem. He could not learn the basic Chinese alphabet. The Chinese letters or ideograms, which singly and in combinations signify both words and concepts, are the medium through which Confucian philosophy is expressed in Korean. Every time he attempted to study these he ended up with a splitting headache. The father failed to make him learn and so did his uncle Chung to whom he was sent. Unable to make any headway with his education, the uncle decided to get him married off. The choice was a good looking daughter of Yi Yoo-shin, a local township administrator. Yi Yoo-shin was perplexed as to why a young man from a high ranking family should want to marry a daughter of a humble township administrator. Perhaps there was a physical problem. A careful examination of the physical attributes of this tall handsome young man, including his "sexual weaponry", could find nothing wrong with him. The marriage took place. The young bride finding that her husband would confine himself to his room and neither go out nor read, thought of testing his intelligence. Perhaps that was the problem. She narrated a story to him. His eyes beamed, and he repeated the story word for word back to her. So, nothing was wrong with his intelligence. Many more narrations of stories followed with the same successful result. In surprise the husband asked his wife from where she got all these stories. "In books," she responded. "May I also learn to read these stories?" asked the husband. So she read the stories pointing to each Chinese character. Ahn-gook swiftly learnt to read. In this project the wife received the help of Ahn-gook's mother and his wet-nurse. What was closed to Ahn-gook earlier now opened up. Stories, not philosophical concepts, became the bearer of enlightenment; and the young man studied, passed examinations with distinctions, and moved up the social ladder to become a high-ranking government official.

Suh remarks that the story is a protest against the Confucian value system that places primary emphasis on "letters" as a medium of communication. Letters represent an indirect medium. The one who reads attempts to understand the thoughts of the one who writes. A story on the other hand is a direct medium which passes from the mouth of one person directly into the ears of the other person and draws the listener into the story.

> Letters (or books) are employed as a medium for formally expressing one's knowledge, that is, the language of the brain, whereas stories are employed as a medium for conveying feelings and matters of daily life. A story is the language of the body. . . . Communication through letters is a method for imposing from the outside and consequently it alienates a person from himself or herself. On the other hand, communication by way of stories is a method for drawing the whole person into the story, for the person willingly accepts the story while being absorbed by the story. In short, the former is oppressive whereas the latter is liberating.[7]

He then goes on to draw attention to the fact that the primary language of God's revelation in the Bible is not letters (theological concepts) but stories about historical events which convey God's acts of redemption. "The discourses of Jesus are replete with stories. The Spirit of the Lord is conveyed through body language, not brain language. . . . The ever-living God's self-revelation continues to be in the events God still performs, so that by saying historical events we do not necessarily limit ourselves only to those recorded in the Old and New Testaments."

> If conventional theology is transcendental and deductive, the theology of story telling is this worldly and inductive. *It is a counter theology (Gegen Theologie).* Moreover, conventional theology is a ruler's theology (*Herrschende Theologie*). Conventional theology soon joins hands with the ideology of domination and justifies the ruling order and blesses such order.[8]

He argues that conventional theology arose in a particular social situation—the slave societies of Greece and Rome—with their dualistic order of free citizens and slaves. Conventional theology has inherited this dualistic tradition which privileges the upper class. It has turned the stories of redemption into a "theology of domination".

Though the story of Ahn-gook as a satire serves to criticise a rigid philosophical and conceptual system, it also has its shortcomings. For, it is trapped in the very system that it tries to contest. While all the major male characters in the story have names, the female characters have none. In actual fact it is the young unnamed bride who is the real protagonist. She together with other unnamed women characters who help him to break through the system are consigned to the background. Patriarchal values entrenched in the Confucian social system remain intact. Furthermore, Ahn-gook becomes literate and climbs the social ladder, utilising the very system which he originally repudiated. How would the story have developed if Ahn-gook remained unlettered, muses Suh. As it stands, it is a story about personal success. It does nothing to critique the social system which story-telling as a counter theology should do. In contrast,

> On November 13, 1970 a sixteen-year old boy named Jeon Tae-il [who also influenced Ahn Byung-mu] immolated himself at the open square in Pyongwha Market, shouting "We are not machines! Labour laws should be obeyed!" He had been working for six years in a small sewing factory. One day he saw a female labourer next to him pass out coughing blood. Deeply shocked, he spent several sleepless nights wondering what he could do. Finally, he decided to take the initiative in forming a labour movement. The shock he experienced marked a turning point in his life.[9]

Suh remarks that Jeon Tae-il did what Ahn-gook would not. Jeon Tae-il's action is symbolic. It demonstrates that unlike analytical and rationally inclined conventional theology, holistic theology that is ingrained in story-telling as a counter theology leads to a bodily response. Suh views Jeon Tae-il's action as sacrificial, in that it embodies the cry for emancipation of the *minjung* workers from an unjust social order and is therefore socially liberative.

The second story he uses concerns a monk named Jee-sung. It comes from the end of the eighteenth century. The monastery to which Jee-sung belonged was located in a faraway mountain; and he was sent with a bag of coins to buy provisions for the monastery to a seashore village a hundred miles away. On the way he met a poorly dressed scholar who was dragging along a small boy and a small girl, both of whom were in tears. The monk pitied the two children and asked the scholar why he was dragging these two along. The scholar replied that the parents of these two owed him money, but were now dead. So, he was taking the children to work for him and pay off their parents' debts. The monk upbraided the scholar saying that these two small ones could not survive in a big city like Seoul where they were being taken. He offered the scholar the money he was carrying in exchange for the children. The scholar asked in surprise, "You want to buy them? What in the world could a monk like you do with the kids?" The monk replied, "I want to free them. Let them decide what they want to do. They can go live with their relatives, if they want to." The money changed hands, a proper document of transaction was written, and Jee-sung gave the document of release to the children, and let them go. He watched them merrily hop away. After some years the two children, now grown and married, saved some money to go visit the monk. At first the monk could not make them out, but was surprised and happy when they introduced themselves. The story ends with a version of the usual traditional ending for such stories: "And they lived happily ever after."

Originally written to depict the plight of poor scholars, Suh derives more meaning from the story. In the original Chinese text there are expressions such as "purchase to free" or "a document of emancipation". Suh comments,

> Here lie two phrases that signify "redemption" and "liberation". Neither redemption nor liberation would have happened had he [the monk] simply purchased them to keep them as his own slaves. But, the monk

purchased the children from their situation of slavery and liberated them to be free persons. In so doing redemption and liberation cannot be separated from one another. Unfortunately, however, the two are divided in Christian theology. On the one hand, redemption as a social act has faded into the background, and it now signifies religious salvation alone. On the other, liberation has lost its religious sense and means only social liberation. Both should be taken together, otherwise both terms deteriorate and become meaningless.[10]

He argues that in the Bible salvation encompasses both meanings, as for instance in the salvation of the Israelites in the exodus from Egypt. In the New Testament the Greek term *lutrō* also carries both meanings as for instance in Luke 24:21, Titus 2:14 and 1 Peter 1:18. "Unless accompanied by social liberation, the salvation of the human soul means nothing more than having a wandering spirit detached from the body." Intrinsic to his argument is the assumption that one is saved—redeemed and set free—from a system or social condition.

[While] Jee-sung redeemed and liberated the two children he did not question the society which enslaved them. . . . He performed an ethical deed, but not a social act to remedy the situation. Jesus Christ redeemed the whole of humankind, not just individuals. How could the redemption of the whole of humankind be effected without taking into consideration the social structure itself that, for instance, permitted the system of slavery? Jesus denied such structures although he did not himself destroy them. In Christianity there can be no individual salvation without social salvation. Human salvation without changing the sinful structure and the system of slavery is quite foreign to the salvation in Jesus Christ.[11]

Contrasting the two stories, he says,

Ahn-gook's enlightenment first led him to gain scholarly knowledge and then social position while Jee-sung's enlightenment first made him act socially on behalf of the children and then to liberate them. In other words, he brought a remedy to the misery he witnessed. In short, the one who learns through books, produces conceptual knowledge, while the one who learns through events produces good praxis. The former is the way of the mind while the latter is the way of the body. The former is the way of theology while the latter is the way of Jesus Christ and his counter-theology.[12]

Suh's concerns as one who proposes a counter theology becomes clearer in his essay "Cultural Theology, Political Theology and Min-jung Theology" in which he criticises C.S. Song's theology. While applauding Song's rejection of western theological approaches that tend to view in polarity the relationship between text (revelation) and context, he has difficulties with the example Song uses to prove this point. In his lecture at a theological symposium in Korea (October 6–21, 1983), Song presented the enlightenment of a Zen Buddhist monk who after much meditation and trying without success can in a sudden moment's enlightenment with one brush stroke bring together both revelation and context. Suh contends that this illustration is the property of Confucianism, and carries the contradictions inherent that system.

> We must realize that from the beginning Confucianism was a political ideology and reflected the social order of the dominating class. I feel that minjung theology in Asia should be as critical of the Eastern culture of Confucianism as it is of the Christian culture of the West.[13]

Suh's criticism of Song's theology is more reflective of his own position as a counter theologian who emphasises the materiality of revelation than of Song's theology. In his book, *In the Beginning Were Stories, Not Texts,*[14] Song sets out his approach encapsulating the various ways in which he uses Asian resources to articulate his theology. In quite a few ways, Song's approach is not dissimilar to that of Suh's. However, Suh has a point with which I am certain Song would also concur. Without a critical assessment of the Asian resources we use, Asian theological efforts could easily become entrapped in the contradictions inherent in the religio-cultural resources we use to express our theologies. Also, there is the danger of simply using the stories of *people* (the marginalised) as mere receptacles for our prefabricated theologies.

ARVIND P. NIRMAL—DALIT THEOLOGY AS A COUNTER THEOLOGY

Nirmal was also a systematic theologian, but unlike Suh stayed largely within that discipline. He even has a stab at constructing the bare bones of a systematic theology from a *dalit* perspective.[15] However, his real contribution lies in contesting the rigid caste system and asserting the rights of the *dalits* to be heard in their own terms in the articulation of theology. To show the rigidity of the caste system Nirmal quotes Rig Veda X, 90, 11–12, which describes humanity as created into pre-defined castes: "When they divided the *Puruṣa* [humanity] how many portions did they make? What do they call his mouth, his arms? What do they call his thighs and feet? The *Brahmin* was his mouth, of both his arms was the *Rājanya* [warrior] made. His thighs became the *Vaiśya* [trader and farmer], from his feet the *Śūdra* [servile class] was produced."[16]

The problem with caste, unlike social class, is that one may not and in fact cannot move upward to a higher caste. However, it is possible to lose caste through some form of moral or social contamination. Manu Dharma Sastra (Laws of Manu)[17] attests not only to the rigidity of the caste system but also to the ontology that underlies caste. Nirmal quotes from Manu Dharma Sastra VIII, 413–14 to illustrate this point with reference to the one who is at the bottom or even outside the caste structure: "But a *Śūdra*, whether bought or unbought, he [the Brahmin] may compel to do servile work; for he [the *Śūdra*] was created by the Self-Existent (*Svayambhu*) to be the slave of the Brahmin. A *Śūdra*, though emancipated by his master, is not released from servitude; since that is innate in him, who can set him free from it?"[18]

Caste Hindus from the first three *Varna* (caste classification) consider those at the bottom of the caste system and those outside the caste system as "untouchables". Any form of contact with them, even the falling of their shadow on a caste person, would require a process of washing and ritual purification. Various attempts have been made to rehabilitate the so-called untouchables. Gandhi called them *harijans* (God's people). However, the *dalits* of India have repudiated the name Gandhi gave them as condescension that does not properly reflect their social situation. Instead, they have embraced the term *dalit*, meaning "broken or crushed" in Marathi, which the Marathi social reformer Jyotirao Phule (1827–1890) used as a truer description of their status as those whose humanity has been repudiated.

Since Indian Christian theology has been the domain principally of the caste converts, Nirmal along with other *dalit* theologians[19] alleges that Indian theology has continued the contradictions inherent in the caste system. He argues that a credible Indian theology cannot emerge unless it takes into account the *dalits* who make up almost seventy percent of the Christian population, and are a sizeable minority in South Asia.

> It [Dalit Theology] will narrate the story of their *pathos* and their protest against the socio-economic injustices they have been subjected to throughout history. It will anticipate liberation which is meaningful to them. It will represent a radical discontinuity with the classical Indian Christian Theology of the Brahminic tradition. This Brahminic tradition in classical Indian Christian Theology needs to be challenged by the emerging Dalit Theology. This also means that a Christian Dalit Theology will be a *counter theology*.[20]

If Suh had to identify himself with and immerse himself in the life-situation and culture of the *minjung* to find his voice as a counter theologian, Nirmal had to embrace an identity from which he could not escape and in fact from which he did not wish to escape to find his voice as a counter theologian.

In some ways similar to Suh's identification of Jesus as part of the *ochlos* (*minjung*) of his time, Nirmal interprets Jesus's table-fellowship with the outcastes of his time as evidence that Jesus himself, though a Jew, was a *dalit* of his time.[21]

Although Nirmal speaks of Dalit Theology as narrating the *pathos* of the *dalits*, he himself does not resort to the genre of story-telling to express that *pathos*. The *pathos* of the *dalits* is similar to the Korean *minjung* experience of *han*, and lies in the indignities they have had to suffer from time immemorial. The closest Nirmal comes to story-telling is his recounting of the humiliation that his ancestors suffered as symptomatic of the continuing *pathos* of the *dalits*; and gives a vivid account of this humiliation in his biography.

> As an outcaste [my dalit ancestor] was cast out of his/her village. The dalit *bastis* (localities) were always and are always on the outskirts of the Indian village. When my dalit ancestor walked the dusty roads of his village, the *Sa Varnas* [upper castes] tied a tree branch around his waist so that he would not leave any unclean foot-prints and pollute the roads. The *Sa Varnas* also tied an earthen pot around his neck to serve as a spittoon. If ever my dalit ancestor tried to learn Sanskrit or some other sophisticated language, the oppressors gagged him permanently by pouring molten lead down his throat. My dalit mother and sisters were forbidden to wear any blouses, and the *Sa Varnas* feasted their eyes

on their bare bosoms. The Sa Varnas denied my dalit ancestor any access to public wells or reservoirs. They denied him the entry to their temples and places of worship. . . . My dalit consciousness, therefore, has an unparalleled depth of *pathos* and misery, and it is this historical dalit consciousness, this dalit identity that should inform my attempt at a Christian dalit theology.[22]

Though such public humiliations are forbidden by law, *dalits* still continue to have various types of indignities heaped on them. Yet, much has happened since the time of his ancestors that would have influenced the thinking of Nirmal, so that he could speak and write with self-confidence as a twentieth century *dalit*. The prominent Indian jurist and writer, Dr. B. R. Ambedkar (1891–1956), also a *dalit*, was instrumental in the drafting of the Indian constitution, which provided constitutional guarantees and protections for a wide range of civil liberties including freedom of religion, the abolition of untouchablity and the outlawing of all forms of discrimination. As a Marathi, Nirmal was also steeped in developments in *dalit* writings and movements in Maharashtra. In June 1972, Namdeo Dhasal, a Marathi writer, together with friends formed the Dalit Panther movement, patterned on the African American Black Panther movement, to express *dalit pathos* as *dalit rage*.[23] Modern *dalit* literature also emerged from Maharashtra.[24]

With this background it is possible to understand what Nirmal intends when he says that it is his *dalitness* that is primary and the adjective "Christian" qualifies his *dalit* identity. In other words, it is as a *dalit* that he approaches his theological task. This approach is evident in his argument that Dalit Theology together with all theologies of *people* (those on the margins) needs to preserve a methodological exclusivism.

This exclusivism is necessary because the tendency of all dominant traditions—cultural or theological—is to accommodate, include, assimilate and finally conquer others. Counter theologies or people's theologies, therefore, need to be on their guard and need to shut off the influences of the dominant theological tradition.[25]

Elsewhere he argues that a methodological exclusivism that is necessary to safeguard a *dalit* perspective does not mean a communal exclusivism.

As a community *dalits* must be open to other communities and other peoples. They must be willing to receive help from all possible sources. They must also promote all horizontal community relationships. But a methodological exclusivism is a different matter.[26]

One part of his approach is to identify the social orientation of Dalit Theology. To do so, he argues for a *dalit* ideology that speaks out of a Christian perspective. After setting aside negative evaluations of ideology and ideological thinking, he fastens on the judgment that an ideology represents the view of a social unit and the action that ensues from it. So, argues Nirmal, "We must recognize that Christian theology, although it is not generated by an ideology, seeks an ideological expression." A. N. Whitehead's dictum was that Christianity was not an ideology generating a religion, but a religion in search of social expression.[27] Furthermore, ideology is an expression of human potentiality. It implies and seeks action that involves risk taking. He quotes with approval what Jan M. Lochman says in his *Church in a Marxist Society*, "Theologically speaking, it [ideology] has to be taken under the judgment, but also the promise, in the Christological perspective to which, for the sake of Christ, nothing human is alien."[28] Nirmal comments, "It is thus the humanity of Christ that makes human ideological quest possible."

> It is when the Word becomes flesh and becomes a concrete historical existence that we can speak meaningfully of the incarnation. It is when the Word assumes and passes through all the stages of humanity redeeming it and renewing it that we have the incarnating process set in motion by God. . . . The Word, the Logos, the Idea becomes historically concrete so that it can transform human history and shape human destiny. And that, it seems to me, is the essential function of an authentic ideology. An authentic ideology is dynamic and no respecter of the *Status Quo*.

He goes on to state,

> Incarnational ideology does not belong to any religion, not to the church, not to any political party. It is meant for the whole of humanity for it is rooted in the humanity of Jesus. The incarnational ideology seeks ideological expression in all times and in all places and beckons us toward the realization of the kingdom of God.[29]

What is perceivable in Nirmal's theology expressed as an ideology is its concern for historical expression that implies movement seeking change. In essence, it is an expression of his *dalit* consciousness in which the story of an individual's *pathos* represents the *pathos* of a whole community seeking liberation. It is liberation that demands change in the whole structure of human community. Dalit theology and ideology have a public orientation. This theological and ideological orientation is evident also in the second part of his approach in which he addresses the subject of Indian philosophy as the bearer of Indian theology.

In his "Towards A Relevant And Contemporary Theology in India," he makes the obvious yet pertinent comment that God neither writes theology nor reads theology. In other words, God has no use for theology, and by implication does not need theology to define or describe the Divine. Rather, the task for theology is to address human life.

> It is human life which raises the question of God and also answers it. By life I mean life in its totality. The primary task of theology, therefore, is to make sense of human life and give it a certain direction and goal. The criteria of theology too then must be derived from human life and not from some other "givens". Any theology which fails to make sense of human life and fails to fulfil it ceases to be relevant and cannot be a living option.[30]

The life situation he has in mind is India, which is in flux between tradition and modernity. As an example he cites the Hindu ceremony (*puja*) when a coconut was broken and a garland placed on the first jumbo jet that flew out of the airport in Bombay. This maybe trivial but is yet a telling example of what happens in India in the interaction between tradition and modernization, "which results in a rediscovery of some of the forgotten emphases of the tradition which make it possible for the tradition to be brought into harmony with modernity and newness." He sees this process of interaction between tradition and modernity as characteristic of "the contemporary Indian consciousness".[31]

Theological construction in this situation would have to deal with this process in which the past is juxtaposed with the present to create a new symbol system where some elements from the past are reshaped and others rejected. Nirmal's intention is to make theological construction as much life-oriented as possible. To do this he brings together two extreme Hindu philosophical systems with opposing world-views that operate in one way or another in "the contemporary Indian consciousness". He then proposes a "middle path" (*madhyamika*) that draws from the best in both.

The two extreme philosophical systems he chooses are *Advaita Vedanta* with the philosopher Śankara as its main proponent and *Lokayatavada* (*Lokayata* teaching) with Brihaspati as its founder.

Advaita Vedanta speaks of three levels of reality. There is the imaginary level which is the extreme level of unreality. The examples it gives are the son of a barren woman or a flower in the sky. This is the level of the absurd. The second level is the level of derived reality or *maya*. This is the empirical level where one sees a rope and assumes it is a snake. Certainly more real than the first level but is yet not actually real. The world belongs to this level of reality. Then there is the level of ultimate reality to which level only *Brahman* belongs. Śankara maintains the absolute identity of the "Universal Self" (*Paramatman*) and the "Individual Self" (*Atman*). One's *moksha*(release) lies in freeing oneself from bondage to the empirical world and realising one's true destiny in *Brahman*. As Nirmal states,

> In the last analysis the empirical reality of the world has no real significance. *Advaita* also removes the individual soul from its conception of the ultimate reality. Ultimately, there is One without a second (*Ekam Advitium*).[32]

Unlike *Advaita Vedanta*, *Lokayata* or *Charvaka* takes the empirical reality of the world very seriously, and denies that there is any reality beyond it. Literally, the word "*loka*" means the world and by extension the ordinary people or masses that inhabit it. This teaching is opposed to the teaching of the Vedas which is the sole property of high caste Brahmins. As is usually the case with dissident writings deemed heretical, the writings of Brihaspati have been destroyed so that the main structure of the philosophy of *Lokayata* has to be derived from what its detractors have to say about it. One of the sources that ridicules *Lokayata*, which Nirmal quotes, states the essence of this teaching in the following words:

> *Lokayata* is always the only *Shastra* [source of knowledge]; in it only perceptual evidence is authority; the elements are earth, water, fire and air; wealth and enjoyment are the objects of human existence. Matter can think. There is no other world. Death is the end of all. Who has seen the soul existing in a state separate from the body? Does not life result from the configuration of matter?[33]

In essence, the *Lokayata* teaching is that all aspects of matter, including humanity, are particular combinations of the four basic elements, earth, water, fire and air. Nirmal draws together various aphorisms of Brihaspati derived from secondary sources to present the tenets of *Lokayata*: "Consciousness arises from matter like intoxicating quality of wine arising from fermented yeast. The soul is nothing but the conscious body. Enjoyment is the only end of human life. Death alone is liberation." At death all matter reverts to its constitutive elements. *Lokayata* refers to the Brahmins, who teach a trans-worldly reality, as "buffoons, knaves and demons" who have created an elaborate system of reality and the various ceremonies associated with the stages of life only for their pecuniary benefit.[34]

Although the written sources of *Lokayata* are lost, Nirmal contends, "It is forgotten only as a philosophical system, but its assumptions and emphases are living."[35]

This is the opinion also of the political scientist, Kancha Ilaiah who views *Lokayata* as the precursor of the modern Dalitbahujan (*dalit mass*) movements.

> The modern Dalit bahujan movements . . . [draw] upon the dialectical materialistic discourses that started in a proto-materialistic form from Indus-based Lokayatas or Charvakas and continued to operate all through history. Lokayatas were the earliest Dalit bahujans who fought against the Aryan invaders who gradually established the brahmanical socio-political and economic system in India. The *vitanda vada satha* (science of dialectical discourse) that the Lokayatas developed was constructed on their interaction with nature in the process of their early agrarian production called *vartakara* (agricultural work).[36]

Hence, instead of viewing *Lokayata* as a bland polemical philosophy that is only to be viewed as anti-brahminical, Ilaiah locates *Lokayata* in a particular worldview—an oral knowledge system (epistemology)—that is concerned with the normal business of living that is evident in the modern Dalit bahujan movements.

The Dalit bahujans have their own theory of knowledge that produces and reproduces itself in the day-to-day interaction with *prakriti* [the common things of life], i.e., land, water, air, seeds, trees. animals, birds, and so on. Dalit bahujans interact with *prakriti* both to produce and reproduce nature and their own beings. In the process, their consciousness produces its own world view (which is closely netted into the process of nature). On the contrary, the brahmanical interaction with nature is anti-production as the brahmanical forces interact with the forces of nature only to consume or destroy them. Their knowledge system is constructed, for example, around consuming and destroying fruits, vegetables, leaves and seeds but not around the process of producing and reproducing the natural elements. They produce and reproduce the brahmanical being and self but not nature, of which they are a part. Hence, their consciousness remains alienated from nature and thrives on idealism. Idealism in its philosophical sense believes that the being and the self exist because of supernatural powers, in specific sense, because of God. Idealism is thus opposed to naturalism and also to the view that the mind and spiritual values have emerged from material products and process. . . . Brahmanical idealism does not have any element of progressiveness like the idealism of the West.[37]

Ilaiah says that through experimentation, Dalit bahujans also study the "nature" (*svabhava*) of plants, insects and animals and relate them to their own nature and decide on what is useful to human beings and what is not. Furthermore, they also experiment with hybridisation, bringing together opposing "natures" again with the test of what is useful and what is not for human beings and animals. Brahmins consume what the Dalit bahujans produce, but with their concentration on *paraloka* (afterworld) view the materials they consume as gifts from God (*paraloka prasada*), and ignore and even denigrate the Dalit bahujans on whose labour they depend and on which they thrive.[38]

Nirmal holds that the positive materialistic philosophy of Lokayata needs to be recovered and allowance made for its extreme positions that were the consequence of its contest with and repugnance of brahmanism, which eventually led to its downfall. As Nirmal notes, "*Lokayata* during its last phase turned hedonistic and therefore lost its appeal."[39] In seeking a "middle path" (*madhyamika*) between the two extreme world views of *Advaita Vedanta* and *Lokayata*, Nirmal brings together disparate emphases that could complement and correct each other while maintaining the primacy of the materialistic base of

Lokayata that acknowledges plurality and values human effort and progress. From *Advaita Vedanta* he accepts the emphasis on morality as a precursor for knowledge of God, but along with *Lokayatavada* discards *karma samsara* (the cycle of births and deaths) as a fatalistic doctrine that places needless emphasis on the importance of the self and its striving for liberation at the expense of the liberation of the community.[40]

As a political philosopher, Kancha Iliah draws upon the epistemology of the Dalit bahujan and pits it against brahminic epistemology which has dominated Indian national political philosophies from the time of Nehru and Gandhi. His approach is polemical. Nirmal on the other hand recognises the fact that brahminic philosophical systems that prescribe proper human action, such as *karma marga* (path of ritual action or disinterested service), *jnana marga* (path of knowledge gained through meditative concentration) and *bhakti marga* (path of devotion and love to God) derived principally from the Bhagavad-Gita, are not likely to disappear from Indian theology. He acknowledges the value in these but holds that if these are indeed to be pertinent the materialistic philosophy of *Lokayata* with its challenge and correction also needs to be taken into account. His approach is not polemical but tactical. It is his way of introducing a *dalit* perspective qualified by Christian belief that the God whom we worship in Jesus Christ is not just a servile God (a *dalit* God) but more importantly a servant God who does not desire the sacrifice of the lowly but through self-sacrifice saves the victim.[41]

To bring together what has been said above, I present with explanatory comments a story from a *dalit* community in a village called Chirakkal in North Malabar, India.

THOTTAM OF POTTAN THEYYAM

In his book, *The Sacred in Popular Hinduism*, Abraham Ayrookuzhiel gives two versions of a *thottam*, or story in song and dance, to the god Pottan (*PottanTheyyam*),[42] which I use to illustrate story-telling as counter theology. In its original version, Pottan is the deaf and dumb god of the Pulayans, the untouchables who are outside the caste structure. Over the years, the Pulayan's *thottam* to *Pottan Theyyam* became so popular that a high caste version was created, as a way both of attracting caste Hindus away from watching the *dalit* performance, and to counter-act the socio-political thrust of the original. In the later version, which is sung in the temples of the high caste and performed by a professional caste of musicians and dancers, the high god Śiva appears in the form of Pottan to challenge the scholar Śankara with his own teaching on *advaita*. In the original version, which is still sung and danced in the shrines of the Pulayans, Pottan himself appears. This god is variously called "vagabond", "idiot", and "loafer god".

In brief, the story goes like this: Pottan with his son in his arms and a pot of toddy (palm wine) on his head walks and dances along a narrow path. He is accompanied by his wife. He is drunk. In the distance comes a high caste Chovar, an aristocrat, with his retinue. He sees the outcaste fellow and shouts at him:

> Give way, give way, you insignificant fellow!
> Give way, give way, you insignificant woman!
> But the fellow retorts:
> In my arms I have my child;
> On my head is a pot of toddy;
> On one side of the path there are thorn bushes;
> On the other side there is a thicket.
> How then can we give way?

This bodily resistance then leads to a discourse on caste:

> When Chovar rides an elephant,
> We ride a buffalo;
> Then why argue over caste?
> When your body is hurt or ours is hurt,
> What gushes out is human blood.
> The blood is the same.
> Must we then quarrel over caste?

> When Chovar wears a garland of lotus flowers,
> We too wear a garland of ordinary flowers.
> When Chovar dances with a bronze idol,
> We dance with vessels of prawns.
> And the rice you eat, and the rice we eat,
> Is it not the same stuff?
> Then, Chovars, what are caste distinctions all about?

By keeping the debate, if one may call it that, on the material level, differences in social status and behaviour cannot deny the simple fact that caste differences are illusory. It is the same blood that both have; and it is the same rice that both eat. The song then becomes more pointed in its sarcasm:

> We planted a plantain tree on a heap of rubbish,
> You take its fruit and make it an offering for god!
> We planted a Tulasi on a heap of rubbish;
> With its leaves and flowers you make offerings to god!
> Then, what really is the difference between us?

The word rubbish, *kuppa*, has a double intention. Its surface reference is to the hill or muck heap in the backyard where the plantain tree and the *tulasi* (the fragrant Ocymum tree) grow. The Pulayans are also derogatorily called *kuppa*. There is a deliberate play on the two meanings to imply that the fruit and *tulasi* leaves that are so piously offered by the high caste Chovars in their temples have their roots in and are nourished by the *kuppa*, the Pulayans themselves. At the very basic material level "untouchablity" has broken down. What then are caste distinctions really about?

The song goes on in the same vein; and finally Pottan speaks with appreciation of the Chovar's calf that is grazing in the field. Caste Hindus do not eat beef, but the Pulayans do; and are often accused of stealing the cattle of the high caste. The implication seems to be that Pottan knows where his next meal is to come from. The Chovar recognises the outcaste fellow as Pottan himself and is terrified:

> Oh Pottan, do not kill my calf!
> Be pleased with my offerings
> As with the offerings made by the . . . Pulayar.

On the surface, the story is about the discomfiture of a high caste Hindu, who finally worships in fear the outcaste vagabond god; and it ridicules caste distinctions. But underneath the satire and merriment, there is the pain of the people that is symbolised in the disfigured, drunken form of Pottan. As a deaf and dumb god, Pottan is no Yahweh, a god who acts: one who hears the cry of his people and comes down to deliver them. Pottan cannot or will not hear; and he cannot or will not speak. But when he does, he expresses through ribaldry and satire the groaning of a people who for centuries have suffered under the intolerable caste system that the high caste claim and maintain as divinely ordained. And through that groaning is expressed a hope not simply for the conversion of the Chovar, which would be short-lived anyway, but for the transformation of society by which the curse of caste will disappear.

However, the high-castes have taken over this story and brahminised it; and have thus neutralised its socio-political impact. Here the contradictions inherent in the caste system are used only to deride the Pulayans. The philosopher Śankara's initial address to Pottan is particularly revealing:

> You have no knowledge of time:
> the past, the present and the future.
> You have no caste;
> You are beyond the law;
> You don't wash;
> You smell of fish and beef.
> You are naturals with no knowledge of God.

Nothing happens in the subsequent dialogue to change this attitude. However, in responding to Śankara's demand that Pottan vacate the path for the learned scholar, the god Pottan challenges the scholar.

> What do you mean by the path,
> And who should get himself out of the path?
> Can you discriminate between Truth and Untruth
> The perennial and the ephemeral
> The sacred and the profane
> The clean conscience and the unclean. . . ?

A recital of high caste Hindu philosophy follows with a pointed challenge to Śankara utilising Śankara's own teaching on *advaita*:

> The inviolable master
> Who has rid himself of the burden
> Of the rope of desire,
> Stands in the heart of Advaita
> It lights itself in you and me,
> In this earth and in the sky.
> If you could reach the original centre . . .
> You reach the sphere of the moon

184 IS GOD CHRISTIAN?

And drink nectar,
You experience sheer ecstasy
And the sense of duality dissolves,
And you experience non-duality.
You know not yourself,
And yet you are cross with me.
It is a matter of pity
That you have asked me to make way,
Poor me, holding the pot of toddy on my head
And managing a little family.

On hearing this learned discourse from the god, who goes on to mimic the original *thottam* of *Pottan Theyyam* as to why he cannot make way for the scholar, Śankara realises that the one who speaks to him with much knowledge cannot be a low-born, but is Śiva himself. He falls at Śiva's feet and praises him. Śiva then reveals the real purpose of his coming incognito to accost Śankara:

I came as a Chandala [low- born] to test you.
I know there is none on earth as learned as you.
Go! You need not be late,
nor should you be crest-fallen.
As the bearer of the snakes blessed him thus,
Śankaracharya resumed his journey.

In the denouement not only are the Pulayans left out, but their god Pottan is also turned into a high god of the upper castes; and permanence is given to this manifestation in a statue:

The Lord said beaming with a smile;
So that the form I assume today
may be visible to the devotees forever,
an image of this form shall be installed on earth.

The earthy flesh and blood approach of the original to the contradictions inherent in the caste system is suppressed in the revised version. The argument here is that all men and women are equal because the same light of *advaita* shines in all. *Advaita* is the post-earthly realisation of non-duality in which all distinctions, including caste distinctions, will disappear. The resolution of the social and religious contradictions that plague humanity is now located, so to speak, in a "heavenly realm". This is high class theology, not counter theology; and it functions the way most high class theologies tend to function. But, Pottan is not Śiva. Instead, may we not say that Pottan is comparable to the Suffering Servant, Jesus the Messiah, whom, however, many of us would prefer to transfigure and worship as the gold-crowned Jesus?

In retelling and expounding the *Thottam to Pottan Theyam,* I have quietly brought the Christian story into an interplay with it, and have also used the brahminised version to show the way in which high-class theologies tend to deal with the stories and experiences that form the matrix of counter theologies. I will bring my exposition of this *thottam* to a halt at this point, and shift my attention to the Christian story.

As pointed out earlier, both in Minjung Theology and Dalit Theology emphasis is placed on the figure and vocation of Jesus in terms of his relationship with *people,* understood as the *ochlos,* whom Jesus described as sheep without a shepherd and to whom Jesus related in compassion. To signify Jesus's response to the condition of the *ochlos,* the gospel writers consistently use the verb *splanchnizomai.* This verb figures only in the words and actions of Jesus in preference to *eleeō* (to have pity or to show mercy). A good example is the narration of the parable of the good Samaritan (Luke 10:25–37) in which this verb occurs in the mouth of Jesus to signify the response of the Samaritan to the one who was robbed and beaten and left by the wayside and ignored by the priest and Levite. When Jesus asks the lawyer as to who proved to be a neighbour, the lawyer responds that it was the one who showed mercy (*eleos*). The lawyer does not use the verb "to have compassion" (*splanchnizomai*). *Splanchnizoma* signifies a gutsy bodily response. It is "to be moved in one's bowels" or better rendered as "his guts went out to them." It is both a maternal response of deep yearning for the abandoned and a paternal response of anger in favour of the down-trodden. In relating to people (*ochlos*), Jesus not only fed them and taught them, but also wept and cursed with them and for them.[43] Jesus represented their deep groaning—groaning like that of the inconsolable Mother Rachel bereft of her children; and the cross is the symbolic concretion of the groaning of Jesus and *people.* The story of Jesus as a counter theology has to be understood and told as the story of that compassion as a bodily response—not a spiritualised mental response that involved Jesus the Messiah physically in the predicament of the people's groaning for salvation. From this perspective, the resurrection is to be understood not so much as a reversal of the crucifixion, taken as an unfortunate but necessary event, but rather as the divine affirmation of the Crucified One—the Lamb that is slain but regnant (cf. Rev 5:11–12).

THE CHALLENGE OF COUNTER THEOLOGIES

Taking a *dalit* perspective that implicitly reflects the challenge presented by all counter theologies, Felix Wilfred remarks:

> Those who rule over and exclude the Dalits [the so-called "untouchables"], in fact, exclude themselves from knowledge and truth. For, they fail to question critically their position and delude themselves with the belief in superiority, which, in reality, is a simple social and cultural construction. This assumed superior position is traded for truth. On the other hand, the unique epistemological advantage of the Dalits could be identified in their multifarious cultural expression. They provide us a window to a reality that is concealed and distorted by the dominators and upper castes.[44]

Speaking to me, a colleague of mine, Abraham Eraly, who is an Indian historian, put the issue more bluntly: "The Brahmins worked out this elaborate con on caste, and the amazing thing is that we have bought into it and held on to it for some three thousand years!"

These critical positions should not lead us to think that *dalits* are *sui generis* good theologians. The call for an epistemological shift should not be confused with a presumed ontological shift! In fact, some of the *dalit* theologians I know have betrayed their ideological position when they moved into positions of power. As I have shown in chapter 2, Mark followed by the other Evangelists sees the possibility of acquiescing to the temptation of power as something that the disciples of Jesus also faced. Jesus had to remind them constantly that the Empire of God as an alternative to the Empire of Caesar calls for a reversal, where the least would be counted as the greatest. Any attempt to aspire to positions of greatness in the Empire of God could be disastrous (cf. Luke 14:7–11).

On the obverse side, the challenge of all counter theologies to those engaged in the articulation of "public theology", and not simply "churchy" theology, is that a radical change of perspective is imperative if the doing of such theology is to be inclusive. Implied in this challenge are the positions of both Suh Nam-dong and Arvind P. Nirmal: theology is about life and the materiality of human existence. This, in essence, is the redoubtable strength of the second story as a counter theology. The temptation to succumb to the allure of power and high class theology remains.

Notes

1. Suh Nam-dong, "Theology as Story-telling: A Counter-theology," *CTC Bulletin* 5, no. 3—6, no. 1 (1984–85): 4–11.

2. Suh Nam-dong, "Cultural Theology, Political Theology and Minjung Theology," *CTC Bulletin* 5, no. 3—6, no. 1 (1984–85): 12–15. Unfortunately this volume of CTC Bulletin is not readily available. Suh Nam-dong's essay, "Towards A Theology of Han," in *Minjung Theology: People as the Subjects of History*, ed. CTC–CCA (Singapore: Christian Conference of Asia & New York: Orbis, 1983), 55–69, is a good example of his method.

3. For Suh Nam-dong's understanding of *han*, see "Towards A Theology of Han," 55–69. See also the discussion in chapter 1 of this book.

4. Suh, "Cultural Theology," 15. Emphasis added.

5. Ahn Byung-mu, "The Transmitters of the Jesus-Event," *CTC Bulletin* 5, no. 3—6, no. 1 (December 1984–April 1985): 30.

6. Hyun Young-hak, "Theology as Rumormongering," *CTC Bulletin* 5, no.3—6, no. 1 (1984–85): 40–48.

7. Suh, "Story-telling," 6.

8. Ibid., 7. Emphasis added.

9. Ibid., 8.

10. Ibid., 9.

11. Ibid., 10.

12. Loc. cit.

13. Ibid., 14.

14. C.S. Song, *In the Beginning Were Stories Not Texts: Story Theology* (Cambridge: James Clarke & Co., 2012).

15. "Towards A Christian Dalit Theology," in *A Reader in Dalit Theology*, ed. Arvind P. Nirmal (Madras: Department of Dalit Theology, Gurukul, no date), 63–69.

16. Nirmal, "Towards Dalit Theology," 53.

17. Codified around 500 BCE, the Laws of Manu define the norms for domestic, social, and religious life from a brahmanic perspective.

18. Nirmal, "Towards Dalit Theology," 53.

19. Sathianathan Clarke, Deenabandhu Manchala, and Philip Vinod Peacock, eds., *Dalit Theology in the Twenty-first Century* (New Delhi: Oxford University Press, 2010). See especially Clarke's introductory essay interpreting Dalit Theology, 19–37.

20. Nirmal, "Towards Dalit Theology," 58–59. Emphasis added.

21. Ibid., 67.

22. Arvind P. Nirmal, *Heuristic Explorations* (Madras: Christian Literature Society, 1990), 147.

23. Lata Murugkar, "Dalit Panthers: A Militant Movement in Maharashtra," in *Indigenous People: Dalit Issues in Today's Theological Debate*, ed. James Massey (Delhi: ISPCK, 1998), 96–110.

24. Arjun Dangle, ed., *Poisoned Bread: Translations from Modern Marathi Dalit Literature* (Bombay: Orient Longman, 1992).

25. Nirmal, "Towards Dalit Theology," 59.

26. Arvind P. Nirmal, "Doing Theology from a Dalit Perspective," in *A Reader in Dalit Theology*, ed. Arvind P. Nirmal (Madras: Department of Dalit Theology, Gurukul, no date), 142–43.

27. Arvind P. Nirmal, "Developing A Common Ideology: Some Theological Considerations," in *Towards A Common Dalit Ideology*, ed. Arvind P. Nirmal (Madras: Gurukul Lutheran Theological College, no date), 123.

28. Jan M. Lochman, *Church in a Marxist Society* (New York: Harper & Row, 1970), 146.

29. Nirmal, "Common Ideology," 124–26.

30. Arvind P. Nirmal, *Heuristic Explorations*, 98–99.

31. Nirmal, *Heuristic Explorations*, 99.

32. Ibid., 101–2.

33. Ibid., 104.

34. For a brief account of Lokayata teaching, see Wendy Doniger, *The Hindus: An Alternative History* (Oxford University Press, 2009), 185–86.

35. Nirmal, *Heuristic Explorations*, 106.

36. Kancha Iliah, *The Weapon of the Other: Dalit Bahujan Writings and the Remaking of Indian Nationalist Thought* (New Delhi: Doring Kindersley,

2010), 5.

37. Ilaiah, *The Weapon*, 3.

38. Ibid., 4–5.

39. Nirmal, *Heuristic Explorations*, 116.

40. Ibid., 100–119.

41. Nirmal, "Towards Dalit Theology," 63–64.

42. A.M. Abraham Ayrookuzhiel, *The Sacred in Popular Hinduism* (Madras: CLS, 1983), 170–81.

43. For a fuller exposition, see my book *From East and West: Rethinking Christian Mission* (St Louis: Chalice, 2001), 78–81.

44. *Dalit Empowerment*, (Bangalore: NBCLC, 2007), 3. See also his *The Sling of Utopia*, (Delhi: ISPCK, 2005).

The Exploration Continues:
Some Concluding Remarks

As I indicated in the introduction, it is not my intention to pull the discussions in the previous chapters in this book into a tight conclusion. I leave what I have said as they are with gaps for further exploration—for additions and corrections. This would be in keeping with my conviction that all theology is theology *en route*; and no theological position or articulation should pretend to be the final word. All that I want to say at this point is that the theological methods in public theology, which I have explored, on first reading may seem independent of each other. Actually they complement each other as they tackle in different ways the problem of the two stories, relating what we have received as the Christian story with the story of our Asian traditions, which we have inherited. The acceptance of plurality is implicit in these approaches.

TOWARDS A WIDER ECUMENISM

One of the consequences of these approaches is that we seek a wider ecumenism that goes beyond mere inter-confessional Christian conversations. In his essay, "Changing Paradigms of Asian Christian Attitude to Other Religions,"[1] S. Wesley Ariarajah makes a plea for a wider ecumenism, and presents several challenges for the doing of theology in the context of religious plurality that characterises our world today. I single out and comment on two of the important challenges he raises.

First, cross-textual reading in particular and cross-textual hermeneutics in general require

> ... that almost all Christian doctrines have to be re-thought and re-for-mulated in the light of religious plurality. Recognizing that much of the official doctrines of the church are themselves products of theological reflection that took place in a particular time and culture and to meet the challenges of a particular time, it is argued that the core of the doctrines of the church is badly in need of a restatement in the context of dialogue and the advances made in Christian relationship to other faiths.[2]

In his book, *Your God, My God, Our God*, Ariarajah makes an initial foray into tackling this challenge by recasting the doctrines of God, Sin, Christology and Salvation, so that these may be more hospitable to other religious traditions. For example, to recast the doctrine of God in a religiously plural world, Ariarajah shows that initially the belief in One God in the so-called monotheistic Semitic religions was a call for a single-minded devotion to the One God who is the source of all life. However, in placing the stress on "Oneness",

> The result is that in actual practice the God(s) of the three monotheistic traditions has emerged as three mutually exclusive tribal gods. The Jew-ish-Islamic-Christian trialogue has begun to deal with this problem by looking at the significance of the claim that their God(s) is the God of Abraham, assumed to be their common spiritual ancestor. But they are yet to make up their mind about the relationship of the One God to all other peoples. In popular Christian thinking, Hindus and Sikhs and oth-ers worship their gods even as we worship God in Jesus Christ. Despite the verbal claim to monotheism, an unacknowledged polytheism is at work in popular Christian theology and piety.[3]

The challenge raised in this book, "Is God Christian?" or better "Is there a Christian God?" remains to challenge Christian piety. If the exploration of methods in Christian public theology could contribute to a recasting of Christian dogma as it impinges on Christian faith, much would have been accomplished. And the plea is that if the God whom we worship in Jesus Christ is the God of "all people", then the recasting of Christian dogma with its implications for Christian piety needs to be done with "all people". As Ariarajah notes, if the first Jerusalem council described in Acts 15 involved the transition and exposition of the Christian faith from a purely Jewish milieu to a

Greek milieu, then a second Jerusalem council is needed to signal the next move to a multi-faith milieu.[4]

Second, western missions, both Catholic and Protestant, have sought to displace other faiths and religious traditions with a Christ centred religion and theology. This approach has not only attempted to turn converts against other religious traditions, but has also inculcated in them the attitude that only their particular denominational or confessional position is right. Ariarajah says,

> There was a time when the main traditions of the church saw themselves as strict alternatives. Even within a single branch of the church, like the Protestant tradition, being a Methodist, an Anglican, or a Lutheran, was so well defined that one would not worship in another's church or *engage in any form of common social action*. The Christian ecumenical movement, over the years, has helped the churches to get to know each other and grow together.[5]

I wonder whether this statement is as true as one would like to believe. While global, regional and national ecumenical bodies have done much to bring churches together, time and again "common social action" has been scuppered by what I would call "confessionalism" that promotes one of several brands of missionary religion as the most appropriate practice of the Christian faith in Asia. Western denominational centres sometimes tend to reinforce this attitude, which gives the impression that confessionalism is in fact colonialism in religious guise. What is particularly invidious about this phenomenon is that it not only denies plurality, but assumes that a particular confessional tradition holds all the answers to address the difficult human predicaments and problems on the ground. There is a mismatch between what Christians in the pew experience living in a pluralistic world and what the local church centres advocate.

I give as an example the article of A. W. Jebanesan, the former president of the Methodist Conference in Sri Lanka, "Hopes and Uncertainties: Sri Lanka's Journey to Find Peace and Justice in the Midst of Religious Conflict."[6] The article begins with an extremely strong analysis of the political and religious situation in Sri Lanka, then leads to a Methodist initiative to deal with the problem of conflict.[7] From this point onwards the reference to "church" is the Methodist Church. Why, one may ask, has this initiative not involved other churches in Sri Lanka which are also vexed with this problem as it affects all Christians besides others?

The challenge is to go beyond ecumenism as a notion, to which one gives lip service, to ecumenism in practice. Aloysius Pieris, S.J., succinctly states the challenge facing all churches:

> Ecumenism is an urgent evangelical imperative in Asia. It is time we cease projecting the image of a dismembered Body of Christ, which is a counter witness to the Good News we proclaim. But the ecumenism we seek is neither a fruit-salad Christianity nor a monolith resulting from one powerful church swallowing the others, but a mega-community composed of churches that complement one another, each with its own historical identity, its unique tradition, its own doctrinal emphasis, and its particular worship form; in short, a Pentecostal communion of communities that understand and speak one another's tongues.[8]

Both these challenges call for further exploration and practice to help Christians live and work meaningfully in a religiously plural world.

THE ABIDING TASK FOR PUBLIC THEOLOGY

I end this book with two statements on the function of theology, which I have quoted earlier. One is from R. S. Sugirtharajah, a postcolonial biblical critic:

> Theologians often assume the role of legislators, and expect that their hermeneutical treatises will change the world. The task of theologians is not to change the world but to understand it. Theology does not create revolution; it changes people's perceptions and makes them aware of the need for revolution. Its function is to make people see more, feel more and rekindle the fire of resistance.[9]

The other is from the Dalit counter theologian Arvind P. Nirmal, who having noted that God neither writes theology nor reads theology, says:

> It is human life which raises the question of God and also answers it. By life I mean life in its totality. The primary task of theology, therefore, is to make sense of human life and give it a certain direction and goal. The criteria of theology too then must be derived from human life and not from some other "givens". Any theology which fails to make sense

of human life and fails to fulfil it ceases to be relevant and cannot be a living option.[10]

In my opinion, these two theologians from opposite ends of the Asian theological camp aptly state the task for theology in Asia. It is my hope that the explorations in this volume will contribute to this continuing quest.

Notes

1. S. Wesley Ariarajah, "Changing Paradigms of Asian Christian Attitude to Other Religions," in *The Oxford Handbook of Christianity in Asia*, ed. Felix Wilfred, (Oxford: Oxford University Press, 2014), 347–67.

2. Ariarajah, "Changing Paradigms," 363–64.

3. S. Wesley Ariarajah, *Your God, My God, Our God: Rethinking Christian Theology for Religious Plurality* (Geneva: WCC Publications, 2012), 45.

4. Ariarajah, *Your God*, 21–32.

5. Ariarajah, "Changing Paradigms," 365.

6. A.W. Jebanesan, "Hopes and Uncertainties: Sri Lanka's Journey to Find Peace and Justice in the Midst of Religious Conflict," *Current Dialogue* 55 (September 2013): 55–62.

7. Jebanesan, "Hopes and Uncertainties," 59.

8. Aloysius Pieris, S.J., in the back cover to *Footprints of an Ecumenical Pilgrimage: National Christian Council of Sri Lanka (1914–2014)*, ed. G. P. V. Somaratna, (Colombo: NCC Sri Lanka). See also his article in the same volume, "Ecumenism and Inter-faith Relationship: The Sri Lankan Experience," 131–40.

9. R. S. Sugirtharajah, *Postcolonial Reconfigurations: An Alternative Way of Reading the Bible and Doing Theology* (Louisville: Chalice, 2003), 125.

10. Arvind P. Nirmal, *Heuristic Explorations* (Madras: Gurukul and Christian Literature Society, 1990), 98–99.

Index of Names and Places